Organized Labor in the Twentieth-Century South

Edited by Robert H. Zieger

The University of Tennessee Press

Knoxville

Library of Congress Cataloging in Publication Data

Organized labor in the twentieth-century South / edited
by Robert H. Zieger. — 1st ed.
        p.   cm.
    "Six of the papers . . . were presented during the University
of Florida Department of History's Institute in March 1989"— Pref.
    Includes index.
ISBN 0-87049-697-2 (cloth: alk. paper)
    1. Trade-unions—Southern States—History—Sources.
2. Southern States—Race relations—Sources.
I. Zieger, Robert H.
HD6517.A13074   1991
331.88'0975'0904—dc20   90-22448   CIP

Contents

Preface

Six of the papers in this collection were presented during the University of Florida Department of History's Institute in March 1989. Robert J. Norrell's contribution to the collection is on a different subject from the one he treated at that time. My own was written just after the institute. Two papers were subsequently solicited by the editor from scholars who did not participate in the institute. The authors of two of the institute papers chose not to make their work available for this project.

The editor and contributors are grateful to the Department of History for its generous support of the institute and its invaluable services during the editorial and production processes. Those involved also owe debts to Ray Jones and Sam Gowen of the University Libraries for making meeting facilities available and to the Department of History's staff for its assistance in holding the institute. Betty Corwine and Ann McDaniel played crucial roles in preparing the manuscript for publication.

Robert H. Zieger

Introduction

Organized labor has played an integral role in the history of the twentieth-century South. During the past decade, labor and social historians have made substantial progress in documenting the experiences of the southern working class but as yet their work has received little recognition in general historiographical circles.[1] In bringing together recent examples of scholarship in the field, *Organized Labor in the Twentieth-Century South* is an effort to counter this neglect.

The papers that make up this volume are diverse in subject, perspective, and focus. Contributions were canvassed on the basis of the editor's knowledge of the authors' previous work and reputations. He sought, first, excellence in scholarship, and, second, diversity in subject matter and perspective.

Although the essays derive from no pre-set agenda, they do exhibit several common themes. They all assume that the story of organized labor is an important component of twentieth-century southern history. In addition, all of the essays, either directly or by implication, address the recurrent problem of the alleged distinctiveness of the southern working class and southern patterns of labor relations. And, finally, most of the essays highlight the role of race in recent southern labor history.

The first of these themes—the importance of labor history in the study of the recent South—hardly needs separate documentation. A host of recent works springs readily to mind; the citations for this introduction suggest the scope and focus of recent literature. "Southern labor history," observes a leading practitioner, "has emerged as a cottage industry, at the least, and probably as a major trend" in the past decade.[2] Most of the contributors to the current volume have not specialized in southern history in their more general work but rather have found southern labor history a rich and productive field of investigation in which they might examine broad questions about the behavior of workers and the activities of organized labor. The South, historians are learning, abounds in rich records, both archival and oral, for the study of workers and unions. The Southern Labor Archives in Atlanta, the oral history collections at the University of North Carolina, federal archives at East Point, Georgia, and individual and specialized collections at Duke, the University of Alabama, the University of Virginia, the University of Texas–Arlington, and elsewhere have helped historians to generate an increasingly sophisticated and wide-ranging body of work. The awarding of the Philip A. Taft prize in 1988 to a book dealing with the quintessential southern labor history topic, the millworkers of the Piedmont, perhaps marks the coming of age of the field.[3]

Debate over the putative distinctiveness of southern workers has characterized much of the existing popular, social scientific, and historical literature concerning Dixie's workers. The primal question of race, the peculiar circumstances under which large-scale industrial development occurred in the South, and the relative ethnic homogeneity of the region's white working class have led generations of observers to treat the South as a distinctive regional entity insofar as labor is concerned. The textile mill villages, the intense legal and extralegal opposition to union organizing, and the inventiveness of local clergy, law enforcement officers, and business leaders in sustaining a "union-free" environment have been the twentieth-century equivalent to the nineteenth-century South's "peculiar institution." Southern states, for example, have pioneered in the passage of "right-to-work" legislation. Southern states stand at the bottom of the list in terms of percentage of workers belonging to unions. As organized labor became increasingly entrenched in other areas of the country in the New Deal–World War II era, the South clung to (and indeed intensified) its status as an antilabor island, passing anti-union laws, smashing the labor movement's ambitious postwar organizing campaigns, and inventing ever more ingenious means of circumventing national labor policy, which in theory privileged collective bargaining. Combined with the South's ongoing white racism, this anti-union tradition seemed to fix the region as the glaring exception to liberal national norms.

Yet, increasingly, this view of southern workers and southern traditions of labor policy has come under criticism. Historians such as James Green, Eric Arnesen, Charles Martin, Delores Janiewski, and Melton McLaurin have called into question the image of southern workers as distinctively non- or anti-union in character. Documentation of energetic unionism among longshoremen, textile workers, coal miners, and steel, paper, tobacco, rubber, communications, and other industrial workers has proliferated. In recent years, teachers and other public employees have made substantial gains in the South and it appears that in the past two decades of organized labor's protracted decline, southern unions have held their own better than their counterparts elsewhere. Today southern workers constitute the highest percentage of the labor movement's ranks in history.[3]

Several of the essays in this collection speak eloquently to this point. Thus as Joe W. Trotter demonstrates, militant biracial unionism was a significant part of the repertoire of West Virginia's black coal miners even in the dismal 1920s. Mary Frederickson's account of women activists documents a long and continuing tradition of union commitment from turn-of-the-century textile mills to the coalfields of Virginia in the 1980s. Colin Davis's southern rail strikers in the 1920s exhibited no less a degree of fervor and tenacity than did their counterparts elsewhere. Michael Honey, for Memphis, and Rick Halpern, for Fort Worth, document patterns of aggressive unionism among food processing, furniture, rubber, and meatpacking workers during the heyday of the CIO, and Judith Stein highlights the efforts of rank-and-file unionists in Birmingham to compel their international union to bring national standards to the southern steel center's operations. Perhaps most telling on the question of alleged southern distinctiveness is the evidence that Gilbert Gall draws upon in his analysis of the electoral behavior of southern workers in early right-to-work referenda in Florida and Arkansas.

The theme of southern distinctiveness comes under a different kind of assault when historians turn their attention to the other side of the equation: the role of management and the state in establishing and sustaining the particular kind of industrial relations "regime" prevailing. Thus as patterns of anti-unionism continue to elaborate in post-1960s America, practices and strategies that once seemed southern aberrations have become increasingly standard nationally. True, southern textile employers may have pioneered in the manipulation and frustration of national labor legislation,[4] but in the past generation employers everywhere have, in effect, adopted the southern strategy, rendering the National Labor Relations Act increasingly useless for the labor movement it was designed to benefit. The other prong in the southern anti-union strategy, namely that of attracting and retaining industry on the basis of low-wage and "union-free" environments, has found wide support in former union strongholds as cities, states, and entire regions find themselves emulating southern pioneers in their efforts to create a "favorable business climate" in an era of intense regional and international competition.

Several of the collection's essays address the theme of the importance of the state and business leadership in creating this climate in the South. The textile manufacturers that Gary Fink describes, for example, took ready advantage of the new wave in industrial espionage and quickly perceived in it a means not only of forestalling unionism but of gaining critical information about their own operations as well. The actions of the southern railroad executives featured in Colin Davis's contribution exhibited the full range of strategies—from determined efforts to crush the unions to sponsorship of programs of union-management cooperation—practiced nationally during the 1922 shopmen's strike. Likewise, public authorities in some locations enlisted energetically in union-busting but elsewhere, as Davis's account of Jacksonville's pro-labor city administration reveals, joined union activists in ridding their communities of scabs and imported thugs.

In the South, the combination of union-baiting public officials and employers determined to keep the low-wage advantage was reinforced by the powerful planter elite. This troika of anti-unionism is particularly evident in the brutal opposition to efforts to organize Memphis's industrial workers, an example of the frankly repressive nature of much anti-unionism, North and South, in the 1930s and 1940s. Hostility toward organized labor was no less intense among local authorities in Birmingham, as described by Judith Stein. Here, however, the fact that the major employer was part of a national corporation coming to terms with its union, along with the lingering effects of regional labor markets, forced local anti-labor activities into more indirect channels. The early "right-to-work" campaign engineered by Florida politicians, and business, public relations, and agricultural elites, as outlined in Gall's essay, provides still another variation on this theme. Robert H. Zieger's survey of the historical literature dealing with the cotton textile industry suggests that the full range of anti-union strategies that Piedmont manufacturers employed—paternalism; repression; reliance on political and electoral instruments; legalistic manipulation of federal labor law—has in recent years become the national norm.

Indeed, the theme that emerges clearly from examination of the roles of both business and government in shaping American patterns of unionism and industrial relations, North or South, is that of hostility. Even as Memphis's business elite and public authorities conspired in the 1930s in the beating of United Automobile Workers organizers, Henry Ford's "servicemen," under the benevolent eye of Dearborn police, were meting out equally brutal punishment to the organizers' comrades in Michigan. Paternalism and stretch-out in the southern textile mills had their counterparts in the northern-based petroleum and shoe industries. And, increasingly, the public relations and political initiatives that gave the South its primacy in "right-to-work" legislation found enthusiastic imitation and elaboration in the post-1960 proliferation of union-busting consulting firms and nationwide patterns of redefinition of the country's labor laws.

Race is another subject on which the distinctiveness of southern labor requires qualification. Until recently, of course, the concentration of blacks in the South has been weakening and historians' examination of the processes of union development in other areas has increasingly focused on the role of black workers. The story of organized labor's relationship to black America, regardless of the region of the country under investigation, is a troubled and often unedifying one. Did racism act in distinctive ways to impede labor organization in the South? Examples of its poisonous effects are not difficult to find. South Carolina's cotton-mill workers in the 1910s, for example, did engage in occasional class-based protest but they clearly reserved their greatest cohesion and militancy for the cause of barring black workers from the mills and enforcing a rigidly segregationist social and political code. Railroad unions ruthlessly victimized black workers who presumed to claim jobs on the trains or in the repair shops. Pulp and paper workers' unions relegated blacks to the most dangerous and difficult jobs, forced them into segregated locals, and subordinated these organizations to the priorities of the white workers.[5]

Yet the story may not be so monolithic as it once seemed. Evidences of biracial unionism among miners, dockers, and even building tradesmen early in the century establish what is at the very least a vigorous tradition of opposition to presumed southern industrial norms. One of the distinctive contributions in this volume is Halpern, Honey, and Stein's suggestion that biracial unionism, despite heavy odds, was part of the heritage of the CIO in the South, a theme advanced elsewhere by students of the tobacco, iron-mining, and post–World War II textile industries as well.[6]

But, some recent scholarship suggests, perhaps historians and other observers have overemphasized the regional component of race. Recent scholarship, even as it has highlighted the racial dimension to twentieth-century labor history generally, has also abounded with documentation of organized labor's failures in regard to race, in the North as well as in the South. Thus, for example, when African Americans moved into the Pittsburgh area seeking work in its heavy industry, they encountered only hostility and discrimination from a labor movement intent on retaining the minimal privileges it had achieved. Even the successes of the more egalitarian CIO in the 1930s and 1940s did not come close to achieving racial justice, as white-led unions that identified with the civil rights movement in the national arena also proved unresponsive to the claims of black workers in the shops and union halls. Recent articles by former NAACP labor secretary Herbert Hill indeed have bitterly castigated even the most "progressive"unions for their racial failures and for their subservience to the racism of their white memberships, spurring a sharp debate among scholars and activists on the subject.[7]

Distinctive southern labor markets and patterns of racial control, of course, remained important at least into the 1960s. Judith Stein's essay on Birmingham steelworkers, for example, establishes the critical significance of separate regional labor markets and the repressive political environment in shaping black steelworker goals and tactics in the effort to bring industrywide standards of wages, working conditions, and job access to the Alabama mills. Robert J. Norrell's account of white workers' hostility to civil rights in Alabama, while acknowledging resonances in northern cities, stresses the pervasive racism peculiar to the Deep South.

Having only recently recognized the centrality of race to the American working-class experience, historians are not close to any resolution of the interpretive problems it poses. But the focus on race is in itself salutary. The contradictions, ambiguities, and painful crosscurrents of racial juxtaposition, so critical to our general American labor history, are amply and imaginatively analyzed from diverse perspectives in the essays by Trotter, Honey, Halpern, Stein, and Norrell. It is a strength of this collection that these essays, reflecting as they do the diversity and vigor of recent labor history scholarship, lead in different directions and, taken together, implicitly challenge one-dimensional treatments of this key subject.

"As always with the South," writes journalist Howell Raines, "things circle back around to race and class."[8] And so it would seem in the matters thus far highlighted in this introduction. But what of the third leg of the social historian's necessary triptych—gender? Here perhaps the current collection can at once acknowledge a limitation and suggest an agenda.

It is not that our selections fail to take gender into account. Indeed, Mary Frederickson's imaginative survey of the relationships between southern women and their unions may well serve as a guide to subsequent scholars. Robert H. Zieger's essay, in addition, takes particular note of the important contributions of Jacquelyn Hall in the redefinition of the ground on which textile history, at least, is staged. Still, gender is not integrated into this collection as intimately as is race, to say nothing of class. In the words of a critic of the collection's prepublication prospectus, gender is "not problematicized" with the same force as are the other two central elements.

Must all significant scholarship in labor and social history "problematicize" gender in this way? Social and labor historians have always assumed the centrality of class, and few who have come of age over the past thirty-five years would fail to award race at least coequal importance. Despite two decades of the new women's history, however, it has only been with the 1988 publication of Joan Wallach Scott's *Gender and the Politics of History*[9] that practicing historians have felt compelled to confront the implications of the gender dimension directly. Southern labor, with its high proportion of female workers, its historic reliance on agriculture, textiles, and other female-centered occupations, and its recent successes in occupations such as teaching and public employment with clear gender components, may prove a particularly rich field for the regenderization of the past. If such is the case, perhaps *Organized Labor and the Twentieth-Century South* will prove a bridge between the "old" new labor history and an even newer, gender-conscious labor history.

Those participating in the publication of this volume hope to acquaint the scholarly community and the interested public with some good examples of recent scholarship in the field of southern labor history and thereby perhaps to further the ongoing discourse over the place of organized labor in American history generally. They believe that these papers, responsive as they are to recent historiographical and methodological initiatives, yet each following its own agenda, make a

real contribution to the fields of labor and southern history, as well as
to the general literature of the recent past. It is our hope that these
forays into the mines, mills, union halls, and polling places of the
working-class South will at once provide solid evidence of the South's
vigorous laborite traditions as well as encouragement for other scholars
to press on with the task of documenting and interpreting them.

Notes

1. Standard citations include F. Ray Marshall, *Labor in the South* (Cambridge,
    MA: Harvard Univ. Press, 1976); Gary M. Fink and Merl Reed, eds., *Essays in
    Southern Labor History: Selected Papers, Southern Labor History Confer-
    ence, 1976* (Westport, CT and London: Greenwood Press, 1977); and Gary
    M. Fink, Merl Reed, and Leslie Hough, eds., *Southern Workers and Their
    Unions* (Westport, CT and London: Greenwood, 1981). Of the various essays
    edited by John B. Boles and Evelyn Thomas Nolen in *Interpreting Southern
    History: Historiographical Essays in Honor of Sanford W. Higgenbotham*
    (Baton Rouge and London: Louisiana State Univ. Press, 1987), covering the
    post–Civil War period, only Jacquelyn Dowd Hall and Anne Firor Scott's
    "Women in the South" contains a substantial body of references to labor
    (454–509, esp. 481–87).
2. Jacquelyn Hall, Comments, "Prospects in Southern Studies: A Symposium,"
    Southern Research Report [Faculty Working Group in Southern Studies,
    University of North Carolina at Chapel Hill] 1 (Spring 1990): 32.
3. Jacquelyn Dowd Hall, James Leloudis, Robert Korstad, Mary Murphy, Lu
    Ann Jones, Christopher B. Daly, *Like a Family: The Making of a Southern
    Cotton Mill World* (Chapel Hill and London: Univ. of North Carolina Press,
    1987).
4. Hall, Comments, 31–32, suggests that some of the alleged distinctiveness of
    the southern working class may be more a product of the conventions of
    scholarly periodization and focus than of objective social circumstances.
5. James Green, *Grass-Roots Socialism: Radical Movements in the Southwest,
    1895–1943* (Baton Rouge: Louisiana State Univ. Press, 1978; Daniel
    Rosenberg, *New Orleans Dockworkers: Race, Labor, and Unionism, 1892–
    1923* (Albany: SUNY Press, 1988); Delores E. Janiewski, *Sisterhood Denied:
    Race, Gender, and Class in a New South Community* (Philadelphia: Temple
    Univ. Press, 1985); Charles H. Martin, "Southern Labor Relations in
    Transition: Gadsden, Alabama, 1930–1943," *Journal of Southern History*
    47:4 (Nov. 1981): 545–68; John G. Selby, "'Better to Starve in the Shade
    than in the Factory': Labor Protest in High Point, North Carolina, in the Early
    1930s," *North Carolina Historical Review* 64:1 (Jan. 1987): 43–64; Robert
    David Ward and William Warren Rogers, *Labor Revolt in Alabama: The*

Great Strike of 1894 (Tuscaloosa: Univ. of Alabama Press, 1964); Robert Korstad and Nelson Lichtenstein, "Opportunities Found and Lost: Labor, Radicals, and the Early Civil Rights Movement," *Journal of American History* 75:3 (Dec. 1988): 786–811, esp. 790–93, 801–6; Robert H. Zieger, *Rebuilding the Pulp and Paper Workers' Union, 1933–1941* (Knoxville: Univ. of Tennessee Press, 1984), 142–52; Robert H. Zieger, "The Union Comes to Covington: Virginia Paper Workers Organize, 1934–1952," *Proceedings of the American Philosophical Society* (1982): 51–89; John N. Schacht, *The Making of Telephone Unionism, 1920–1947* (New Brunswick, NJ: Rutgers Univ. Press, 1985), 134–35; Ray Marshall, "Southern Unions: History and Prospects," *Perspectives on the American South: An Annual Review of Society, Politics and Culture*, vol. 3, ed. James C. Cobb and Charles R. Wilson (New York: Gordon and Breach, 1985), 163–78; Melton A. McLaurin, *Paternalism and Protest: Southern Cotton Mill Workers and Organized Labor, 1875–1905* (Westport, CT: Greenwood, 1971); Horace Huntley, "Iron Ore Miners and Mine Mill in Alabama, 1932–1952" (Ph.D. diss., Univ. of Pittsburgh, 1976); and William Edward Regensburger, "'Ground into Our Blood': The Origins of Working Class Consciousness and Organization in Durably Unionized Southern Industries, 1930–1946" (Ph.D. diss. [Sociology], UCLA, 1987).

6.   See James Hodges, *New Deal Labor Policy and the Southern Cotton Textile Industry, 1933–1941* (Knoxville: Univ. of Tennessee Press, 1986), and Barbara S. Griffith, *The Crisis of American Labor: Operation Dixie and the Defeat of the CIO* (Philadelphia: Temple Univ. Press, 1988), 40–41, 69–70, 94–95, 101–2.

7.   David L. Carlton, *Mill and Town in South Carolina, 1880–1920* (Baton Rouge and London: Louisiana State Univ. Press, 1982); Hugh B. Hammett, "Labor and Race: The Georgia Railroad Strike of 1909," *Labor History* 16:4 (Fall 1975): 470–84; Zieger, *Rebuilding the Pulp and Paper Workers' Union*, 112–16.

8.   Huntley, "Mine Mill in Alabama"; Korstad and Lichtenstein, "Opportunities Found and Lost," 790–93, 801–6; Eric Arnesen, "To Rule or Ruin: New Orleans Dock Workers' Struggle for Control, 1902–1903," *Labor History* 28:2 (Spring 1987): 139–66; Mary Frederickson, "Four Decades of Change: Black Workers in Southern Textiles, 1941–1981," *Workers' Struggles, Past and Present: A "Radical America" Reader*, ed. James Green (Philadelphia: Temple Univ. Press, 1983; paperback), 62–82.

9.   Peter Gottlieb, *Making Their Own Way: Southern Blacks' Migration to Pittsburgh, 1916–1930* (Urbana and Chicago: Univ. of Illinois Press, 1987), 146–82; Dennis C. Dickerson, *Out of the Crucible: Black Steelworkers in Western Pennsylvania, 1875–1980* (Albany: SUNY Press, 1986); Robert J. Norrell, "Caste in Steel: Jim Crow Careers in Birmingham, Alabama," *Journal of American History* 73:3 (Dec. 1986): 669–94; Zieger, "The Union Comes to Covington," 81; William Gould, *Black Workers in White Unions: Job Dis-*

crimination in the United States (Ithaca, NY: Cornell Univ. Press, 1977); Nelson Lichtenstein, "Uneasy Partners: Walter Reuther, the United Automobile Workers and the Civil Rights Movement" (paper delivered at the annual meeting of the American Historical Association, Cincinnati, Dec. 28, 1988; in Zieger's possession); Herbert Hill, "Race, Ethnicity and Organized Labor: The Opposition to Affirmative Action," *New Politics* 1:2 (new series, Winter 1987): 31–82; Discussion of "Race, Ethnicity and Organized Labor" (symposium), ibid. 1:3 (Summer 1987): 22–71; Herbert Hill, "Myth-Making as Labor History: Herbert Gutman and the United Mine Workers of America," *International Journal of Politics, Culture and Society* 2:2 (Winter 1988): 132–200; "Labor, Race and the Gutman Thesis: Responses to Herbert Hill" (symposium), ibid. 2:3 (Spring 1989): 361–403.

10. Howell Raines, "Getting to the Heart of Dixie" (review of *Encyclopedia of Southern Culture*, ed. Charles Reagan Wilson and William Ferris), *New York Times Book Review*, Sept. 19, 1989, p. 3.

11. Joan Wallach Scott, *Gender and the Politics of History* (New York: Columbia Univ. Press, 1988).

1. Efficiency and Control

Labor Espionage in Southern Textiles

Gary M. Fink

The experience of both workers and managers at Fulton Bag and Cotton Mills in Atlanta during the early years of the twentieth century provides insight into the early efforts of southern textile manufacturers to gain shop floor control while at the same time resisting the development of vigorous trade unionism. An examination of labor-management relations at this large urban factory provides an unusual opportunity to examine the functions of detective agencies during periods of conflict as well as relatively peaceful industrial relations. Moreover, such an examination illustrates the close linkage that existed between labor espionage, welfare capitalism, and scientific management.[1]

Between the late 1890s and the mid-1920s, the twin juggernauts of scientific management and welfare capitalism fundamentally altered industrial relations in the United States. Although largely unrecognized, a third force, labor espionage, contributed significantly to that revolution. Students of American labor history long have recognized the presence of undercover operatives in the labor-management conflicts of the period, but they have considered it as more of an aberration than a serious component in the evolving pattern of industrial relations. Most scholars have assumed that undercover operatives functioned solely to disrupt union-organizing initiatives and to break strikes. Historians and more polemical investigators have generally seen labor espionage as a treacherous anti-union practice, but one that management reverted to only during periods of crisis when other means of subduing their employees had failed.[2]

David Montgomery's pathbreaking book, *The Fall of the House of Labor*, contains a penetrating analysis of the impact of the scientific management revolution on labor-management relations, but his only acknowledgment of American industry's use of espionage firms is contained in a passing reference to the role of Pinkerton detectives in the Homestead strike of 1892.[3] Daniel Nelson's important studies of scientific management also are silent on the subject.[4] Similarly, students of welfare capitalism and industrial paternalism, such as David Brody and Stuart D. Brandes, fail to tie labor espionage into the introduction of that new system of labor control.[5]

Nevertheless, the objectives of scientific management, welfare capitalism, and labor espionage were highly interrelated and often interchangeable: management autonomy in the workplace, efficiency in production, and the pacification of labor. Management often did not explicitly recognize this linkage, but labor espionage firms clearly did, and they geared their pitch to employers in terms of how they could assist their clients in achieving those objectives.

As a result by the early years of the twentieth century, a new-style detective agency had emerged that tailored its services to the needs of industrial management. Responding to the growing interest in efficiencies in production spurred by the scientific management movement, they employed undercover operatives who were not only skilled at infiltrating union organizations and gathering labor intelligence but were also "efficiency men" capable of suggesting ways of improving labor productivity while at the same time keeping an eye on shop floor supervisors and other low-level management personnel. This arrangement rationalized and stabilized the labor espionage business, making it essentially peace-proof, for during periods of relative labor-management harmony, undercover operatives simply emphasized "efficiency work."

Unlike their notorious nineteenth-century ancestors, these companies maintained a very low profile, and their operatives differed significantly from the crude, criminally inclined thugs of the nineteenth-century stereotype. These newer agents shared the American work and success ethic and clearly thought of themselves as loyal, upstanding citizens. Although most agents were working class in origin, a surprising number espoused upwardly mobile values and projected a distinctly middle-class perspective. Their educational backgrounds varied, but they were literate enough to write detailed, reasonably coherent reports. The vocabulary and writing style exhibited by some evidenced a relatively advanced level of education. Others were quite obviously well read. Most operatives were relatively stable, hard-working people, who shared the American dream and saw themselves as providing a valuable service.[6]

The great wave of industrial violence that accompanied the surge of labor organization at the turn of the century and American industry's continuing efforts to rationalize production through the introduction of scientific management deflected attention from these new developments that were subtly changing the nature of labor espionage. Between 1897 and 1904, union membership doubled and redoubled as the number of workers who joined affiliates of the American Federation of Labor soared from 260,000 to 1,676,200. With their plans to rationalize production threatened, employers counterattacked with a vigorous open-shop movement. Led by the National Association of Manufacturers, employers' organizations throughout the country vowed to resist union organization and to avoid collective bargaining. The result was an unprecedented period of labor-management conflict. When the smoke had cleared, the labor movement's great organizing initiative obviously had been halted. Nevertheless, although checked, the labor movement was not subdued. It held its gains among skilled workers, but the effort to expand organization into the unskilled, industrial sector had been stymied.

Meanwhile, spurred by the growth of industrial violence, the Congress, in 1912, created the U.S. Commission on Industrial Relations to study labor-management relations. Frank Walsh, a Kansas City labor lawyer with headquarters in New York, chaired the Commission, and Dr. Charles McCarthy, the Wisconsin reformer, directed the research effort from Commission offices in Chicago. McCarthy sent investigators to such trouble spots as the coalfields of Colorado, the garment centers of New York City, and the textile mills of Lawrence, Massachusetts, and Atlanta. After investigations were completed, Frank Walsh held public hearings to gather further testimony and to publicize the sources of labor-management tension.[7]

Commission investigators blamed labor espionage agencies for much of the violence. In a report entitled "Policing the Industry: How Does Violence Originate?" written shortly before the Commission ended its work, investigator Inis Weed concluded that the employment of labor spies "creates a feeling of distrust among employees, which is a natural forerunner of acts of violence."[8] Investigators found the use of spies to be so pervasive that McCarthy and Walsh assigned Daniel T. O'Regan, a Commission agent, to draft a proposed federal statute to regulate the activities of detective agencies.[9]

The involvement of private detective agencies in labor disputes, of course, was well known and had even become something of a political issue earlier. After conducting an investigation of the activities of such agencies in connection with the 1892 Homestead strike, a U.S. Senate Select Committee concluded that professional strikebreaking and espionage firms had created "an utterly vicious system" of labor-management relations.[10] Nevertheless, as the report of the Commission on Industrial Relations clearly documented, such practices had not only continued but had become even more insidious.[11]

Commission investigators, however, focused their attention on labor-management confrontations; consequently, they observed only one aspect of the work performed by labor espionage firms. These investigators probably would have been startled to learn that many companies used undercover operatives even during periods of peaceful labor-management relations. At Fulton Bag, owner Oscar Elsas and his managers employed espionage agents long after the initial labor agitation, for they found undercover reports of great value in monitoring shop-floor activity and in increasing the efficiency of their operations.

Although Fulton Bag had experimented with the use of undercover operatives earlier, the first documented record of labor espionage in the mills dates to the spring of 1914. Since the previous October, labor unrest at the facility had been growing steadily after the settlement of a short-lived, inconclusive strike. Subsequently, workers organized Local 886 of the United Textile Workers of America. Thereafter, the systematic discharge of workers active in the new union and management's refusal to adjust any of the grievances that had inspired the October strike led the union's rank-and-file members as well as some of its leaders to demand a showdown with the company.[12]

With a potential strike looming on the horizon, Oscar Elsas listened as H. N. Brown, vice president and general manager of the Railway Audit and Inspection Company, Inc. (RA&I), recommended putting experienced operatives inside his Fulton Bag and Cotton Mill Company plants to carry out "secret service work." The Philadelphia-based RA&I was a large, full service anti-labor agency that could furnish security guards, provide strikebreakers, conduct espionage operations, and install "efficiency men" in a factory of mill to make recommendations for improving productivity. Even before World War I, RA&I had become a major purveyor of strikebreaking and labor espionage services.[13]

Despite RA&I's impressive credentials, earlier experience with such firms had left the Fulton Mills' president skeptical. In the past, he complained, these companies had employed operatives who believed their jobs depended on keeping "trouble always brewing"; they simply were not suited to the purpose of quietly monitoring employee activities and had a tendency to stir up strife and create unnecessary trouble.[14] Nevertheless, Elsas told the general manager of the labor espionage agency to make a proposition covering a yearly service contract and they might have something to discuss.[15] Brown responded immediately. RA&I had two good weavers currently available and, he assured Elsas, the Atlanta industrialist would quickly discover that these "operatives work a little differently than those employed by the ordinary Detective Agency."[16]

RA&I used a sliding scale to set its rate for agents. Compensation for operatives was six dollars per day along with a small allowance for incidental expenses incurred while "knocking around" with mill employees. If an agent was employed for less than six months, the detective company added a transportation charge from Philadelphia to Atlanta and return, and for less than thirty days, the charge was seven dollars per day, transportation, and time en route both ways. The wages an agent earned while working alongside other employees would be deducted from the amount charged to the company. General manager Brown listed three references, two of whom owned textile mills in Augusta. The third had important Atlanta business interests.[17] As was his practice, Elsas checked the references and received a very positive report from his correspondents. This endorsement and the deteriorating labor-management relationship in his mills convinced him to utilize the RA&I operatives.[18]

The professionalism apparent in RA&I's approach to its business obviously influenced Elsas's decision to select it to do his espionage work. In fact, RA&I was chosen from among many such companies that operated in the South during the first quarter of the twentieth century. Southern capitalists actively shared information about these companies and the range and quality of services they provided. The larger companies, most headquartered in the North, maintained branch offices in major southern cities. Much of the secret service work done in the South, however, was performed by relatively small agencies consisting of one or two operatives who had left one of the larger firms—Burns, Pinkerton, RA&I—to establish their own business. Lower prices gave these often short-lived enterprises a competitive advantage over the older firms, but they were fragile concerns for which industrial peace and prosperity was no blessing. None of these smaller agencies—at least five of which were employed by Fulton Bag before the end of World War I—were among those in the lists that the Commission on Industrial Relations compiled.[19]

Unlike most of these smaller firms, RA&I adapted the newest technology to its enterprise. Shortly after the outbreak of the strike at Fulton Bag and Cotton Mills in May 1914, for example, RA&I district manager E. G. Myers approached Elsas with the idea of maintaining electronic surveillance of union headquarters and the hotel room of UTWA organizer, Charles Miles. Elsas agreed, and RA&I operatives placed a transmitter in the union meeting hall wired to a Dictograph machine in a small room in a nearby building. The microphone in Miles's room was connected to a Dictograph in an adjoining room. The hotel room "bug" worked well, but background noises, electric fans, and a variety of other problems reduced the effectiveness of the device in the union hall. Moreover, the transmitter had an unfortunate habit of squealing. Despite these problems, RA&I agents eventually provided Elsas with detailed transcripts of union meetings as well as the confidential conversations of union organizers.[20]

But on Tuesday morning, June 9, shortly after organizer Miles had called the daily union meeting to order, the Dictograph transmitter emitted a piercing shriek. Outraged union men quickly located the device and began tracing the wire. Alerted, the RA&I agents hurriedly packed up their equipment and abandoned the listening room. Upon returning to their hotel room, they contacted their Atlanta supervisor who told them to leave town immediately. Atlanta police detectives sympathetic to the strikers had already traced the wire to a small retail shop where, within a few hours of the discovery of the device, they were busily leafing through purchase orders in an attempt to identify the wiremen. Meanwhile, the two agents, after first stopping at nearby Marietta, quickly concluded "that Marietta was too close for our good health," and continued on to Cartersville, Georgia, where they awaited instructions.[21]

The undercover operatives employed by RA&I also differed dramatically from their nineteenth-century counterparts in the range of skills they brought to their tasks. Most of their agents working in southern textiles were skilled operatives who could perform virtually every job in a mill, but most identified themselves as loomfixers or weavers. Because of the nature of their job, loomfixers wandered freely throughout the plant, thus facilitating the task of gathering intelligence. For their part, weavers were traditionally among the most militant workers in the textile work force, making a weaving room an ideal place to identify troublemakers and sniff out potential problems.

The typical undercover agent in southern textiles had few prior contacts inside or outside the mill. At the Fulton Bag and Cotton Mill Company new agents contacted company president Oscar Elsas or general manager Gordon Johnstone immediately upon arriving in Atlanta. A meeting was then arranged at Elsas's private residence where he and Johnstone instructed the agent concerning the type of information they wanted. Elsas and Johnstone were the only people in the company aware of the agent's identity, and all communicated through assigned numbers. Thus, Johnstone, the principal contact for undercover operatives, was identified as Operative No. 20.[22]

These security measures reduced the likelihood of accidental or unconscious exposure of an undercover operative. They also facilitated performance evaluations of shop-floor supervisors, but they complicated the life of the agent. The task of gathering information and identifying potential agitators required the operative to socialize on and off the job and often to initiate provocative conversations. Both activities attracted the attention of shop-floor supervisors who, once their suspicions were aroused, might conclude that the new hires were union agitators. Operatives who pursued their task too aggressively could soon find themselves discharged. One indiscreet RA&I operative was fired his first day on the job, and two others did not finish their first week before being dismissed as union agitators.[23]

Discharged operatives sometimes had the option of identifying themselves as union sympathizers and continuing their work on the outside, their dismissal investing them with a degree of legitimacy among strikers and union officials. For reasons only too obvious, most operatives preferred the more relaxed life on the outside, although a continual shortage of operatives greatly increased the value of those who were also skilled textile workers. Moreover, outside operatives were useful primarily during periods of labor unrest and strikes.

Considering the number of hours they put in each day, effective inside operatives needed a union as much as the workers they were betraying. Agents at Fulton Bag typically worked from 6:00 A.M. to 6:00 P.M., Monday through Friday. They worked half days on Saturday and normally had Sundays off. The end of daily mill hours, however, did not mean the end of the workday for these undercover operatives. After regular work hours, they socialized with workers from the mill, picking up whatever information might be of value to mill management. They made lodging arrangements at boardinghouses patronized by millworkers whom management viewed with suspicion. One agent, for example, was lodged with a group of weavers imported from a nearby mill to keep the Fulton Bag mills operating during a strike until permanent weavers could be recruited. With some justification, management worried about the loyalty of these workers.[24]

Weekends provided no respite for the hard-working labor spies. Saturday afternoons and Sundays were ideal times to socialize, expand contacts, and skillfully direct conversations into areas that might yield useful information. Each evening, usually after everyone else had gone to bed, the agent wrote a long, detailed report of the day's undercover activities. After agency personnel had typed up these reports, they were sent directly to the company employing the operative. Daily operative reports averaged one to two single spaced pages, although they varied in length and content with the personality, intelligence, and language proficiency of individual agents.

The activities of Operative 457, who had secured work as a weaver, illustrate the extent to which some agents were prepared to go in completing their assignments. Suspecting that agitators were at work in one of the folding rooms, No. 457 requested a transfer to cloth work, but owing to a shortage of weavers and a surplus of cloth workers, the transfer was denied. Undaunted, the dedicated agent deliberately slashed his thumb, and, after being treated in the infirmary, gained reassignment to the cloth room. Some time later, responding to reports that oilers were idle several hours each day, management instructed him to use his injury to request an oiler's job. In his daily report, Operative 457 noted that the thumb had pretty much healed. Ever the masochist, however, he said he would "squeeze it and cut it somehow or other before Thursday, making it too sore for the weaving job . . . then there won't be any suspicion, and I can knock a big piece of skin off of my thumb, which, when dressed, will leave me unable to tie a knot, and will then have a good excuse for . . . oilers job." But such dedication had its limits, and when it came time to agitate the wound, No. 457 confessed a loss of courage.[25]

Clearly it took special people to be effective undercover operatives. Not only did they work fourteen to fifteen hours a day, seven days a week, but they had to cope with the continual stress of being exposed as a management spy or mistaken for a labor agitator. Along with a variety of industrial skills, the successful agent also needed both oral and verbal communication facility, physical stamina, a keen understanding of human nature, and the psychological toughness and moral insentience to live in a world of endless betrayal.

Beyond any psychic satisfaction such work may have brought, there were material rewards. Inside operatives earned a regular wage as weavers, loomfixers, or the like—usually the better paying jobs in the mill—along with a second wage as undercover operatives. Moreover, they could save much of the money they earned. With the exception of room and board, most of their incidental expenses were paid, and they had little time to spend money. Many of these operatives dreamed of opening their own agencies while others found possibilities for advancement within the agency of their employment.[26]

RA&I employed a variety of undercover operatives at Fulton Bag before and during World War I. Collectively, they comprised a diverse and intriguing group, belying the nineteenth-century stereotype of the labor spy as thug or cynic, and many brought special talents, skills, and ambitions to their tasks.

Most agents had a "hook" they used to gain credibility among workers and entree to the union leadership. An English accent was one of the more effective ruses. A new worker who identified himself as an English worker won almost immediate acceptance from co-workers and union leaders alike. Perhaps native-born workers could not imagine employers or detective agencies using foreign workers to spy on them, or they simply assumed English workers were more faithful to their own class interests than were their American counterparts. One agent used his singing talent to become the union's song leader and to ingratiate himself to union leaders; another was a lay preacher who claimed the title of "reverend"; and a third was a dance teacher who said he was working in the mill in order to save enough money to open a studio.[27]

Still others exhibited a wide range of attributes useful to their work.

One agent had a youthful enough appearance to pass as a child laborer, his seeming youth and innocence providing an effective cover.[28] Another, R. W. Oglesby, was a heavy drinker who converted an unfortunate habit into an employment asset. Using the general manager of the nearby Exposition Mill as a reference, Oglesby applied for undercover work at Fulton Bag while a strike was in progress in the fall of 1914. Albert Johnson, Exposition's general manager, wrote Elsas a positive, if somewhat peculiar, endorsement. Along with other attributes, he noted that Oglesby "seems to stand in with the burglars, yeggs, and poor room bums, and probably does a good deal of drinking with them."[29] Drinking was Oglesby's forte. He regularly took susceptible union leaders out for a night on the town, got them roaring drunk, and then pumped them for information about union plans and tactics. Then he returned to his boarding house and wrote surprisingly coherent reports on what he had learned.[30]

At other times Oglesby sought to have union leaders jailed for disturbing the peace. On one such occasion, he reported that he had gotten Local 886 president W. E. Fleming "so drunk he could not walk, and he was disorderly but Officer Whitley stood for it and allowed Murphrey [another union official] to take Fleming home." Similarly, he tried to keep union pickets "tanked up on whiskey and beer to make them more offensive to the public and the aggressors in various disputes." Perhaps as a result of the many hours he spent in bars and taverns, Oglesby had good contacts with a petty criminal element with which some strikers who lived in and around the mill district had become associated. Through Elsas and Johnstone, Oglesby fed Atlanta police a constant stream of information about planned robberies, the location of stolen goods, and violations of city ordinances involving prostitution, liquor, and gambling. Most of this was done so as to discredit striking workers and their union.[31]

Although mill managers obsessively concerned themselves with the morality of their employees, particularly females, Elsas and Johnstone willingly used undercover operatives to compromise union organizers and sympathizers sexually. In one such case they suspected a company informer named Lillie Priest of being a double agent. Hoping to learn the truth, company officials gave undercover Operative 429 the task of seducing Miss Priest and discovering her true loyalties. Posing as a union sympathizer, No. 429 finagled an introduction and arranged several meetings with the suspect. Miss Priest, however, had an irritating habit of bringing a friend along on all dates, thus frustrating the operative's designs. Nevertheless, after several conversations, the undercover operative was convinced that Priest had ties to local labor organizers and would prove a valuable source of information once he was able to gain her complete confidence. The shrewd Miss Priest, however, continued to avoid Operative 429's elaborate entrapments. The frustration is evident in his October 1, 1916, report: "I met Lillie Priest and her chum Miss Annison at 5 P.M. I was compelled through circumstances to entertain them both which left me no room for conversation alone with Miss Priest." The operative left Priest and her friend at 8:45 P.M., telling the subject he would drop her a line when he wanted to see her again, but would "no longer tolerate having a third party in [their] company again." She said she would move near the center of the city, and they would be alone on future occasions.[32] Operative 429's recall to Philadelphia a few days later ended his liaison with Miss Priest, her true loyalties still unknown.

Efforts to discredit John Callen, however, were much less subtle than those used in the Lillie Priest affair. Callen, a Methodist minister and textile union organizer, previously had been a target of several efforts to destroy his effectiveness, including an arrest in Columbus, Georgia, as a German spy. A female agent identified only as Mrs. G. Newton (Operative No. 2) was ordered to take a room in the Atlanta boarding house in which Callen had lived since the dismissal of the spy charges against him. Mrs. Newton's assignment was to establish a relationship with Callen. Previous experience, however, suggested that discrediting the prudent organizer would not be easy. Mrs. Newton observed that such measures as planting dynamite and whiskey in his room had already been tried. While she doubted such maneuvers would work, she promised to employ them as a last resort. "I prefer incriminating him with a woman," Mrs. Newton stated, and she described her plan with surprising candor: "I am thoroughly convinced that it will not be a hard matter to get acquainted with a man [of] his type and nine times out of ten our plans work out to perfection when the operation is properly worked." Newton hoped to talk Callen into taking her into Tennessee where authorities would be alerted to arrest him as soon as he crossed the state border. She would then supply the necessary evidence to convict him. "It may require however a tremendous intimacy with him here," she declared, "and after he sees he can confide in me I am certain from previous experience I had that should he be a man who is strong for the women I will be able to trap him up."[33] Clearly, then, these anti-labor espionage firms were as resourceful as they were unscrupulous in their efforts to gather intelligence or discredit an effective union organizer. Neither morality, legality, nor personal feelings could interfere with an agent in pursuit of his or her assigned objectives.

Ironically, however, the activities of these nefarious undercover operatives sometimes benefited the workers against whom they were directed. Although these agents spent little time worrying about the welfare of workers, their activities nevertheless sometimes improved factory conditions. Following the Triangle Shirt Waist Factory fire in 1911, most undercover operatives were especially sensitive to safety hazards and frequently made suggestions on how to avoid accidents in the mills. They reported on blocked fire escapes, unsafe elevators, and dangerous machinery. Agent 185, for example, recommended that smoking be restricted in areas containing combustible materials, and another agent suggested that safety-first reminders be posted around the mills, especially in areas adjacent to dangerous machinery.[34]

Similarly, spy operatives reported on unsanitary conditions both inside and outside the mills. Boardinghouse conditions attracted special attention. Operative G. J. Manuel, reporting during the 1914–15 strike, found that the quality of boardinghouse food and the dirty condition of the rooms he and his cohorts had been assigned so upset several imported weavers that they were threatening to leave or join the union. Manuel clearly empathized with the disgruntled workers. He noted that even most workers who had not joined the strike believed the union was providing better housing than the company. Meanwhile, accounts of unsanitary conditions inside the mills laced the reports of undercover operatives. Filthy, "repulsively smelling" toilets were often cited, along with the need for improved ventilation and better climate control.[35]

Working incognito beside regular mill employees, undercover operatives suffered the same supervisory abuse as other workers and clearly did not like it. Undercover agents' reports contain numerous complaints about the inappropriate conduct of shop floor supervisors and overseers. An operative working as a loomfixer found much objectionable in the work of the second hand in the card room, who was a "chronic grouch," while another agent reported that the overseer in the rope department "certainly keeps his help working, [but] I doubt very much whether the results are any better from his bull-dozing methods, which I have seen him use on three different occasions to-day." Such conduct on the part of supervisory personnel, he observed, precipitated most strikes. Experience proves, he said, "that most textile strikes are not deliberately planned in advance, but that it is usually [the result of] some little dissatisfaction . . . coupled with a lack of tact in proper handling of the situation on the part of Over-seer, Sup't, and possible lack of fore-sight on the part of Management."[36]

Operatives also reported instances of sexual harassment of female employees by foremen, overseers, and fellow workers. Charges that department heads, supervisors, and the like were forcing their attentions on female employees were often relayed to management. The extent of this problem was revealed during the 1914–15 strike when an agent reported that a female organizer, Mrs. E. B. Smith, had spent a day taking testimony from sexually harassed women. Another agent reported that the "men here have no respect for women whatever. They seem to think that women are for them to do with as they please. The men are the dirtiest talking men I have ever met."[37]

Hoping to discourage such behavior, mill managers suspended some employees for harassing women verbally and fired others for abusive behavior.[38] Nevertheless, at least one agent urged restraint in exercising such disciplinary action. More inclined to blame the victim than the offender, he argued that women often initiated or encouraged flirtations. "Since I have been here, I have been invited to accompany so and so and hardly pass one that she doesn't smile or jest with me, and as a man of their society it would be hard to resist their temptations and might insult them."[39] Another agent worried about the attire of the black women who worked in the mills as sweepers and scrubbers. These women, he observed, "could wear more clothing while at work without hurting them. One in particular, in Mill No. 1 card room, wore so little, that at times, she was a very good imitation of 'September Morn,' or rather 'September Night.'"[40]

Management took agents' reports of potential health and safety hazards seriously, and Oscar Elsas often instructed his general manager to correct the problem. Similarly, mill foremen and superintendents who were accused of abusive treatment of employees were sometimes reprimanded or discharged. For example, when Operative 457 reported that supervisors in the cloth room were verbally abusing employees, Oscar Elsas wrote "This should be stopped" on the margin before passing the report along to Gordon Johnstone. To be sure, corrective actions were clearly motivated more from a desire to increase productivity and to pacify labor than from a regard for workers' welfare. No matter how abusive a foreman was, if productivity in his department was satisfactory, he was likely to escape disciplinary action.[41]

Ultimate priorities were obvious not only in the operatives' determination to undermine any effort at labor organization but also in their effort to secure total management hegemony over the workplace. Agents often commented on the amount of work time being lost as a result of employees reporting late, taking unauthorized breaks during the day, and leaving early. These agents made it clear, moreover, that such conduct on the part of employees was deliberate and self-conscious. An operative working during the winter of 1914–15 reported worker reaction to a notice posted by management instructing employees to remain in the work area until the factory whistle blew. "One of them said she had worked here nine years and it was the first time any one had ever said anything to her about going out before the whistle blew." It was also suggested that a gong be installed in the cutting room that would be rung at set times, "as they are very tardy in beginning work and leave off work very early."[42]

An agent's report three years later suggests the degree to which management failed to impose time discipline upon the work force. Shortly after Operative 185 began work at Fulton Bag, an employee named Mildred informed him that he "should quit 10 minutes before 12. That they always did." He noted that "at 5:30 we closed shop, foreman had his overalls off and ready to go."[43] A few days later this agent reported that time was being lost by employees lunching between the hours of 9:30 and 10:00. "Negroes are sent out for Coca Cola and about quarter to twelve they prepare to go to lunch. The same at 5:30, washing and dressing to go home and at twenty minutes of 6:00."[44] Other forms of resistance to management imperatives were also evident. Informal production limits existed in many areas of the mill, apparently with the acquiescence of some shop foremen. An agent working the cutting and folding room noted that the machines could cut a good many more bags than currently was being done, but the women who operated the machines would "not put in more than Co asks and never have, for fear the Co will change the amount." As a result, they often shut their machines down well before closing time.

All of this was done, the agent reported, with the knowledge and tacit approval of the foreman.[45]

The personal habits of mill employees was another matter to which undercover operatives devoted considerable space in their reports. Drinking on and off the job was a matter of concern, and the drinking habits of supervisors attracted particular attention. Reporting on a new shop floor supervisor, an undercover operative noted that the man drank a good deal, "but I never saw him the worse for it." The new supervisor, he observed, was experienced, had a good understanding of the "vogaries" of human nature, and had the respect of those working under him, but at 6:30 every evening he can [be] found lined up at the bar of Johnson's saloon at Decatur St."[46] Another agent reported on a conversation with a loomfixer who declared that he took a flask of whiskey to work with him each day. He said he simply could not get through the day without it. Still another undercover operative, a heavy drinker himself who spent much of his time in the bars and taverns of the mill district, regularly reported on the drinking habits of mill employees—both shop-floor workers and their supervisors.[47]

Unfamiliar with Atlanta customs, many of these agents were bewildered by the seeming addiction to Coca-Cola of so many Atlantans. "I have never seen people so fond of Coca Cola as they are in this mill," reported Operative 457. "They cannot get along without it; they long for it as some people do for beer and whiskey. They spend nearly as much for Coca Cola, 'Dope,' as they call it, as they do for food."[48]

Fulton Bag's managers had their own unquenchable thirst, an insatiable appetite for knowledge about the habits and activities of their employees. They were especially eager to learn what their employees thought of them. The reports from undercover operatives could not have been reassuring. One agent, who solicited opinions from workers shortly after his arrival at the mills, was surprised at the level of animosity that mill employees voiced. "It was rather singular," he observed, "that I did not strike even one man with a good word for the management." A few employees, he said, had expressed the opinion that "mill officials were so crooked they could hide behind a corkscrew or go through a barrel of fish hooks without getting caught." Another observed that "any man with any grit at all, left as soon as he found how the mill was run."[49] Another agent generally agreed with this assessment. "Nobody ever says anything good about Fulton Bag," he said. Most of the workers' complaints focused on the often arrogant and sometimes ruthless general manager, Gordon Johnstone, who raised the ire of mill laborers more than did company president Oscar Elsas.[50]

Undercover operatives did not hesitate to tell management things it would rather not hear. Fulton Bag used an employment contract under which the company withheld one week's pay and required employees to give one week's notice of their intention to quit. Their failure to do so resulted in the forfeiture of the withheld wages. Although Elsas cherished the contract and vowed never to relinquish it, at least three different operatives concluded it was causing more trouble than it was worth. In the most critical evaluation of the contract, Operative 457 explained that workers had learned how to manipulate the contract to their advantage. A worker who wanted his money immediately simply began loudly praising the union and advocating organization. He was immediately discharged and paid off without having to give five days' notice. This procedure, the operative argued, not only kept union agitation alive but actually contributed to the turnover problem it was supposed to help solve. Several agents pointed to general manager Johnstone's brusque and arrogant behavior as a source of discord. Thus Operative 185 noted that Johnstone's open criticism of a newly installed bonus system was undermining the effectiveness of the incentive plan. A short time after the submission of this report, Elsas replaced Johnstone with Frank Neely, a formally trained scientific manager.[51]

Along with a competency in breaking strikes and gathering intelligence, these spies performed a variety of tasks that were generally subsumed under the label of "efficiency work." Though they lacked any formal training in scientific management, they clearly had a familiarity with the concepts of efficiency and management control associated with that movement. Much of that knowledge was practically acquired. Because of the nature of their occupation, these operatives typically had worked in a great many textile mills, North and South, where they had observed a variety of alternative methods of organizing work and managing employees. Moreover, they were skilled workers with a wealth of knowledge about production techniques in almost every department of a textile mill.

Ultimately, the ability to do efficiency work became an important consideration to many of the firms that employed labor espionage agencies, and it did much to stabilize and rationalize the labor spy business. When, for example, in 1914 a newly organized agency approached Oscar Elsas about putting an undercover operative into his mills, Elsas responded that he would want a man capable of reporting "not only to the possibility of union disturbances, but also efficiency work, etc."

By temperament and training, Oscar Elsas, earlier than most textile manufacturers in the South, subscribed to the tenets of scientific management. He had studied management methods at the Massachusetts Institute of Technology, which he attended for three years before transferring to the Georgia Institute of Technology where he became a member of that institution's first graduating class. Elsas then studied textile production methods and traveled extensively in Europe. Meanwhile, his brother, Benjamin, first vice-president of Fulton Bag and Cotton Mills, had studied efficiency methods at Harvard.[52]

Among the suggestions made to management by undercover operatives at Fulton Bag, many involved the rearrangement of equipment and machinery on the mill floor to reduce the strain on employees and thus ultimately to increase productivity. Operative 470, for example, suggested that the bobbin holder on the cone machine be raised six to eight inches. This change, he observed, would eliminate much of the stooping required of the women working in the twine room.[53] Another agent recommended a reorganization of the cloth room to "increase output." He suggested that the skid tables, which were located across the room from the cutters and folders, be moved to a more convenient location. He also recommended that folding and cutting machinery be cleaned and serviced more regularly and that more suitable wrenches of various sizes be provided.[54]

Operative 457, whose own productivity had been compromised by the continual snapping of warp yarn, concluded that the primary problem was a lack of humidity in the weave room and offered many ways of correcting the problem. At times this operative's advice was quite technical. In a report that reflected the range of experience he brought to his task, he noted that a woman working in the spinning room was running eight sides of waste yarn and could not keep their ends pieced up half the time. He asked her if they creeled it single or double, and she said single. He noted that he had seen the same class of yarn creeled double in mills in which he had worked, and it spun just as good as the better grades of cotton: "Instead of sluber size roping, the card is to intermediate size, which raises the cost in the carding department, but reduces the waste in spinning, as it takes less sides to get the same production in creeling double with intermediate size roping then it does when creeling double with sluber roping, and the increase in the cost in the carding department, and decrease in spinning, will about balance."[55]

After five weeks on the job, Operative 470 reviewed mill improvements made since he had arrived. He reported that waste had declined and production had increased. Overseers were attending to business with less socializing among the bosses, and machinery was in better shape, allowing the loomfixers to sit down and rest on occasion. While 470's assessment was hardly disinterested, management had ready means of testing its accuracy. Moreover, the agent himself was inclined to give a new supervisor the credit for much of the improvement.[56]

An examination of industrial relations at Fulton Bag reveals much about the character of southern textile workers and the role of the labor espionage in subduing them. The willingness of some workers to operate undercover as management informants provides another chapter in the long history of American working class disunity. One student of labor spy activities concluded that most such operatives were tricked into becoming spies and then, after being so compromised, were locked into the system.[57] In contrast, most undercover operatives employed at Fulton Bag were recruited from the work force, but they felt little sense of remorse about what they were doing. They not only identified with management but clearly thought themselves superior to the workers with whom they associated. Moreover, the dedication, determination, and creativity with which these agents went about their tasks belied any sense of reluctance or shame. Quite simply, they were ambitious, opportunistic, and upwardly mobile people on the lookout for the best chance.

The activities of undercover operatives varied greatly from time to time and place to place. When they were not ferreting out union organizers or sympathizers, they reported on the performance of shop-floor foremen or lower-level supervisors, critiqued company policies, observed the implementation of new management procedures, and made suggestions for improving productivity. Meanwhile, they gathered intelligence on worker attitudes, reported on the habits of employees both on and off the job, watched for employee pilfering, reported on the condition of machinery, noted unsafe or unsanitary working and living conditions, and warned their employers about conditions in the workplace, such as abusive overseers or sexual harassment, that could cause future trouble.

The manner in which labor espionage activities were carried on at Fulton Bag appears typical of the industry in the South. Oscar Elsas corresponded with officials of other southern firms, sharing information on the qualities and capabilities of espionage companies. Company managers employing these espionage firms thought they were effective. Oscar Elsas was a hardheaded businessman who did not spend money frivolously, yet he spent thousands of dollars each year on "secret service work." These espionage activities were carried on not only in his Atlanta mills but also in Fulton Bag plants in New Orleans, St. Louis, New York, and elsewhere.

At Fulton Bag at least, management got its money's worth. The employment of undercover operatives had a chilling effect on labor organization. At Fulton Bag, everyone knew spies were at work. The resulting climate of suspicion and fear made union recruitment extremely difficult and forced union organizers to function so secretly that worker involvement in the union-building process was virtually precluded.[58]

Although the anti-union activities of espionage agents had the greatest notoriety and were the easiest to evaluate, efficiency work, over time, had a greater impact on industrial relations in the United States. Throughout this period of bitter ship-floor conflict, employers resorted to scientific management to wrest from workers the secrets of their skills so as to enable them to routinize work and increase both productvitiy and shop floor control. While Fulton Bag espionage operatives were not scientific managers, they were very much involved in the transfer of knowledge from labor to management. Most undercover operatives were highly skilled workers and intelligent observers who told management everything they knew. In terms of the evolution of industrial relations, these co-opted workers served as transitional figures in the shift from worker control of production in the nineteenth century to management hegemony over the workplace in the twentieth century. By the second quarter of the new century, they, themselves, were being co-opted by professionally trained management consultants. With the great wave of union organization during the 1930s, espionage agencies reverted to form, breaking strikes and busting heads.[59]

Notes

1. The Fulton Bag and Cotton Mills papers provide unusually full documenta-
    tion of employment practices and labor policies. For a description of the
    collection, see Robert C. McMath, Jr., "History by a Graveyard: The Fulton
    Bag and Cotton Mills Records," *Labor's Heritage* 1 (April 1989): 4–9.
2. Rhodri Jeffreys-Jones characterized such agents as incipient entrepreneurs
    who identified a need and provided a valuable service for their employers
    ("Profit over Class: A Study of Industrial Espionage," *Journal of American
    Studies* 6:3 (1972): 233–48). In a more recent study, Charles Hyde examined
    labor espionage activities in the copper mines of Michigan and concluded
    that the companies that employed labor spies largely wasted their money
    ("Undercover and Underground: Labor Spies and Mine Management in the
    Early Twentieth Century," *Business History Review* 60 [Spring 1986]: 1–27).
    While concentrating on legislative efforts to outlaw such practices in Wis-
    consin, Darryl Holter found espionage activities an insidious practice in the
    industrial relations of that state ("Labor Spies and Union Busting in Wiscon-
    sin, 1890–1940," *Wisconsin Magazine of History* 68 [Summer 1985]:
    243–65). The Pinkerton and Burns agencies are the best known, and their
    activities, especially during the nineteenth century, have come to symbolize
    the role of espionage firms. See, for example, Frank Morn, *The Eye That
    Never Sleeps: A History of the Pinkerton National Detective Agency* (Bloom-
    ington: Indiana Univ. Press, 1982), and Gene Caesar, *The Incredible Detec-
    tive: The Biography of William J. Burns* (Englewood Cliffs, NJ: Prentice-
    Hall, 1968).
3. David Montgomery, *The Fall of the House of Labor: The Workplace, the
    State and American Labor Activism, 1865–1925* (Cambridge: Cambridge
    Univ. Press, 1987), 38–39.
4. Daniel Nelson, *Managers and Workers: Origins of the New Factory System
    in the United States, 1880–1920* (Madison: Univ. of Wisconsin Press, 1975);
    Milton J. Nadworny, *Scientific Management and the Unions, 1900–1932: A
    Historical Analysis* (Cambridge, MA: Harvard Univ. Press, 1955).
5. David Brody, *Workers in Industrial America: Essays on the Twentieth-
    Century Struggle* (New York: Oxford Univ. Press, 1980), ch. 2; Stuart
    Brandes, *American Welfare Capitalism: 1880–1940* (Chicago: Univ. of Chi-
    cago Press, 1976).
6. These generalizations are largely drawn from the information about some 40
    undercover operatives employed by the Fulton Bag and Cotton Mills Co.
    from 1914 through 1918 appearing in the Fulton Bag and Cotton Mills
    Company Papers, Georgia Institute of Technology Archives, Atlanta, Boxes
    1–11 (hereafter cited as Fulton Bag Papers). One of these operatives, a
    former Socialist, penetrated the Atlanta Socialist movement and engaged his
    unsuspecting comrades in lengthy discussions of Marxist principles, im-
    pressing them with his familiarity with radical literature. (Operative 429,
    Aug. 22–Oct.7, 1916, Fulton Bag Papers).
7. Graham Adams, Jr., *Age of Industrial Violence, 1910–15: The Activities and*

Findings of the United States Commission on Industrial Relations (New York: Columbia Univ. Press, 1966).

8. U.S. Commission on Industrial Relations Papers, State Historical Society of Wisconsin, Microfilm, P71–1683 (cited hereafter as CIR Papers, Wisconsin).

9. Ibid.

10. Report of U.S. Special Senate Committee, 1892, p. 13, quoted in CIR Papers, Wisconsin, P71–1683.

11. CIR Papers, Wisconsin, P71–1683.

12. Report of Alexander M. Daly, July 31, 1914, Papers of the U.S. Commission on Industrial Relations, RG 174, National Archives; report of John B. Colpoys and Robert M. McWade, commissioners of conciliation, Aug. 18, 1915, U.S. Mediation and Conciliation Service Records, RG 180, National Archives.

13. Weed, "Preliminary Report," CIR Papers, National Archives. In the years to come, it would rival the Burns and Pinkerton agencies in that line of work. By the 1930s, investigators for the LaFollette Civil Liberties Committee identified the Railway Audit and Inspection Company as one of the major labor espionage firms in the nation. See Leo Huberman, *The Labor Spy Racket* (New York: Modern Age Books, 1937), 34, 53–55, 102.

14. Oscar Elsas to H. N. Brown, May 15, 1914, Fulton Bag Papers.

15. Ibid.

16. Brown to Elsas, May 18, 19, 1914, Fulton Bag Papers.

17. Ibid.

18. Elsas to Wickersham, Raworth, and Thomas, May 22, 1914; Wickersham to Elsas, May 23, 1914; Thomas to Elsas, May 23, 1914, Fulton Bag Papers.

19. "Detective Agencies," CIR Papers, National Archives.

20. Operative 10, May 30–June 9, 1914, Fulton Bag Papers.

21. Operative 10, June 9, 10, 1914, Fulton Bag Papers.

22. The Operative Reports in the Fulton Bag Papers provide numerous examples of the detailed instructions given new undercover operatives.

23. See, for example, Operative HAH, June 1–11, 1914, and Operative HJD, June 1–10, 1914, Fulton Bag Papers. Boxes 1 and 2 of the Operative Reports contain numerous examples of such problems.

24. Operative GJM, June 7–July 29, 1914, Fulton Bag Papers.

25. Operative 457, Nov. 21, 1914–Jan. 31., 1915, Fulton Bag Papers.

26. An especially notable example of the latter is Harry Preston, who as an undercover operative during a 1914–15 strike at Fulton Bag infiltrated the local textile union and ultimately became something of an advisor to United Textile Workers of America president John Golden. A few years later he was appointed southern district manager of the Railroad Audit and Inspection Company in Atlanta. See Gary M. Fink, "Labor Espionage and Southern Textiles: The Fulton Bag and Cotton Mill Company Strike of 1914–15," *Labor's Heritage* 1 (April 1989): 11–35.

27. See the reports of Operatives 16, 115, 185, 429, and 457, Fulton Bag Papers.

28. Operative GJM, June 7, July 29, 1914, Fulton Bag Papers.

29. Albert Johnson to Oscar Elsas, Dec. 17, 1914, Fulton Bag Papers.
30. Operative 16, Dec. 27, 1914–Feb. 5, 1915, Fulton Bag Papers.
31. Ibid.
32. Operative 429, Oct. 1, 1916, Fulton Bag Papers.
33. Operative 2, June 7, 8, 1918, Fulton Bag Papers.
34. See, particularly, the reports of Operatives 185, 429, 457, and 470, Fulton Bag Papers.
35. Operative GJM, June 7–July 29, 1914, Operative 115, June 17–Dec. 9, 1914, Fulton Bag Papers.
36. Operative 457, Dec. 18, 1914, Operative 429, Sept. 9, 1916, Fulton Bag Papers.
37. See the reports of Operative HJD, June 2, 1914, Operative HAH, June 2, 1914, Operative 115, July 8, 1914, Operative 457, Dec.14, 19, 1914, Fulton Bag Papers; *Journal of Labor*, June 12, 1914.
38. See the reports of Operatives HDJ, June 2, 1914, HAH June 2, 1914, Operative 115, July 8, 1914, and Operative 457, Dec. 14, 19, 1914, Fulton Bag Papers.
39. Operative 185, April 30, 1918, Fulton Bag Papers.
40. Operative 470, Aug. 14, 1914, Fulton Bag Papers.
41. Operative 457, Dec. 17, 1914, Fulton Bag Papers. Initialed comments such as this on the margins of operative reports reflect the seriousness with which management received these disclosures. Elsas often instructed his general manager to correct the problems that occasioned his marginal comments.
42. Operative 457, Dec. 16, 1914, Fulton Bag Papers.
43. Operative 185, April 16, 1918, Fulton Bag Papers.
44. Ibid., April 26, 1918.
45. Ibid., May 3, 1918.
46. Operative 470, Sept. 5, 1914, Fulton Bag Papers.
47. Operative 457, Jan. 30, 1915, Fulton Bag Papers. See also the reports of Operative 16.
48. Operative 457, Nov. 26, 1914, Fulton Bag Papers.
49. Ibid., Nov. 21, 1914; Operative 470, Sept. 5, 1914; Operative 429, Sept. 19, 1916; Operative 185, May 22, 1918, Fulton Bag Papers.
50. Operative 457, Dec. 14, 1914, Fulton Bag Papers.
51. Operative 185, April 20, May 7, 1918, Fulton Bag Papers.
52. Elsas to Day's Detective Agency, Sept. 4, 1914, Fulton Bag Papers.
53. Operative 470, Aug. 14, 1914, Fulton Bag Papers.
54. Operative 185, April 26, 1918, Fulton Bag Papers.
55. Operative 457, Dec. 22, 1914, Fulton Bag Papers.
56. Ibid.
57. Huberman, *Labor Spy Racket*, ch. 3.
58. Cf. Hyde, "Undercover and Underground," 1–27.
59. Kim Dawson, "From Paternalism to Scientific Management" (M.A. thesis, Georgia Institute of Technology, 1989).

2. Textile Workers and Historians

Robert H. Zieger

Two central questions have occupied serious investigators of twentieth-century southern textile workers: what has been the distinctive character of the culture of the millworkers?; and why has unionism been so unsuccessful among them? Recent historical scholarship speaks eloquently to the first question, with a prize-winning book's controversial portrayal of a rich and humane Piedmont-wide community in place of the desolate and employer-dominated mill villages of much previous scholarship serving as the basis for spirited reexamination. On the second question, the recent literature also suggests revision, but of a more somber kind. The failures of organized labor and the successes of anti-unionism in the South once seemed the exception to national patterns of industrial relations. Now, however, in a period of chronic union diminishment, the experience of the textile South seems prototypical rather than exceptional. The mill villages themselves, whether seen as prisons or inspiring communities, were clearly a unique part of a distinct regional past. However, as a once-powerful labor movement recedes from even its traditional centers of the strength in other regions, the southern textile industry's defeat of organized labor seems as American as apple pie.

The centrality of textiles to the economic life, social character, and historiography of the twentieth-century South is obvious. With its modern origins in the post-Reconstruction determination of southern boosters to modernize their region and exploit its abundant natural resources and generous supplies of cheap labor, cotton textiles expanded slowly in the late nineteenth century and then with increasing tempo around the turn of the century, primarily along a three-hundred mile corridor extending from south-central Virginia along the Piedmont regions of the Carolinas and into northern Georgia and Alabama. By the 1920s, when southern spindlage surpassed that of the northern textile industry, Piedmont mills had long since established regional manufacturing leadership in terms of employment, capitalization, and value of product. The proliferation of employer-owned and -controlled mill villages, in which at least 80 percent of the Piedmont's textile workers lived in the 1920s, and outbreaks of labor rebellion, notably the stretch-out protests of the period 1929–1934, brought southern textile workers forcefully into national attention. Even in the depressed 1930s, cotton textiles led all southern industries in value of product, extent of labor force, aggregate wages, and other key indices of size and vigor. Between the late 1930s and the mid-1960s, organized labor renewed its efforts to bring mill workers into its fold in the face of relentless employer opposition. Renewed growth in the 1960s and 1970s enabled the textile industry to retain its place among the ten largest in the United States in terms of dollar volume of product. Despite rapid development of labor-saving technology, it still employed over three-quarters of a million workers, the vast majority of them in the South.[1]

The social and political significance of the industry has matched its economic importance. As the most numerous and cohesive elements in the southern working class, textile workers have played—either through active participation or, more usually, through lack of participation—critical social and political roles. "[O]rganized labor's failure to unionize the southern textile industry was one of its most critical defeats," observes historian Tom Terrill. Since workplace organization usually is associated with liberal political activity, Terrill speculates that "the Democratic party in the region might have been significantly different" had the unions been successful.[2] Certainly, another historian, Dale Newman, is correct in claiming that "to understand southern labor history, one must understand the southern textile workers."[3]

The volume of printed observation, commentary, and scholarship concerning the industry and its workers in the twentieth century testifies to its importance. With the exception of coal miners and perhaps more recently, autoworkers, no body of workers has received more attention than the textile operatives of the Piedmont. Employers, reformers, labor activists, journalists, and social scientists have created a rich body of observation and analysis.[4] Still, until recently, historians have largely neglected this phase of southern society. In the 1980s, however, they began to remedy this neglect and are creating an evocative and challenging new literature.[5] As the most recent entrants into the stream of scholarship, historians have been employing previously unexamined archival materials, conducting broadly conceived oral history interviews, applying econometric tools, and exploiting new vocabularies of discourse in efforts to rescue millworkers from "the enormous condescension of posterity" and to arrive at definitive understanding of these key participants in twentieth-century life.[6]

Until the past decade, there was little sophisticated historical scholarship available dealing with southern textile workers. Students of southern labor history relied on the accounts of participants and contemporary observers, as supplemented by a few early dissertations and monographs. Thus in their broad surveys of southern labor history at various times in the twentieth century, F. Ray Marshall, George Brown Tindall, and Irving Bernstein, duly awarding southern textiles serious consideration, drew heavily on labor activist Tom Tippett's firsthand 1931 account, *When Southern Labor Stirs*; the pioneering work of economists Broadus and George Mitchell; Liston Pope's classic 1942 account of the 1929 Gastonia strike, *Millhands and Preachers*; and dissertations by Robert R. R. Brooks and Herbert J. Lahne, both solid and informative but written without access to archival material.[7] Until recently, the revolution in labor and social historiography dating from the mid-1960s seemed to have passed the mill villages by.

But newly available archival materials and intensive programs of oral interviewing have brought the mill villages and their inhabitants into the purview of labor and social historiography. Thus, David L. Carlton in *Mill and Town in South Carolina, 1880–1920* (1982), I. A. Newby in *Plain Folk in the New South: Social Change and Cultural Persistence, 1880–1915* (1989), and James A. Hodges in *New Deal Labor Policy and the Southern Cotton Textile Industry, 1933–1941* (1986) move beyond the stereotypes of mill-village life to depict communities whose internal dynamics, cultural integrity, and cultural dynamics sharply qualify the images of paternalism and passivity projected by most social observers. Thus, for example, Carlton's South Carolinians combined intense racism, fierce resistance to would-be reformers, and strong political allegiance to their statewide champion, governor and perennial candidate Cole Blease, with grudging acquiescence to mill operators in the day-to-day operation of the factories. Sporadic labor activism did erupt in the South Carolina mill regions; however, its most consistent and most effectively pursued goal was the prohibition of black labor from the mills, an achievement embodied in a 1915 legislative enactment.[8]

Newby's *Plain Folk in the New South*, a close-to-the-bone survey of the mill villages and their inhabitants, stresses the determination of a premodern folk to preserve their culture in the face of rapid modernization. Little concerned with the agenda of most labor historians, Newby writes from a perspective of deep sympathy, if not with the actual values and behavior of his subjects, at least with their tenacity and plight as human beings. From his perspective, "unions and the model of labor-management relations they provided were [not] promising means for resolving the problems of mill workers" in the New South era. Even in the few instances when workers sustained mass protests, the very qualities of egalitarianism and individualism that represented the best of their culture militated against the ability to sustain the disciplined concerted action that alone might have successfully challenged their employers. Much in their lives, by his own account, was unattractive, even ugly. The same tenacious commitment to family and culture that enabled them to retain a coherent world view in the face of vast social forces made Piedmont textile workers susceptible to paternalism, racism, fatalism, and physical debility. Newby relies heavily on traditional archival, newspaper, and manuscript sources, as well as on previously collected oral histories, but interprets the millworkers' lives through the lens of modern scholarship in anthropology and social psychology. His account examines the various strands of mill culture in fascinating detail, focusing always on the folk's ability to survive even their own pathologies of physical debility, ignorance, and poverty.[9]

Hodges, drawing on the insights developed by historian John Bodnar in his studies of immigrant families in Western Pennsylvania, moves beyond the paternalism-rebellion axis, noting that "many southern cotton mill workers . . . assessed with considerable intelligence the means of survival and adaptation in their world." Life in the mills was harsh and the power of the mill owners and their political allies was great, but "Mill village life in the Piedmont generated an indigenous culture common from village to village." Neither docile nor foolhardy, millworkers relied primarily upon themselves, regarding the plans of union organizers and the programs of government bureaucrats skeptically, forever weighing these instruments of change against the likelihood of deterioration in their circumstances.[10]

Hodges's book illustrates the importance of new sources and insights in accounting for millworkers' behavior. Building on Louis

Galambos's pioneering exploitation of governmental and business archives in his 1964 monograph on the cotton textile trade association,[11]
Hodges uses the massive government and labor archives of the New
Deal era to suggest a subtle and complex picture of labor policy in the
1930s. Federal labor policies, widely viewed by historians as positive
stimuli to union growth, were problematic when applied to southern
textiles. During the National Recovery Administration period (1933–
35), they followed industry's priorities, as the Cotton-Textile Institute
dominated the NRA's code writing and administration processes. The
huge 1934 general strike in textiles, in which over 200,000 supposedly
docile southern mill hands participated, ended in disaster for organized
labor, embittering millworkers with regard both to the government as
an agent of positive change and the ill-led and outmaneuvered United
Textile Workers. The wave of firings and other reprisals that followed
in the wake of the strike insured that even when better led and better
financed textile workers' unions sought to renew the battle, and even
when more potent federal labor law in the form of the 1935 Wagner
Act promised with greater plausibility to protect union activists, southern workers responded warily. And with good reason, Hodges con-
cludes, for even the CIO's Textile Workers Organizing Committee and
the New Deal's National Labor Relations Board were no match for
sophisticated and ruthless anti-union strategies, especially in view of
the powerful political influence that southern politicians exerted in the
waning days of the New Deal. Thus the story of the failure of organized labor, aided by New Deal measures, to organize southern textiles
is no simple tale of docility or perversity. Rather, it is the logical result
of a mill village culture whose caution, insularity, and conservatism
were rational and appropriate responses based on shrewd understanding of where ultimate power lay. Hodges quotes one woman who
assessed the lineup of forces in a campaign to organize the Cone mills
in Greensboro, North Carolina, in the early thirties: "'No, sir,' she
said, 'no union for me . . . the Cones is still totin' the keys to the
mill.'"[12]

Also resting on newly available archival materials and extensive
oral interviewing, Barbara S. Griffith's 1988 monograph *The Crisis of
American Labor: Operation Dixie and the Defeat of the CIO* benefits
as well from the rapid expansion of labor and social historiography.
The failure to organize southern textiles in the 1930s did not end
labor's hopes. Indeed, during World War II, the CIO Textile Workers

Union of America (TWUA), with the strong support of federal authorities eager to forestall labor unrest, made important breakthroughs in the South. By the end of 1945, the TWUA counted nearly 400,000 members, with about one-fifth of them located in the South. In 1946, the CIO announced the launching of "Operation Dixie," a bold new drive to exploit its wartime victories in the South. And the Piedmont's millhands were the crucial target for this vast undertaking, for "when you organize the textile industry of the South," declared the drive's director, "you have practically all industries in the South under the banner of the CIO."[13]

Alas for labor's hopes, the drive collapsed soon after it began. Defeat at the large Cannon Mills facilities at Kannapolis, North Carolina, in the fall of 1946 spelled doom for the CIO's high hopes, though the Southern Campaign hobbled along for several years after. Griffith's account exploits the large CIO Operation Dixie collection at Duke University and other archival sources relating to the industrial union movement of the 1930s and 1940s, most of them available only in the past twenty years. Dozens of oral interviews with labor activists, most of them native southerners, graphically reveal both the strength of union activism among some southerners and the difficulty of the task they faced in the postwar Piedmont. Her work exhibits the sensitivity to questions of race and radicalism characteristic of recent labor historiography and, in its criticism of the weakness of federal labor relations protections and the CIO's anti-communist fixations as factors in Operation Dixie's failure, calls sharply into question the conventional industrial relations wisdom of an earlier generation.

However, it is the culture of the mill communities and its contribution to union defeat that are at the heart of Griffith's account. In Kannapolis, for example, the many mistakes and limitations of the CIO campaign became evident. Fixated on the dramatic northern victories that had characterized the birth of the CIO in the 1930s, union strategists inappropriately applied the lessons of Flint, Michigan, and Akron, Ohio, to the highly decentralized textile industry. Despite its unprecedented war chest, Operation Dixie was grotesquely underfunded for the enormous task of bringing unionism to the South. Union officials were unclear in their plan of action and organizers too often substituted pious wishes for realistic reports on their activities. Racial discord proved insurmountable in some areas while the hostility of southern clergymen and local officials proved crippling in others. The appeal of industrial unionism, backed up by the federal labor relations machinery forged in the thirties, was no match for intransigent employer power, bolstered by the South's one-party, anti-union political system.

Always, however, Griffith comes back to the problem of the mill workers themselves, just as the CIO's organizers did. "Had the union encountered a part of America that was organically resistant to it?," she asks. Was the Piedmont tradition of "submission and defeat, or resignation and apathy" simply too powerful for organized labor? In Kannapolis and other textile centers, CIO organizers simply could not achieve the first step in the program, the forming of indigenous in-plant committees. Workers were too fearful or too loyal to company president Charles Cannon. Or perhaps fear and loyalty were so intertwined that no one, least of all the earnest labor organizers who tramped the streets and knocked on the doors of the workers in the company-dominated town in the hopeless task of recruiting union members one by one, could separate them. "The 'fear' that organizers frequently referred to was . . . oddly compounded of workers' belief that they were part of Charlie Cannon's family . . . alongside a deep anxiety about opposing him." In the end, she suggests, long-lived southern traditions of dominance and subordination were insurmountable. "The naked mechanisms of social control that enforced inherited class and caste relations in Southern mill villages were of a kind and type that went beyond the imagination of most Americans." The Piedmont was not Detroit or Aliquippa; it was another country.[14]

The most ambitious reexamination of mill culture, however, challenges both the older stereotypes and, by implication at least, the pessimistic and instrumentalist view of it exhibited in the work of Carlton, Hodges, and Griffith. In *Like a Family* (1987), a group of historians centered at the University of North Carolina employs the results of a decade of oral interviewing in an effort to reveal the core of mill village life. Resting largely on some 200 interviews with mill-workers and residents, *Like a Family* joins Hodges and Newby in viewing the mill communities as rational responses to intrinsically unenviable conditions of life and labor. But whereas other recent scholars stress the narrowness of the workers' necessary accommodations, the authors of *Like a Family* celebrate the achievement of a rich and vigorous communal life. Millworkers, they argue, were indeed dependent but they were not servile. "The mill village," conclude the authors, "undeniably served management's interests, but it also nurtured a unique workers' culture" and sustained "communal values [that] . . . distanced mill folk from the acquisitiveness that characterized middle-class life in the New South towns."[15]

Millworkers brought with them from the rural countryside traditions of self-help and mutual support, as well as notions of moral economy and self-respect that put sharp boundaries around the claims of the mill operators. Despite the rhetoric of harmony purveyed by employer apologists—and that of despair and debility emanating from would-be reformers and sympathizers—millworkers largely disdained welfare schemes, fought tenaciously and often effectively against wage cuts and stretch-outs, and created a Piedmont-wide culture of mill-village life that confounded the all-embracing goals of their employers. In their family celebrations, their folk arts and domestic crafts, their skills of musicianship, midwifery, and storytelling, and their strong networks of kith and kin, millworkers "create[d] a new industrial world in the Piedmont South."[16]

In the late twenties and during the early New Deal, millworkers conducted some of the most dramatic and extensive strikes in American labor history. They fought the stretch-out, forged their own local unions that embodied a millworker version of sturdy republican protest, and joined national textile worker unions to implement the promise of the labor provisions of the National Industrial Recovery Act. Ultimately, however, the authors locate the heart of workers' resistance not primarily in these spectacular episodes but rather in the refusal of mill folk to internalize the subordination required by their employers on and off the job. The textile workers found outsiders—the Communist National Textile Workers Union, the AFL's United Textile Workers, and the federal officials who administered the cotton textile code under the NRA and who mediated the great 1934 general strike—unreliable and insensitive to their needs. The workers whom the authors interviewed showed little desire to talk about these strikes, exhibiting a "social amnesia" that contrasts sharply with their vivid and positive recollections of mill village life. But the Franklin D. Roosevelt Library yielded hundreds of communications that millworkers wrote in the wake of the savage 1934 textile strike in which at least 20 cotton-mill workers were killed. Bitterly denouncing the NRA for its broken promises and poignantly reaffirming notions of republican moral economy that survived despite union mismanagement and employer triumph, argue the authors, these brave and poignant letters reveal mill communities unbowed by defeat even if the workers resolved never again to trust outside unions and government agencies.[17]

In rescuing millworkers and their families from more pessimistic assessments, the authors run the risk of appearing to romanticize their subjects. As John Bodnar has recently pointed out, oral interviews are apt to fall into preconceived narrative patterns, casting a golden glow around certain phases or episodes, for example. *Like a Family*'s virtual silence on the question of race contrasts with Carlton's and Newby's forthright confrontation of the racial consciousness that appears to have been central to the world view of their otherwise sympathetically portrayed millworkers. In stressing the richness of mill communities' culture and mutuality, the authors elide some of the social pathologies that other scholars have documented, notably low levels of education, anomie, constricting insularity, and even physical debility.[18]

Nor does *Like a Family*'s discussion of the problem of union organizing do more than relabel an often observed phenomenon, namely the penchant of millworkers for alternating spectacular episodes of protest with rapid retreat. After all, despite the claims made on behalf of the efficacy of the anti–stretch-out protests, relatively minor reforms in the methods with which increased work loads were introduced seem to have appeased Piedmont workers in the thirties and forties. Workers "demonstrated a marked degree of cooperation and flexibility" in the introduction of new work arrangements, declares the historian of the cotton textile industry; in the post-1929 decade the industry showed an impressive forty-percent growth in man-hour productivity. True, the inept UTW and ineffective federal labor law enforcement caused legitimate worker disillusionment, but after all, workers in coal, steel, auto, and other industries who did build enduring unions in the 1930s also suffered bitter defeats along the way. Perhaps after all, the Piedmont, for all the richness of the private and familial lives it encouraged, did not permit, as Harry Boyte suggested, "the social terrain on which workers could establish independence."[19]

In contrast to the North Carolina historians, economic historian Gavin Wright views the textile industry primarily through the prism of econometric concerns. His focus on the parameters of economic performance lead to conclusions that both supplement and challenge recent social history initiatives. In a series of articles and in a chapter of his influential book, *Old South, New South: Revolutions in the South-*

ern Economy since the Civil War (1986), Wright contends that the crisis in southern textiles that triggered the strikes of 1929–1934 had sharply different origins than those identified by most historians and contemporary observers.

The southern mill-village system, Wright argues, was not an employer conceit foisted upon an unwilling rural labor force. Virtually all agrarian societies resort to some form of subsidized housing and child labor during the start-up period in textile production. The need to tap the labor of youthful females in the American South paralleled similar necessities in early nineteenth-century New England and in late nineteenth-century Japan. Given the poverty of the rural population, the isolation of most mill sites, and the need for this segment of the labor market, the mill village was an eminently rational institution whose social control functions were, at least initially, incidental.[20]

Labor force changes during the critical 1900–1920 period, however, drastically changed the industry's manpower patterns. Child labor laws, the seepage of teenage males out of the industry, and the declining fortunes of Piedmont agriculture caused increasing numbers of adult males to regard millwork as permanent. Nor did employers particularly lament the passing of the old child-labor system, for even in an industry with relatively low skill requirements, experience and maturity were positively associated with productivity, a growing concern as southern mills began to compete with northern manufacturers in finer grades of textiles. Hence, an industry which had been over one-half female in 1880 had become over two-thirds male by 1920. Moreover, in the early twentieth century, the expanding southern mills experienced a severe labor shortage, one aggravated by the increases in demand that World War I created. Labor shortages and the increasingly male, breadwinner character of the labor force in turn caused a sharp increase in southern wage rates. By the early 1920s, these two key factors—rising real wages and an increasingly male labor force—had combined to bring southern textiles in line with national industrial patterns.[21]

Wright by no means ignores the social dimension. Indeed, concepts of "moral economy" associated with labor historians E. P. Thompson and Herbert Gutman, critical to the analysis of the *Like a Family* group, are also central to his understanding of the events of the 1920s. For mill-village life, despite all its limitations, did permit a certain solidarity among Piedmont cotton-mill workers. Male textile operatives, who dominated the industry's more stable, skilled, and full-time positions and who embraced the nationally encouraged role of bread-winners, saw the wage increases of the 1910s decade as essential parts of the bargain they had made by becoming permanent citizens of the textile industry and its communities. When in the deflationary postwar period, operators imposed wage cuts, millworkers fought back fiercely in a wave of strikes that rippled through the Piedmont. These strikes did not result in permanent unions but they did moderate the wage cuts. More importantly, they taught southern operators that efforts to cut monetary wages, even if theoretically justified by general defla-tionary tendencies and by the fact that a depressed southern agricul-tural sector actually increased the supply of surplus labor, were a no-win proposition, for "cuts in the money wages could be counted on to generate a cohesive response because they were taken as acts of class warfare, violations of the 'moral economy' of labor relations."[22]

This moral economy functioned as well in worker resistance to the stretch-out that culminated in the strikes of 1929 in Gastonia and Marion, North Carolina, and in South Carolina, the protracted Dan River Mills walkout of 1930–31, and the Great Textile Strike of 1934. Ironically, however, at the heart of the stretch-out lay the factor of sticky wage rates. For despite the postwar cuts, Wright's figures show that "hourly real wage levels in Southern textiles were 60 to 70 percent higher in the 1920s than they had been before World War I."[23] Employ-ers could not cut wages and they did not wish to return to the child-labor system, for that would have deprived them of the "fifty years of progress in labor skills and socialization" that they had achieved. Instead, they turned to new technologies and managerial initiatives that workers perceived as increasing the work load. As a result of the resultant stretch-out, the Piedmont flared into rebellion once again in the legendary strikes of the late 1920s and early 1930s.[24]

Wright's stress on the econometric balance sheet is a welcome addition to southern historiography. Appreciative of the concerns and insights of the social historians, Wright himself stresses to the econo-mists in his readership the central importance of nonquantitative fac-tors in the creation of economic patterns and institutions. Thus, for example, he insists that in back of the graphs that show rising propor-tions of male workers lies a whole bundle of assumptions on the part of textile workers about the bargain they are making in becoming full-time, career-long, waged workers. Nor did workers suffer from the "money illusion" as such; rather, they *expected* rising standards and, absent unions or other independent vehicles for the expression of their interests, they quite rationally focused first on the money bargain, then on the work-load issue, as critical to their rational conception of moral economy. As the authors of *Like a Family* do, Wright highlights the critical role that the mill community played in mobilizing workers in defense of their interests, although unlike the North Carolina group, Wright emphasizes the extent to which millworkers in fact used these devices primarily in behalf of acquisitive, as opposed to intrinsically communal, aspirations. Thus the mill community that emerges (largely by implication, since it per se is not the focus of his investigations) from Wright's analysis does share many of the positive features posited in *Like a Family*. However, in part by the very nature of Wright's research agenda, this community assumes a far more instrumental and defensive character than it does in the book.[25]

These recent historiographical initiatives, based as they are on newly available archival material, careful econometric investigation, and imaginative oral history gathering, have added much to our understanding of the southern textile industry, its workers, and its communities. In large part, however, they remain wedded to traditional questions and employ familiar vocabularies. Recent work by Jacquelyn Hall, the major figure in the *Like a Family* group, however, suggests new foci of investigation and even new languages of discourse in her examination of the subtexts of labor struggle in the Piedmont. Building in part on radical feminist notions of the centrality of gender in all social discourse, Hall, in an impressive recent article on the 1929 Elizabethton, Tennessee, textile strike and in a provocative paper dealing with labor activist Ola Delight Smith, repaints the landscape in which labor conflict occurred in the textile South.[26]

Hall's article on the Elizabethton strike, an episode familiar to labor historians from their reading of Tippett, Bernstein, and other chroniclers of Piedmont protest, seeks to recontextualize the familiar. Unconcerned with retelling the story of grievances, demands, negotiations, and repression, Hall offers "a fresh reading of an important episode, . . . employing a female angle of vision . . . [and taking] a close look at women's distinctive forms of collective action." In part, this entails setting the record straight: female strikers against the J. P. Bemberg and Glanzstoff companies were, contrary to much contemporary testimony and subsequent accounts, far from the demure, sun-bonneted Elizabethan anachronisms who inhabit the standard tableaux of Piedmont labor history. These were young women for whom factory work represented liberation from the hardscrabble farms and mountain hollows that drained their mothers of energy and hope. Eschewing Appalachian calico, they copied modern styles of dress from the mass-circulation magazines they read and the Hollywood films they devoured. Devotees too of radio programs and familiar with the liberating possibilities of the automobile, these young women, while not repudiating their families, saw their work as a means of entry into a new and more exciting lifestyle.

Nor did they follow the script that Department of Labor mediators and national union leaders offered. Outraged at the companies' high-handed and unfair treatment, they displayed innovative and distinctively feminine strategies of protest. They were "inventive, playful, and shrewd," asserts Hall. They flirted with with sober national guardsmen sent in to protect scabs. Learning that the guardsmen's rules required that, upon seeing the American flag displayed, the men were to stop in their tracks and perform and hold a rigid salute, the young women delighted in taunting the soldiers with minor rule-breakings and then, as the men began to pursue them, unfurling a flag to bring their pursuers repeatedly to snappy attention. They presented the guardsmen with bouquets of wild flowers, inquired about their girl-friends back home, hinted at rewards for those who exhibited sympathy or support for the strikers. In contrast to the grim and often deadly atmosphere that usually accompanied the entry of the military in labor disputes, "the women's tactics encouraged a holiday spirit" in Elizabethton. Indeed, Hall posits, "they may also have deflected violence."[27]

Hall also highlights a dramatic trial that took place in the strike-beset town when two women—outsiders who were more experienced, outspoken, and sexually insouciant than the rest—were charged with disturbing the peace. These strikers, Trixie Perry and "Texas Bill," had openly defied the soldiers and had used foul language and explicit sexual gestures to embarrass and ridicule them. Disconcerted officials offered them up as warnings to their younger co-strikers, but the tactic backfired. True, the younger country women did not emulate the two "disorderly women," but neither did they repudiate them. Strikers took encouragement from the public testimony offered by these feisty, unintimidated women. The courtroom audience, strikers and townspeople alike, found the spectacle of sassy and assertive females at first amusing, then sobering as the women's testimony eloquently specified their grievances and the difficulties that they and their fellow workers faced. The very fact that women were daring to protest so openly impressed observers. "Since, presumably, only extraordinary circumstances call forth feminine aggression," Hall comments, "women's assaults against persons and property constitute a powerful witness against injustice."[28]

As with virtually all the great Piedmont strikes, the Elizabethton walkout ended in defeat for the strikers. But Hall measures the effect of the strike on the women who participated by a different calculus than that normally applied in labor history. The women whose interviews provide the basis for the article have forgotten many of the specific grievances and the precise terms of settlement. What is important to them is their common struggle, the female bonding that predated the strike and was powerfully reinforced during its course. Combined with the experience of industrial employment itself and the powerful impact of the commercial culture of the 1920s, the Elizabethton strike helped these young women to forge identities as agents of their own lives and as comrades in the ensuing struggles in life in modern America.[29]

Hall's paper on gender and protest gives intriguing hints that southern textiles may yield even more subtle and provocative readings of the map of social conflict. The central figure in her paper, an energetic and iconoclastic labor organizer and publicist named Ola Delight Smith, played a major role in a protracted 1914 strike at the Fulton Bag and Cotton Mills in Atlanta. On one level, Hall's account rescues a fascinating female activist, one whose career spanned over fifty years, from obscurity. However, Hall's examination of the ways in which Ola Delight Smith and her opponents—company spies, progressive religious friends of organized labor, public authorities, and her husband—both described and interpreted her life yields tantalizing clues about the subtext of language, gender relations, and even epistemology. For example, sober representatives of Men and Religion Forward, seeking public support for the humble textile workers, invariably described the women strikers as simple, demure flowers, clad in print dresses; Smith's vivid photographs, which she took and circulated for strike support purposes, depict strong, rawboned women, clad in men's overalls. They are fully industrialized citizens of a commercial republic, not Victorian sisters inexplicably trapped in a cotton mill.

More sinister, though, are the various descriptions of Smith's behavior as seen through the eyes of her various tormenters. To her
outraged husband, her associations with male strikers and unionists
signified sexual misconduct. The judge who granted him a divorce
concurred, imposing strict prohibitions against her remarriage and
proclaiming his repugnance not so much for her alleged moral transgressions, which the judge, however much he disapproved, understood, but rather for her inexplicable behavior as an autonomous and
confrontational activist, which he simply did not. A zealous company
spy tracked Smith's every move, trying with limited success to understand the actions of a southern woman who failed to conform to the
pre-existing stereotypes of white femininity. Even Smith herself, reflecting on her plight and pleading for understanding, reverted to a
Victorian vocabulary of outraged womanhood, contradicting the testimony of her actions. For Hall, Smith's story, as seen through these
various lenses, offers compelling evidence of changing gender roles in
a southern urban context and illustrates the gains to be reaped by
historians sensitive to the mythology and iconography of gender and
social protest.[30]

Clearly, recent historical scholarship has enriched understanding of
the nature of the textile communities, the behavior of workers, and the
course of labor relations. New sources, new applications of older
methodologies, and new languages of discourse, of course, do not
guarantee any definitive conclusions about these matters. More important, however, than the elusive bottom line is the fact that the scholarship of the 1980s at last brings southern textiles into the mainstream of
labor, social, and regional history. For decades after autoworkers, coal
miners, steelworkers, and other bodies of industrial workers had attracted gifted historians whose sophisticated scholarship generated
lively and fruitful exchange, textile workers languished in their geographical backwaters, visited only occasionally by a dissertation-seek-
ing historian. After the work of scholars such as Hodges, the North
Carolina group, Gavin Wright, and Jacquelyn Hall, however, they
have joined Detroit's car builders and Pittsburgh's steelworkers in the
front ranks of historical subject matter, even if most of them did not
join their northern counterparts in the CIO.

For a brief moment in the late 1970s, it *did* seem that southern
textile workers might at last join the ranks of organized labor and
perhaps even play a leading role in laborite resurgence.[31] Changes in

the industry, which rebounded from its post–World War II doldrums to record production and profits in the 1960s and 1970s, along with a surge of black membership, the possibility of federal labor law reform, and seeming political liberalization in the South encouraged organizers and textile activists. In 1963, the Textile Workers' union launched a new drive directed at the South's second-largest textile employer, J. P. Stevens. Despite this company's uncompromising resistance, unionists found encouragement in NLRB and court rulings that vindicated victimized activists and narrowed the scope of anti-union harassment.

The entry into the industry for the first time of large numbers of black workers was a particular source of optimism. Union organizers and social investigators alike quickly noted that blacks were more militant, more pro-union, and far less susceptible to company threats and blandishments than their white counterparts. Many had lived in the North and had acquired familiarity with organized labor and other forms of collective action. The triumphant civil rights movement, building as it did on the cohesive black religious and civic traditions, legitimated aggressive social activism. Many blacks entered the textile mills under the cover of the equal opportunities provisions of the Civil Rights Act of 1964 and were convinced that only through continued struggle could they continue to make gains. Meanwhile, the industrialization and urbanization of the South brought thousands of heavy industry and high technology jobs to Dixie. Along with the expansion of education, this development raised wage levels in the South closer to national norms and offered alternatives to workers who normally would have resigned themselves to life in the low-wage mills.

Stirrings among veteran textile workers also bespoke a new activism in the Piedmont. Surveys indicated more positive views of unions than investigators had expected on the basis of past experience. As the effects of byssinosis (or brown lung disease), a widespread and disabling affliction associated with the inhalation of cotton fibers, became publicized in the mid-1970s, once-quiescent textile workers began to stir. Encouraged by the passage of federal occupational safety legislation in 1970 and by the support of social activist medical professionals, they formed regionwide networks of brown lung clubs, confronted textile executives in public meetings, and testified eloquently in Washington on behalf of compensation for themselves and rigorous cotton-dust standards in the mills.

North Carolina textile worker Crystal Lee Sutton, an appealing and articulate victim of Stevens's tactics and principal in a widely publicized unfair labor practices case, provided unionists with a heroine reminiscent of the stalwarts of yesteryear. The sweeping legal victory of the Amalgamated Clothing and Textile Workers Union over Stevens in October 1980 vindicated Sutton, who received $25,000 in back wages and penalties and made a triumphal return to the Roanoke Rapids plant from which she had been dismissed. This victory, the product in part of innovative boycotting and public relations tactics on the part of ACTWU, held out the hope that just as the auto and steel industries had succumbed to organized labor thirty-five years before, now southern textiles could at last be organized.[32]

Alas for labor's hopes, the Stevens case quickly proved not to be readily transmutable into other victories. Southern textile executives remained obdurate. Growled company executive Whitney Stevens after the settlement, "We haven't succumbed in any way, and I doubt that this agreement will be the first step toward any further unionization." Other textile manufacturers, angry with Stevens for pursuing blatantly illegal and unpopular tactics, resolved to step up their own more indirect campaigns of co-optation, human relations management, and harassment of unionists.[33]

Nor did the other briefly positive indicators prove decisive. Organized labor could not take advantage of the brief Carter presidency to rebuild the New Deal–Great Society coalition. Labor law reform proposals, inspired in good part by labor's experience in southern textiles, failed of passage. A new surge of textile imports, along with plant closings and the growth of multinational operations, created unemployment in the Piedmont and added plausibility to industry spokesmen's warnings against labor unrest or organizing agitation. Old patterns of paternalism and distrust of organized labor remained strong among millworkers, few of whom could bear the expense and anguish that even a successful labor law violation suit would entail. Just as in 1921, 1934, and 1946, the Piedmont remained nonunion territory.[34]

Whatever the tribulations of the labor movement in the Piedmont of the 1980s, historians have been successful in bringing textile workers back to center stage. From the work of Carlton, Newby, Hodges, and the *Like a Family* authors, we have a far more textured and coherent understanding of classic mill-village life than ever before. Informed by the insights of the past generation of social historians, these scholars have restored workers' agency to the Piedmont and have learned to listen to the voices of its inhabitants with a sensitivity all too rare among their predecessors.[35] Perhaps less impressed with the blessings of modernization than an earlier generation of scholars, they exhibit respect for the self-conceptions of a people who seemed to earlier visitors anachronistic—at best quaint, at worst benighted. Especially when this new sensitivity is leavened by careful illumination of the essential economic parameters that also shaped Piedmont life, the new textile history is rich and suggestive indeed.

And what of the union? For decades, laborites and social observers regarded the lack of unionization as both a cause and a symptom of the Piedmont's backwardness. As industrial workers surged into unions in the 1930s, millworkers hung back. As powerful national corporations came to terms with the new labor movement and the New Deal labor law requirements, textile makers continued in their disreputable, if no doubt ultimately futile, resistance. Like their mills, their villages, and their workers, textile operators belonged to an earlier, less enlightened stage of development.

In the 1980s, however, such judgments seem increasingly suspect. After all, who is more typically American, the southern textile workers or the 17 percent of the nonagricultural labor force that belongs to unions? For years, textile employers threatened union-minded workers with plant removals, shutdowns, and relocations.[36] In the past fifteen years, however, these devices have proved increasingly popular with the corporations astride the unionized sectors of the economy. For years, textile employers experimented with and perfected a wide range of anti-union weapons. Far from being throwbacks to the bad old days, it seems, these men have proved tribunes of the future as more and more companies employ these weapons. Where once the flouting of national labor law seemed the unique province of textile employers, now organized labor has come to regard the NLRB as practically useless in recruitment campaigns, as more and more employers embrace the tactics pioneered by textile manufacturers in manipulating the complex and cumbersome machinery. Harassment of union activists, for years the stock in trade of southern textile campaigns, has become rampant throughout the economy. The boosteristic political calculations that enlisted public authorities against unionism in the South have become standard fare wherever apprehensive state and local communities feel threatened with foreign (or regional) competition, plant closure, or relocation. In short, the southern textile industry, it turns out, has not been the laggard in the realm of industrial relations. It has been on the cutting edge.

Indeed, the southern textile experience drives home a sometimes neglected fact of American labor history, namely that the creation and building of unions has always been problematic and risky in the United States. For a generation or so after the New Deal reforms, it was possible to see unions as central institutions, countervailing powers, part of the national mainstream. But lengthening perspective reveals just how special the circumstances of the 1930s and 1940s were. The delegitimation of corporate leadership, the presence in Washington and state capitals of a gifted cadre of legislators and administrators steeped in progressive politics, the fortuitous presence of able young trade unionists, many of them infused with idealistic visions of a more egalitarian society, the patriotic requirements of a world war that put a premium on labor peace and offered full citizenship to immigrant industrial workers—when again would such favorable circumstances occur? For most of American history, unions have been public pariahs. To join a union, even today, is an act of rebellion, often inviting retribution or marginalization. In his or her careful assessment of risks and legitimate fear of employer retribution, the southern textile worker has been far closer to the national norm than earlier observers ever thought.

In his review of *Like a Family*, Gavin Wright applauded the enormous effort and sensitive portrayal of millworker life that the authors displayed. The book, he declared, served as a lesson to those who thought that they could read the history of an industry in the graphs and statistics of econometric analysis. Intangibles—the networks of mutual support; the kinds of expectations that workers brought to their industrial lives; the effect of informal, on-the-job training and shop-floor cooperation on productivity; the sense of moral economy that underlay patterns of acquiescence and resistance—played a powerful role as well, as the authors brilliantly demonstrated. But, he cautioned, the authors, just as millworkers had, ignored the economic parameters, at their peril. Given the unresponsiveness of wages to market conditions and the competitive and profit characteristics of the industry, he declared, some sort of revision in work loads—the hated stretch-out—was inevitable. Thus, applauding the authors for helping the millworkers at last to articulate their expectations and to re-create their lives, Wright warned of the limits of this kind of testimony. In the end, he declared, in a comment that might well serve as an epitaph for generations of students of southern textile workers, "It is up to historical scholars . . . to weave the millworkers' story into a full account of the role of the cotton mills in the history of the South."[37] In the 1980s historians at long last laid the groundwork necessary to carry on this task.

Notes

1. James A. Hodges, *New Deal Labor Policy and the Southern Cotton Textile Industry, 1933–1941* (Knoxville: Univ. of Tennessee Press, 1986), 8–21; Barry E. Truchil, *Capital-Labor Relations in the U.S. Textile Industry* (New York, Westport, CT, London: Praeger, 1988), 1–21; Gavin Wright, *Old South, New South: Revolutions in the Southern Economy since the Civil War* (New York: Basic Books, 1986), 124–155.
2. Thomas E. Terrill, "Southern Mill Workers" (review of Jacquelyn Hall et al., *Like a Family*), *Reviews in American History* 16:4 (Dec. 1988): 597.
3. Dale Newman, "Labor Struggles in the American South," *International Labor and Working Class History*, no. 14/15 (Spring 1979): 43. See also F. Ray Marshall, *Labor in the South* (Cambridge MA: Harvard Univ. Press, 1967), 80–85, 101–33, 167–75, 274–79.
4. Three generations of labor organizers, industrialists, and public relations minions have left always revealing and sometimes insightful accounts of work among southern mill workers. The most important of these are Marjorie Potwin, *Cotton Mill People of the Piedmont: A Study in Social Change* (New York: Columbia Univ. Press, 1927); Paul Blanshard, *Labor in Southern Cotton Mills* (N.p.: The New Republic/League for Industrial Democracy, 1922); Tom Tippett, *When Southern Labor Stirs* (New York: Cape and Smith, 1931); Broadus Mitchell and George Sinclair Mitchell, *The Industrial Revolution in the South* (Baltimore: Johns Hopkins Univ. Press, 1930); Harriet L. Herring, *Welfare Work in Mill Villages: The Story of Extra-Mill Activities in North Carolina* (1929; Montclair, NJ: Patterson Smith, 1968 reprint); Lois MacDonald, *Southern Mill Hills: A Study of Social and Economic Forces in Certain Textile Mill Villages* (New York: Alex L. Hillman, 1928); Ben F. Lemert, *The Cotton Textile Industry of the Southern Appalachian Piedmont* (Chapel Hill: Univ. of North Carolina Press, 1933); Jennings J. Rhyne, *Some Southern Cotton Mill Workers and Their Villages* (Chapel Hill: Univ. of North Carolina Press, 1930); Liston Pope, *Millhands and Preachers: A Study of Gastonia* (New Haven: Yale Univ. Press, 1942); Harriet L. Herring, *The Passing of the Mill Village: Revolution in a Southern Institution* (Chapel Hill: Univ. of North Carolina Press, 1949); John Kenneth Morland *The Millways of Kent* (Chapel Hill: Univ. of North Carolina Press,

1958); John R. Earle, Dean D. Knudson, and Donald W. Shriver, Jr., *Spindles and Spires: A Re-Study of Religion and Social Change in Gastonia* (Atlanta: John Knox, 1976); and Glenn Gilman, *Human Relations in the Industrial Southeast: A Study of the Textile Industry* (Chapel Hill: Univ. of North Carolina Press, 1956). More recent investigations include Patricia Hammond Levenstein, "The Failure of Unionization in the Southern Textile Industry" (M.A. thesis, Cornell University, 1964); Joseph A. McDonald, "Textile Workers and Unionization: A Community Study" (Ph.D. diss. University of Tennessee, 1981); Joseph A. McDonald and Donald A. Clelland, "Textile Workers and Union Sentiment," *Social Forces* 63: 2 (Dec. 1984): 502–21; and Rhonda Zingraff and Michael D. Schulman, "Social Bases of Class Consciousness: A Study of Southern Textile Workers with a Comparison by Race," ibid. 63:1 (Sept. 1984): 98–116. See also the citations in note 30. This literature is the subject of a separate essay in preparation.

5. There is no single source for bibliographical material on the industry, its people, and its unions. Bibliographies in recent historical work provide the best guides to literature and sources. See especially Hodges, *New Deal Labor Policy*, 236–44, and Jacquelyn Dowd Hall, James Leloudis, Robert Korstad, Mary Murphy, Lu Ann Jones, and Christopher B. Daly, *Like a Family: The Making of a Southern Cotton Mill World* (Chapel Hill and London: Univ. of North Carolina Press, 1987), 421–44. Maurice Neufeld, Daniel Leab, and Dorothy Swanson, compilers, *American Working Class History: A Representative Bibliography* (New York and London: R. R. Bowker, 1983), 274–79, is also useful.

6. In addition to works discussed and cited below, see also the historical essays in *Hanging by a Thread: Social Change in Southern Textiles*, ed. Jeffrey Leiter, Michael D. Schulman, and Rhonda Zingraff (Ithaca, NY: ILR Press, forthcoming). See especially Linda Frankel "'Jesus Leads Us, Cooper Needs Us, The Union Feeds Us': The 1958 Harriet-Henderson Textile Strike"; Gary Freeze, "Poor Girls Who Might Otherwise Be Wretched: Society, Gender, and the Origins of Paternalism in North Carolina's Early Cotton Mills, 1836–1880"; and Bryant Simon, "Choosing between the Ham and the Union: Paternalism and Workers at the Cone Mills of Greensboro, North Carolina, 1925–1930."

7. Marshall, *Labor in the South*; George Brown Tindall, *The Emergence of the New South, 1913–1945* (Baton Rouge: Louisiana State Univ. Press, 1967); Irving Bernstein, *The Lean Years: A History of the American Worker, 1920–1933* (Boston: Houghton Mifflin, 1960), 1–43; Irving Bernstein, *The Turbulent Years: A History of the American Worker, 1933–1941* (Boston: Houghton Mifflin, 1970), 298–315 and 616–23; Walter Galenson, *The CIO Challenge to the AFL: A History of the American Labor Movement 1935–1941* (Cambridge, MA: Harvard Univ. Press, 1960), ch. 9; Robert R. R. Brooks, "The United Textile Workers of America" (Ph.D. diss., Yale University, 1935); Herbert J. Lahne, *The Cotton Mill Worker in the Twenti-*

eth Century (New York: Ferrar and Rinehart, 1944). See also the citations to Tippett's and the Mitchells' work in note 4. Bernstein's treatment of textiles in *The Turbulent Years* does make extensive and effective use of manuscript materials in the Franklin D. Roosevelt Library and the National Archives, while Paul David Richards, "The History of the Textile Workers Union of America, CIO, in the South, 1937 to 1945" (Ph.D. diss., University of Wisconsin, 1972), rests on the papers of the TWUA at the State Historical Society in Madison, Wisconsin.

See also vivid left-wing accounts of the labor upheaval of the late twenties and early 1930s, notably Robert W. Dunn and Jack Hardy, *Labor and Textiles: A Study of Cotton and Wool Manufacturing* (New York: International, 1931), and Fred Beal, *Proletarian Journey* (New York: Hillman-Curl, 1937). Partly owing to the timing of its appearance, Robert Sidney Smith's *Mill on the Dan: A History of the Dan River Mills, 1882–1950* (Durham: Duke Univ. Press, 1960), by far the best textile company history, has received little attention in the literature, despite its extensive coverage of labor relations and its exploitation of rich company records.

8. David L. Carlton, *Mill and Town in South Carolina, 1880–1920* (Baton Rouge and London: Louisiana State Univ. Press, 1982), 137–44, 159–60, 249–53, 267–70.

9. I. A. Newby, *Plain Folk in the New South: Social Change and Cultural Persistence, 1880–1915* (Baton Rouge and London: Louisiana State Univ. Press, 1989), quote on p. 562. Another recent account, Cathy L. McHugh, *Mill Family: The Labor System in the Southern Cotton Textile Industry, 1880–1915* (New York, Oxford: Oxford Univ. Press, 1988), focuses sharply on the functional econometric aspects of the New South textile labor system.

10. Hodges, *New Deal Labor Policy*, 26–34.

11. Louis Galambos, *Competition and Cooperation: The Emergence of a National Trade Association* (Baltimore: Johns Hopkins Univ. Press, 1964).

12. Hodges, *New Deal Labor Policy*, quote on p. 34.

13. Barbara S. Griffith, *The Crisis of American Labor: Operation Dixie and the Defeat of the CIO* (Philadelphia: Temple Univ. Press, 1988), 12–21; Richards, "History of the Textile Workers Union," 177–79; Van A. Bittner quoted in Earle, Knudson, and Shriver, *Spindles and Spires*, 178.

14. Griffith, *Crisis of American Labor*, 49–61, 161–76.

15. Hall et al., *Like a Family*. The quotes are from Hall, Korstad, and Leloudis, "Cotton Mill People: Work, Community, and Protest in the Textile South, 1880–1940," *American Historical Review* 91:2 (April 1986): 250, 254.

16. Hall et al., *Like a Family*, 43. Although *Like a Family* and *Plain Folk in the New South* largely overlap in chronological coverage, the former does treat episodically the labor militancy of the 1920s and early 1930s. The Hall group views this activism as a direct extension of the communal and mutualist culture earlier forged in the mill village while Newby's brief allusions to it posit a rater sharp break with traditional mill culture.

17. Hall et al., *Like a Family*, 328–54. See also Janet Irons, "Testing the New Deal: The General Textile Strike of 1934" (paper delivered at the annual meeting of the Organization of American Historians, St. Louis, April 7, 1989, copy in Zieger's possession).

18. See, e.g., Dale Newman, "Work and Community in a Southern Textile Town," *Labor History* 19 (Spring 1978): 204–25; reprinted in *The Labor History Reader*, ed. Daniel Leab (Urbana: Univ. of Illinois Press, 1985), 433–40. "Three generations of employer paternalism had produced an hereditary work force of poorly educated, economically insecure, and socially isolated individuals," claims Newman. "[T]he three-M diet [molasses, meat (fat pork), meal] suggests that the suspicions, mistrust, and hostility exhibited by cotton mill workers toward 'outsiders' may be a product of biological needs as well as class distinctions." See also Dale Newman, "Textile Workers in a Tobacco County: A Comparison between Yarn and Weave Mill Villagers," *The Southern Common People: Studies in Nineteenth-Century Social History*, ed. Edward Magdol and Jon L. Wakeman (Westport, CT and London: Greenwood, 1980), 345–68. Despite the book's title, Newman's essay deals with the period 1915–1935. Many of the contemporary commentators alluded to in note 4 graphically portrayed these pathologies. See, e.g., MacDonald, *Southern Mill Hills*, 52–55, 72–79, 107–8, 141–42. For sophisticated recent discussions of the medical pathologies that afflicted mill workers, see Edward H. Beardsley, *A History of Neglect: Health Care for Blacks and Mill Workers in the Twentieth-Century South* (Knoxville: Univ. of Tennessee Press, 1987), 42–74, 189–242, and Newby, *Plain Folk*, 352–86.

19. John Bodnar, "Power and Memory in Oral History: Workers and Managers at Studebaker," *Journal of American History* 75: 4 (Spring 1989): 1201–8; Jack Blicksilver, *Cotton Manufacturing in the Southeast: An Historical Analysis* (Atlanta: Bureau of Business and Economic Research, Georgia State College, 1959), 97; Harry Boyte, "The Textile Industry: Keel of Southern Industrialization," *Radical America* 6 (March–April 1972): 43. Other recent scholars have echoed early observers such as Tom Tippett in drawing a sharp contrast between the vigor and efficacy of spontaneous local unionism, unconnected with national organizations such as the UTW, and the lethargy, ineptitude, and collaborationist orientation of the latter, suggesting thereby that the root of the failure to establish permanent unions in southern textiles lies in the very nature of the UTW, the AFL, and perhaps the entire labor-New Deal dispensation. See, e.g., Irons, "Testing the New Deal: The General Textile Strike of 1934," and John G. Selby, "'Better to Starve in the Shade than in the Factory': Labor Protest in High Point, North Carolina, in the Early 1930s," *North Carolina Historical Review* 64:1 (January 1987): 43–64.

20. Wright, *Old South, New South*, 124–55; Gary Saxonhouse and Gavin Wright, "Two Forms of Cheap Labor in Textile History," *Technique, Spirit and Form in the Making of Modern Economies: Essays in Honor of William N.*

Parker ("Research in Economic History," Supplement 3; Greenwich, CT and London: JAI, 1984): 3–32. See also McHugh, *Mill Family.*

21. Gavin Wright, "Cheap Labor and Southern Textiles, 1880–1930," *Quarterly Journal of Economics* 96 (November 1981): 608–20.

22. Ibid., 627.

23. Ibid., 623–26. Wright observes that "this development has been nearly overlooked by industry historians" and acknowledges that "readers of an earlier draft [of this published paper] expressed skepticism" as to the validity of his findings. He reports, however, that upon reviewing his data, he remains convinced on the point.

24. Wright, *Old South, New South,* 151–55.

25. See Wright's review of *Like a Family* in the *Journal of Interdisciplinary History* 19:4 (Spring 1989): 697–99, and Gavin Wright, "Labor History and Labor Economics, *The Future of Economic History,* ed. Alexander J. Field (Boston; Durdrecht, Neth.; Lancaster, Eng.: Kluwer-Nijhoff, 1987), 313–48.

26. Jacquelyn Dowd Hall, "Disorderly Women: Gender and Labor Militancy in the Appalachian South," *Journal of American History* 73:2 (Sept. 1986): 354–82; Jacquelyn Dowd Hall, "Private Eyes, Public Women: Class and Sex in the Urban South," *Work Engendered: Toward a New History of Men, Women, and Work,* ed. Ava Baron (Ithaca: Cornell Univ. Press, forthcoming).

27. Hall, "Disorderly Women," 366–69, 378–80.

28. Ibid., 374–78.

29. Ibid., 377–78.

30. Jacqueline Dowd Hall, "Private Eyes, Public Women." See also Joan Wallach Scott, *Gender and the Politics of History* (New York: Columbia Univ. Press, 1988), 53–67. In this essay entitled "On Language, Gender, and Working-Class History," Scott calls for "attempts to bring women as a subject and gender as an analytic category into the practice of labor history." (53). Hall's focus on the theme of gender in these two papers is closely connected to the agenda of the authors of *Like a Family.* The book highlights the roles of women as workers and family members in the Piedmont. See also Linda Frankel, "Southern Textile Women: Generations of Survival and Struggle," *My Troubles Are Going to Have Trouble with Me: Everyday Trials and Triumphs of Women Workers,* ed. Karen Brodkin Sacks and Dorothy Remy (New Brunswick: Rutgers Univ. Press, 1984), 39–60; Valerie Quinney, "Textile Women: Three Generations in the Mill," *Southern Exposure* 3:4 (1976): 66–72; and Marion W. Roydhouse, "'Big Enough to Tell Weeds from the Beans': The Impact of Industry on Women in Twentieth-Century South," *The South Is Another Land: Essays on the Twentieth-Century South,* ed. Bruce Clayton and John A. Salmond (New York, Westport, CT, and London: Greenwood, 1987), 85–106.

31. For a fascinating recent example of textile workers in a vanguard role, see Peter Winn, *Weavers of Revolution: The Yarur Workers and Chile's Road to Socialism* (Oxford: Oxford Univ. Press, 1986).

32. On the new role of black workers, Mary Frederickson, "Four Decades of Change: Black Workers in Southern Textiles, 1941–1981," *Workers' Struggles, Past and Present: A "Radical America" Reader*, ed. James Green (Philadelphia: Temple Univ. Press, 1983; paperback), 62–82; Richard L. Rowan, *The Negro in the Textile Industry*. The Racial Policies of American Industry, Report No. 20. (Philadelphia: Industrial Research Unit, Univ. of Pennsylvania Press, 1970); and Rhonda Zingraff and Michael D. Schulman, "Social Bases of Class Consciousness: A Study of Southern Textile Workers with a Comparison by Race," Social Forces 63:1 (Sept. 1984): 98–116. On the brown lung movement, see Mimi Conway, *Rise Gonna Rise: A Portrait of Southern Textile Workers* (Garden City, NY: Anchor/Doubleday, 1979), Bennett M. Judkins, *We Offer Ourselves in Evidence: Toward Workers' Control of Occupational Health* (New York, Westport, CT, London: Greenwood, 1986), 111–70, and Beardsley, *History of Neglect*, 237–41. Commentaries about changes in the industry and optimistic assessments of the possibilities for textile organizing occur in Boyte, "The Textile Industry: Keel of Southern Industrialization," and Chip Hughes, "A New Twist for Textiles," *Southern Exposure* 3:4 (1976): 73–79. For the post–World War II period, see generally Truchil, *Capital-Labor Relations in the U.S. Textile Industry*. A brief account of the ACTWU case against Stevens is found in Terry W. Mullins and Paul Luebke, "Symbolic Victory and Political Reality in the Southern Textile Industry: The Meaning of the J. P. Stevens Settlement for Southern Labor Relations," *Journal of Labor Research* 3:1 (Winter 1982): 81–88.

33. Mullins and Luebke, "Symbolic Victory," 85–89, quote on p. 85.

34. These developments are treated in Truchil, *Capital-Labor Relations in the U.S. Textile Industry*, 132–50.

35. The voices of millworkers are particularly evident in Victoria Byerly, *Hard Times Cotton Mill Girls: Personal Histories of Womanhood and Poverty in the South* (Ithaca, NY: ILR Press, 1986), and Allen Tullos, *Habits of Industry: White Culture and the Transformation of the Carolina Piedmont* (Chapel Hill: Univ. of North Carolina Press, 1989).

36. Several essays in *Hanging by a Thread*, ed. Leiter, Schulman, and Zingraff, provide recent documentation for the tribulations of the textile industry and its continuing anti-union stance. See John Gaventa and Barbara Smith, "The Deindustrialization of the Textile South: A Case Study," and Rhonda Zingraff, "Facing Extinction?"

37. Gavin Wright, review of *Like a Family*, *Journal of Interdisciplinary History*, 19:4 (Spring 1989): 699.

3. Class and Racial Inequality

The Southern West Virginia Black Coal Miners' Response, 1915–1932

Joe W. Trotter, Jr.

For nearly three decades, research on black life during the industrial era has proceeded apace. Scholars of black urban life are giving increasing attention to the socioeconomic transformation of African-American life during the era of the Great Migration. Our knowledge of the black urban proletariat in northern, southern and western cities grows.[1] The emergence of a black proletariat, however, was not limited to American cities. In large numbers, blacks migrated to the southern Appalachian coalfields of Kentucky, Tennessee, Virginia, and, particularly, West Virginia.[2] The experiences of black coal miners in southern West Virginia between World War I and the early years of the Great Depression reveal the dynamics of class and racial inequality in the bituminous labor force, the black miners' response, and the comparative dimensions of black life and labor in different coal-producing regions of the nation.

As the bituminous coal industry entered the postwar era, racial and ethnic competition increased. African-Americans found it increasingly difficult to retain the precarious foothold acquired earlier in supervisory and skilled positions. As manual coal loaders, they also faced growing discrimination in the assignment of workplaces, a factor that made it hard to keep pace with the production and wage levels of their white counterparts. For the most disagreeable tasks, employers sought blacks in preference to immigrants and American-born whites. The discriminatory policies of employers, however, were repeatedly reinforced by the racial attitudes and behavior of white workers and the state. Operating on the narrow middle ground between these hostile forces, black coal miners eventually developed strategies for combating them.

Although the black proletariat in southern West Virginia had roots in the prewar years, it gained its fullest development during World War I and the 1920s. West Virginia increased its share of the nation's bituminous coal production from 7 percent in 1890 to 26 percent in 1930, while production in the leading northern Appalachian state of Pennsylvania plummeted from 33 percent to roughly 25 percent of total national output. Production from southern West Virginia—nine contiguous counties in the south-central section of the state—generated between two-thirds and three-quarters of the state's coal, employed over 80 percent of the state's black miners, and enabled the Mountain State to displace Alabama as the leading employer of African-American coal miners.[3]

In response to the war and postwar labor demands of the bituminous coal industry, the black population increased from just over 40,000 in 1910 to nearly 80,000 in 1930. At the same time, the number of black coal miners rose from 11,000 in 1915 to 16,500 in 1917, and to an estimated 20,000 by 1930. More importantly, the proportion of black workers increased from 20 percent to over 26 percent of the total labor force, as the proportion of immigrants declined from 31 percent to 12 percent.[4] Even as it grew in numbers, however, the black mining proletariat continued to experience a precarious existence. The economic obstacles that black miners faced caused them to have deep grievances and to develop complex responses to the impact of industrial capitalism in West Virginia's booming mining region.

After the war, black representation among supervisory personnel dropped sharply. Black foremen, for example, increasingly lost ground during the postwar era. In the 1916–1920 period, nearly 10 percent of the supervisory personnel killed or seriously injured were black men. Over the next five years no black fatalities or injuries were reported in this category, indicating a drastic dropoff in the numbers of blacks holding supervisory positions. As early as 1916, attorney W. H. Harris, a *McDowell Times* columnist, complained, "It has been the practice not to employ Colored men as bosses in the mines. This has been . . . a sort of unwritten law as it were—no matter how capable or efficient they were."[5]

In its 1921–22 survey of black miners, the West Virginia Bureau of Negro Welfare and Statistics (BNWS) recorded only seven black foremen and other bosses in the entire state. A similar survey in 1927 produced "only one fire boss." "In late years, many or all of these places were filled by native whites and foreigners," wrote the teacher and political activist Memphis T. Garrison in 1926.[6] Under the impact of the depression, sociologist James T. Laing found, only eleven blacks "were in positions which, even by the most liberal stretch of the term, could be called positions of authority." Two of the eleven were assistant mine foremen; five worked as stable bosses in mines that still used mules; and the remainder held a miscellaneous set of jobs, including foreman over a slate dump, boss mule driver, and head of a "negro rock gang." In practice, employers modified their traditional position that "a Negro is a very good boss among his own color." One contemporary observer noted an emerging pattern when he remarked that "even foreigners are given these positions in preference to native Colored men."[7]

The discriminatory attitudes and practices of state officials reinforced black exclusion from supervisory jobs. To meet the new standards that had been set on the eve of World War I, West Virginia University expanded its mining extension classes for the training of white foremen. During the war years, enrollments reached over 4,500, accelerated during the 1920s, and by 1930 had climbed to over 20,000. These classes not only trained whites for managerial and supervisory positions but also heightened the racial stratification of the mine labor force. Only in the late 1930s did blacks receive similar classes, and then on a segregated and inadequate basis.[8] In the war and postwar years, as in the prewar era, caste restrictions continued to limit the occupational mobility of black workers.

If blacks found it nearly impossible to gain supervisory jobs, they found it somewhat less difficult to secure positions as machine operators and motormen. The employment of blacks in unskilled and semi-skilled jobs was highly sensitive to the specific labor demands of the bituminous coal industry. During the coal strikes of the early 1920s, for example, company officials hired growing numbers of black machine operators and frequently praised them for their efficient labor. In 1921–22, according to the BNWS, employers of skilled black workers stated that "they are as efficient, more loyal, as regular and take a greater personal interest in their work and in the success of the business than workers of other races." Likewise during the economic upswing of the mid-1920s, the bureau enthusiastically reported, "Not only has the Negro made for himself a permanent place as miner and laborer about the mines, but he is being sought . . . by mine owners to fill positions requiring skill and training."[9]

Although some blacks gained skilled positions, their path was nonetheless difficult. During the war years, for example, a Logan County engineer informed operators that "where ever one finds a Colored motorman having a white brakeman or machineman a white helper, he may be sure that there is more or less friction between the two. . . . A white man doesn't care to have a Colored for his buddy." Black workers found it especially difficult to secure jobs as mainline motormen, workers who transported loaded coal cars from underground working areas to the surface. In the mines of Hemphill and Coalwood, McDowell County, Pink Henderson bitterly recalled, during the 1920s "the mine foremen wouldn't let the black[s] . . . run the motor. . . . A white man ran the motor." When the foreman assigned blacks to motormen jobs, he was careful to specify that they were "running the motor extra," as a temporary expedient, thus preserving for whites a proprietary right to the job.[10] Another black motorman agreed: "When a white man came there and wanted the job then . . . you had to get down. . . . A black man had to get down and let the white run."[11]

Highlighting the exclusion of blacks from jobs on the mainline motor was their employment as brakemen and mule drivers. Among skilled and semiskilled jobs, blacks gained their strongest foothold in the dangerous brakeman job, which paralleled the hazardous coupling job on the old railroad cars. They worked behind white motormen but continually complained that white men "would not brake behind a black motorman." Although the use of draft animals steadily declined with the rise of mechanization, some southern West Virginia mines continued to use mules in the underground transportation of coal. During the 1920s, Oscar Davis and later his son Leonard drove mules at the New River and Pocahontas Consolidated Coal Company in McDowell County.[12] Disproportionately black, the mule drivers worked between the individual working places and the mainline rails, where the "mainline motor," usually operated by white men, pulled the cars to the tipple, the outside preparation and shipment facilities. According to the accident reports of the State Bureau of Mines, between 1916 and 1925 African-Americans accounted for over 35 percent of the state's 124 fatal and serious nonfatal accidents involving mule drivers.[13] Gradually, however, the "gathering motors" replaced the mules. The introduction of the gathering motor, which was ancillary to the "mainline motor," provided increasing opportunities for blacks after World War I.

As the coal industry entered the depression years of the late 1920s, white resistance to employment of blacks as skilled workers grew more vocal. Employers increasingly asserted that "the negro is not much good with machinery." At times, according to Laing, "the tone of the employer seemed to imply. . . . A coal cutting machine is a machine—hence, of course, he is no good." At the same time, white workers increased their resistance to the employment of blacks as machinist helpers, men who had privileged entree into machinist jobs. When asked if his black helper was a good worker, one machinist replied, "'Yes, he will do his work and half of mine if I want him to.' He said that he never 'gets familiar' and 'keeps his place.'" The same machinist nonetheless expressed his preference for a white helper, and, as blacks lost such jobs, those who remained worked under reluctant and blatantly exploitative white bosses.[14] While racism indeed shaped the white workers' responses toward blacks, white machinists desired white helpers not because blacks were "lazy," inefficient, or uncooperative, but because they were apparently the opposite and were thus perceived as a threat during a period of increasing mechanization and subsequent economic decline.[15]

In the aftermath of World War I, as racial discrimination excluded blacks from important skilled, semiskilled, and supervisory positions, it blocked their progress in unskilled jobs as well. As coal loaders paid by the ton, blacks faced increasing discrimination in the assignment of work places. To be sure, black coal loaders shared a variety of debilitating working conditions with their white counterparts. Low wages, hazardous conditions, and hard work characterized the experiences of all miners, regardless of ethnicity or race. Yet, according to the testimonies of black miners, racism intensified the impact of such conditions on them. "A lot of those mines had unwritten policies. The blacks would work a certain section of the mines. The [American] whites would work a certain section. The Italians and the foreigners would work a certain section," recalled Leonard Davis. Describing his father's experience during the 1920s and later his own, Davis also said, "At times . . . in certain conditions blacks would have a good place to load coal. But mostly they were given places where there was a lot of rock, water, and some days you worked until you moved the rock. You didn't make a penny because they weren't paying for moving rock then. You didn't make anything."[16]

During the mid-1920s, black miners repeatedly complained of poor working conditions. The seams they worked were characterized by excessive rock, water, low coal content, and bad air. They sometimes loaded three to four cars of rock before reaching the "good" coal. From the mid-1920s through the early 1930s, Roy Todd recalled, black miners lost a lot of time and money through "dead work." If there was a rock fall in your area, he said, "you had to clean it up for nothing." The cleanup sometimes took two or three days.[17] Although many observers emphasized the water-free nature of West Virginia mines, in fact work in excessive water was a common problem. Some men loaded coal in hip boots. Even where water was no problem, black men were disproportionately assigned low seams. They frequently worked in seams as low as two or three feet, loading coal on their knees. "I like it high. . . . I don't like it low," one black miner exclaimed. "You got to crawl in there."[18] Although they used pads when loading low coal, some men developed calluses on their knees that "looked like they had two knee caps." According to Lawrence Boling, poor ventilation also hampered the black coal loader's progress: "Sometimes the circulation of air or no air would be so bad you'd have to wait sometimes up to two hours before you could get back in there to load any coal. I have been sick and dizzy off of that smoke many times. . . . that deadly poison is there. . . . It would knock you out too, make you weak as water."[19]

Compounding the problems of bad air, low coal seams, and water were the difficulties of unmechanized mines. While few mines used pick mining exclusively, traditional methods persisted in portions of mines where use of machines was difficult and unprofitable. During the late 1920s, in one of the few mines relying upon pick methods, black miners outnumbered the combined total of immigrants and American-born white workers. In such cases the coal was undercut and loaded by hand, thus employing the traditional skill of pick and shovel mining. Recalling his father's employment as an occasional pick and shovel miner, one black miner said, "My dad would tell me many times that I was [a]sleep when he went to work and [a]sleep when he came back." Another black miner, Willis Martin of Gary, McDowell County, recalled, "We used to go to work so early in the morning and come home so late that on Sunday morning you'd see a little baby start to crying when he saw the strange man in the house."[20]

While these conditions indeed characterized the experiences of all miners to some extent, racism undoubtedly intensified their impact on blacks. Surveys of employer attitudes and practices during the late

1920s confirm the role of racism in shaping the black coal loader's experience. "The best points of the colored coal loader are that he will work in wet places and in entries where the air is bad with less complaint than the white man," claimed an employer in the Kanawha-New River field. Another employer declared that "in this low coal I would rather have a negro than any other loader."[21]

Reflecting the immigrants' ability to outbid blacks for the better working areas, one employer exclaimed that "if they [immigrants] do not get the best places in the mine they will not work. . . . That is one thing about the colored man—he will work anywhere." Like American-born whites, immigrants in competition with black workers increasingly adopted anti-black attitudes and practices. According to blacks, some of them exceeded "native whites in this respect." When one immigrant foreman lost his job, black miners rejoiced, one of them stating, "I just can't stand being Jim-crowed by one of those fellows."[22]

Few workers of either race worked in the less hazardous outside positions, relatively safe from the dangers of explosions, coal dust, poisonous gases, and slate falls. Yet, even more than inside labor, the racial stratification of outside labor increased during World War I and its aftermath. Blacks dominated jobs in the coke yards, the hot, difficult, and most disagreeable of the outside positions, while whites dominated the less demanding phases of outside work, such as the preparation and shipment of the coal. In 1910, blacks had made up 47 percent of all the state's coke workers, but in southern West Virginia during World War I and the 1920s, blacks constituted 65–80 percent of all coke workers, with immigrants and American-born whites making up only 20–35 percent.[23]

Racial discrimination gained concrete expression in the lower average earnings of black miners. During the economic downturn of the late 1920s, the racial wage gap widened. In 1929, the payrolls of three coal companies revealed an average semimonthly wage of $118.30, with the earnings of whites, both immigrant and American, exceeding those of blacks by nearly $20.[24] No doubt racial discrimination exacted a similar toll on the earnings of black miners throughout the postwar period.

Despite the debilitating effects of class and racial inequality, black miners took a hand in shaping their own experience. They developed strategies designed to vitiate the effects of various discriminatory practices that white employers, workers, and the state devised to subordinate them. These strategies included high levels of productivity in the face of white worker competition, solidarity with white workers in the face of capitalist exploitation of all workers, and a growing alliance with black elites in the face of persistent patterns of racial inequality. Thus at times their actions appear contradictory and at cross purposes with each other. Yet, within the highly volatile class and racial environment of southern West Virginia, the black coal miners' responses in fact had an underlying coherence and logic. As time passed and evidence of white hostility persisted, black miners placed increasing emphasis on racial solidarity with black elites as their primary strategy.[25]

In their competitive encounter with white workers, black miners targeted job performance as one of their most telling mechanisms of survival. Seeking to secure their jobs, black miners resolved to provide cooperative, efficient, and productive labor. During his career, one black miner set a record for handloading. He loaded 90,000 tons of coal, an amount equal to a seventeen-mile long train of 1,750 cars, each containing fifty tons.[26] More ordinary black coal miners also related with pride the number of tons they loaded in a day or week, and ultimately over a lifetime. Lawrence Boling later offered crucial insight into the black miner's contributions to the coal industry, the use of productivity as a strategy of survival, and the black miner's mentality, when he stated, "As far as I am concerned back in those days, the black miner was the backbone of the mines. . . . I am proud of my life. . . . I may have worked hard. It was honest."[27]

Up through the job hierarchy, black miners exhibited a similar resolve to perform well. At the Weyanoke Coal Company, Charles T. Harris transformed the dangerous brakeman job into a status symbol, as well as a mechanism of survival. "I liked the brakeman best . . . because the guys . . . would get together in the pool rooms . . . to see who was the best brakeman and [to] show of[f]. . . . In fact I done it mostly for a name. . . . They said that I was one of the best brakemen . . . and they called me 'Speed Harris.'" Harris even developed a joke around his job, which captured the inter- and even intraracial competition in the coal mining labor force: "I said, very few colored people can do what I do but no white at all."[28]

In the face of white competition, black machine cutters and motormen also worked to improve their productivity. In the early 1920s, William Beasley alternated between jobs as a motorman and machine cutter. Later in the decade, using an old standard Godman machine, he set a record on the undercutting machine, cutting twenty-eight places in eight hours. At times, coal operators used the performance of black men to raise standards for white workers. The general manager of a large company in McDowell County said, "We try to standardize our work as much as possible. One day one of the groups of [white] coal cutters at a certain mine decided that five places were all that any one man could cut in a day. I went to one of my Negro cutters and told him to go down to that place and we would give [him] all the places he wanted and a $100 [bill] besides. That night this Negro cut 25 places. We standardized at seven."[29]

Black miners not only worked to increase tonnage; they aimed to do so with minimal damage to their health. Even as they pushed to increase output, they sought to avoid lost-time accidents. Like whites, black miners participated in company-sponsored safety contests. Through such contests, but most of all through day-to-day attention to their own safety, black miners honed their survival and safety skills. Roy Todd later recalled that he worked in the mines "47 years without a lost time accident." Another black miner recalled that his father worked in the mines "51 years and he never had a lost time accident."[30] After over 50 years of coal mining, Charles Harris recalled that his father "never was what you might say sick and he didn't have no bad back, and he didn't have no beat up hands. . . . That's right. I am telling you the truth now." No doubt Harris exaggerated this claim, but it nonetheless suggests insight into the black miners' attention to their own health and safety. Other black men simply refused to work in the most dangerous places, reflecting the constant tension in the black miners' effort to provide productive labor while simultaneously protecting their lives and health. Columbus Avery said, "I's goin to a place in the morning and inspect it. If it was bad, I wouldn't have anything to do with it. I never was hurt. I just wouldn't go into a dangerous place. They could fire me if they wanted to, but I wouldn't risk my life on a bad top."[31]

Refusal to work in dangerous places was an aspect of the chronic transiency of southern West Virginia's black coal miners. "They fired me at Pidgeon Creek once because I refused to go into a place I thought was dangerous," Avery said. Like their white counterparts, in efforts to improve working conditions, increase wages, and gain greater recognition of their humanity, black miners frequently moved between one mine and another within the region. They regularly traveled through southern West Virginia and farms in other parts of the South. Gradually, they made their way to the mines and steel mills of northern West Virginia, Pennsylvania, and Ohio. "I moved once ten times in ten years. I was high tempered. I would not take nothing off of anyone. I had a lot of pride," North Dickerson recalled. Another black miner said, "I would always be looking for the best job and the most money."[32]

Much of the black miner's geographic mobility was involuntary, generated by cyclical swings in the coal economy. Moreover, even during good times, coal operators and their supervisory personnel were often arbitrary and callous in their hiring and firing decisions. As Walter Moorman recalled, when miners complained about pay, one foreman retorted, "Don't grumble and stay, grumble and be on your way." In good and bad times, many black miners took this advice. When one mine foreman told a black brakeman that he had other brakemen tied up outside "with a paper string, if it rain[s] they'll come in," the brakeman reached upon the motor board, got his lunch bag, said "you get em," and quit.[33]

Roy Todd's travels typified the geographical mobility of black miners. In 1919, he took his first job at the No. 1 mine of the McGregor Coal Company at Slagle, Logan County. He worked there for one year before moving to Island Creek Coal Company at nearby Holden. Beginning at the firm's No. 1 mine, Todd soon moved to No. 8, before going to Trace Hollow for six months, working as a brace carrier on a company-constructed high school building. During the mid-1920s, he worked at several mines in McDowell County, including those of the Carswell Coal Company and the Houston Colliery Company at Kimball. During the late 1920s and early 1930s, Todd spent short periods mining in Washington, Pennsylvania, the Fairmont District of northern West Virginia, and Lance and Wheelwright, Kentucky.[34] Thus, Todd, in common with other black miners, traveled widely, not only from company to company but from mine to mine within the same company, always seeking better seams and safer conditions throughout the multistate eastern bituminous region.

In response to the intrinsic hazards of coal mining, black coal miners sometimes developed close bonds with white miners, especially during crises surrounding such catastrophes as explosions. Echoing the sentiments of many, one black miner exclaimed that "When that mine [explosion or accident] come everybody seem like they were brothers. . . . If one man got killed it throwed a gloom over the whole mine." Even under ordinary circumstances, black and white miners slowly developed bonds across racial and ethnic lines. Such ties were apparently most prominent among blacks and immigrants of Italian origins, whom blacks called "Tallies." Pink Henderson recalled that a "certain bunch of whites would not work with a black man," but immigrants and blacks got along "pretty well." Lawrence Boling recalled, "They seemed like they'd rather be with the blacks than with the whites." While black coal miners made few comparable remarks about their relationship with American-born white miners, some suggested that blacks got along better with the West Virginia "mountain whites" than with white workers who migrated into the coalfields from Mississippi and other Deep South states.[35]

However uneven the relationship between black and white coal miners, union struggles brought about a substantial degree of interracial solidarity among the southern West Virginia coal miners. During World War I, districts 17 and 29 of the United Mine Workers of America (UMWA) expanded dramatically. Covering the Kanawha-New River and Williamson-Logan coal fields, including Kanawha, Fayette, Logan, and Mingo counties. District 17, the larger of the two, increased its membership from 7,000 in early 1917 to over 17,000 within a few months. By the war's end, it claimed over 50,000 members. Union membership in District 29—covering the southernmost Pocahontas and Winding Gulf fields, including McDowell, Mercer, and Raleigh counties—increased during the period from fewer than 1,000 to over 6,000. Black coal miners were prominent among the rank and file, frequently held office in local unions, served on the executive boards of districts 17 and 29, worked as district organizers, and served as delegates to the biennial meetings of the national body.[36]

Because of language barriers, immigrants sometimes deferred to black leadership. At the 1921 meeting of the national body, for example, black delegate Frank Ingham of Mingo County eloquently addressed the gathering on conditions in his area: "I will first say that I am happy to be permitted to speak, not for myself but for Mingo county. . . . The real truth has never been told of Mingo county. It cannot be told. The language has not been coined to express the agonies the miners of Mingo county are enduring today. The world is under the impression that martial law exists there. That is not true. What exists in Mingo is partial law, because it is only brought to bear upon the miners that have joined the union." Even T. Edward Hill, the staunch anti-union director of the Bureau of Negro Welfare and Statistics, confirmed the positive character of interracial unionism in the area: "Negro members of the Executive Board . . . were elected in conventions in which white miner delegates outnumbered negroes more than five to one. The Negro union miners . . . are as staunch and faithful supporters of their organization as any other class of workers."[37]

George Edmunds of Iowa, a black international organizer, played a key role in helping to unionize black miners in southern West Virginia. In 1916 Edmunds wrote to West Virginia comrades, expressing intimate knowledge of conditions in the region: "I know so many of you, brothers. We have had some good times and hard times together. On Paint Creek and Cabin Creeks; from Gauley to the Ohio River, I have passed and repassed among you and . . . I always did my best for you and your cause." On one occasion, Edmunds addressed "a large and enthusiastic gathering" at Bancroft, West Virginia, where miners from several other mining towns in the Kanawha-New River district had gathered. On another occasion, he helped to organize a "rousing meeting" at Winnifrede, also located in the Kanawha-New River area. In the early postwar years, Edmunds continued to appear among the slate of speakers at the UMWA membership drives in the region.[38]

The immediate postwar years produced the most dramatic expression of working-class solidarity, culminating in the coal strike of 1921 and the "Armed March" of miners on Logan and Mingo counties. When coal companies denied workers the right of collective bargaining, armed conflict erupted in Logan and Mingo counties between more than 5,000 union miners on the one hand and over 1,200 local law enforcement officers, strikebreakers, and company-employed detectives on the other. The conflict killed more than 100 men and led to the declaration of martial law on three different occasions, once in 1920 and twice in 1921. Only the intervention of federal troops ended the savage warfare. Before the conflict ended, however, many black coal miners had demonstrated solidarity with their white brothers. The march on Logan and Mingo counties included an estimated 2,000 black miners, mainly union men from the Kanawha-New River field. The movement eventually attracted black adherents in the violently anti-union strongholds of Mingo, Logan, and McDowell counties as well.[39]

In their violent confrontation with capital, black and white miners developed reciprocal loyalties. Their commitment to each other was sometimes demonstrated in dramatic ways. When law officers and Baldwin-Felts guards dispersed a meeting of union men at Roderfield, McDowell County (leaving four dead and four wounded), black miner R. B. Page organized a contingent of seventy-five men and marched to help his union brothers. Although the police thwarted his plans, his actions were a testament to the interracial character of the mine workers' struggle. At the height of class warfare, according to the *Charleston Gazette*, "One of the [white] deputies who was killed was John Gore. He was scouting through the woods near Blair [Mountain] and encountered a Negro scout. The negro [sic] opened fire on Gore and the latter fired in return. The negro was killed." When a white miner "came upon Gore who was bending over the body of the negro searching for identification marks," he shot the officer "through the heart." In an enthusiastic letter to the *United Mine Workers Journal,* a white miner summed up the interracial character of the miners' struggle in southern West Virginia: "I call it a darn solid mass of different colors and tribes, blended together, woven, bound, interlocked, tongued and grooved and glued together in one body."[40]

Given before a U.S. Senate investigation committee, headed by Sen. William S. Kenyon of Iowa, the most potent evidence of black participation in the "Mingo War" was the testimony of black coal miners themselves. Black miners stood firmly with white workers and their testimonies reflect the complicated blending of class and racial consciousness. Black men also suffered a large, perhaps disproportionate, share of the violent reprisals from law enforcement officers and private Baldwin-Felts guards. For his union activities, Frank Ingham lost his job and house on several occasions. A veteran miner of fourteen years, in the early postwar years Ingham resisted efforts to divide workers along racial lines. The superintendent at his Mingo County mine fired Ingham when the black miner urged his fellow workers to ignore the company's promise to reward them for abandoning their white co-workers. "He told me to get out when I told the colored people not to take the white people's places," Ingham told the senators.[41]

Nor was dismissal and eviction Ingham's only punishment. Arrested several times by both federal and local authorities, he was brutally beaten and denied visiting privileges. On one occasion, he testified, a local officer suggested that "what we ought to do with

[Ingham] is not take him to jail; but to riddle his body with bullets." At midnight, law officers removed him from jail, stole his money and belongings, took him to an isolated spot, and beat him nearly to death. Federal and state authorities were no less brutal. Ingham said that Maj. Thomas Davis of the West Virginia National Guard denied him visitors and informed his wife, relatives, and friends that "the next nigger that came over and asked him anything about me that he would put them in [jail] as well." Through it all, however, Ingham emphasized his working-class activities as the fundamental cause of attacks upon him. Even following his brutal beating, he testified, saying, "They asked me what I had been in the hands of the mob for and I told them because I belonged to the Union."[42]

Still, basic to Ingham's support of the union was his commitment to his race. When he joined the union and resisted the use of black strike-breakers, he revealed consciousness of both class and race. Of his decision to oppose efforts to divide black and white mine workers, he declared, "I did not think that would be a very safe thing to do, from the fact that it would terminate in a race riot, and I would not like to see my people in anything like that, because they were outnumbered so far as Mingo County" was concerned. Ingham said further, "My motive in advising the people was, I am a pioneer colored man in that creek. Before that they had been denied the privilege of working in these mines, and since they have got well established in there, many of them had found employment there. I did not want them to make enemies of the white race by taking their places."[43]

Other black miners confirmed Ingham's commitment to working-class solidarity within the framework of black unity. George Echols, a union miner, local UMWA officer, and striker said, "The United [Mine] Workers of America have privileges which are guaranteed by the United States, we have rights to protect us, both black and white, but they [operators and law officers] do not regard those rights at all. They take those privileges away from us. Now we are asking you to give them back to us. Let us be free men. Let us stand equal."[44] Born in slavery, Echols articulated a distinctive African-American perspective. "I was raised a slave," Echols related. "My master and my mistress called me and I answered, and I know the time when I was a slave, and I feel just like we feel now." The remarks of another black miner, J. H. Reed, likewise expressed the blending of class and racial consciousness. Reed linked his arrest, incarceration, and mistreatment to his activities both as a union man and a black: "The thing here is that a man here is the same as being in slavery."[45]

Still, in West Virginia as elsewhere, working-class solidarity was a highly precarious affair. White workers and employers coalesced to a substantial, even fundamental, degree around notions of black inferiority.[46] In its contract with employees, under a provision on workmanship and methods, the Carbon Fuel Company stipulated that "The miner shall load his coal in every case free from shale, bone, *niggerhead* [i.e. worthless coal] and *other impurities* [my italics]."[47] When the *United Mine Workers Journal* reprinted a racist joke from the operators' *Coal Age*, the racial consensus between operators and coal miners was made even more explicit: "Sambo, a negro [mule] driver . . . was able to gather his trips without speaking to his mule . . . Mose, another driver [presumably black] . . . went to Sambo for help and asked Sambo what was needed to teach such tricks. Sambo said all that was necessary was to know more than the mule."[48] Further high-lighting the white racial consensus were distasteful and often vicious stereotypes of black women.[49]

Cross-class white unity helped to engender a growing bond between workers and black elites. The activities of the Bureau of Negro Welfare and Statistics, the black press (especially the *McDowell Times*), and the McDowell County Colored Republican Organization (MCCRO), all evidenced aspects of the growing black worker-black elite alliance. Through the strikebreaking activities of T. Edward Hill of the BNWS, for example, some blacks gained jobs during the massive coal strikes of the early 1920s. The bureau proudly claimed credit for deterring over 100 black miners from joining the "Armed March." Under Hill's leadership, the BNWS nonetheless pursued its strike-breaking function with care, seeking to avoid racial violence. As an added measure of protection for black workers, Hill, with some success, advocated the use of small, interracial contingents of strikebreak-ers. "The coal companies that are bringing in workers are having them sent in bunches of not more than 25 and in all crowds brought in to date there have been whites as well as negroes," he reported in 1922.[50]

Hill not only tried to avoid racial violence in the short run, he also sought long-run job security for the black miner. Keenly aware of traditional dismissal of blacks after strikes, Hill attempted to pry protective agreements from owners. In a letter to the local secretaries of the Coal Operators' Association and the president of the West Virginia

Coal Association, Hill wrote that it would be "manifestly unfair to use negro miners in this crisis and then displace them when workers of other races are available."[51] In the coal strikes of 1921–22, Hill secured an agreement from owners and managers, "that, however the strike is settled, the negro miners now being employed" would be retained; or, if they voluntarily left their jobs or were "discharged for cause," their places would be filled by other blacks. In case operators could not secure other blacks to take the vacant places, the State Bureau of Negro Welfare and Statistics would "be requested to supply qualified Negroes." M. S. Bradley, president of the West Virginia Coal Association, Hill reported, promised to "lend his personal assistance in seeing that justice is done." The secretaries of the Kanawha and New River Coal Operators' Association endorsed the agreement. Hill believed the operators would keep their word and, until the Great Depression, most of them did.[52]

Such economic concessions, however, were purchased at a substantial price. They were achieved not only at the expense of interracial working class unity, but at the expense of greater racial pride and self-assertion. Although based upon the interplay of concrete class and racial interests, the relationship between blacks and coal operators was mediated through the increasing rhetoric of welfare capitalism, conditioned by the operators' paternalistic and racist notions of black dependency. In a 1920 advertisement titled "Discrimination Against the Negro," the Logan County coal operators hoped to convince blacks that they, not the United Mine Workers of America, were best suited to protect the interest of black workers. "Colored miners in the Williamson field who have been induced to become members of the United Mine Workers," the operators lamented, "were doubtless not informed about the discrimination practiced against their race in the unionized fields."[53]

The following year the same operators sponsored a pamphlet directed toward black workers. Again the owners informed blacks that only the company had their best interest at heart. "First," the *UMWA Journal* warned black miners, "when they open up a new mine they think of the things that will lead you and your children to the better land. . . . So we can plainly see how kind and true the operators are to the colored people in Logan fields." As late as 1928, before the U.S. Senate's coal investigation committee, a local coal operator testified that "the negro is not responsible for his position in America. It is the duty of the white man to treat him with justice, mercy, and compassion. . . . I do believe in providing the negroes with every economic and industrial [as opposed to social] opportunity possible."[54]

The black press supported the operators' portrait of themselves as just and paternalistic employers. In doing so, they also adopted aspects of a larger progressive tradition, which urged corporate America to take a more humane interest in the welfare of its workers. In a detailed description of the Carter Coal Company, the popular *Times* columnist W. H. Harris presented a telling contrast between what he called the old and new captains of industry: "The old time captain of industry was ob[sessed] with just one idea to get as much labor as possible for the smallest amount of money. . . . In late years the industrial captains have found that . . . the best investment is an intelligent, satisfied class of employees."[55] During the 1920s, the popular Bluefield columnist S.R. Anderson reiterated the same theme in his recurring column "News of Colored People," printed in the white *Bluefield Daily Telegraph*. On one occasion, Anderson reinforced the idea of welfare capitalism "as an expression of the human element in corporate interest upon which we may rely as a 'savor of life unto life' against the wreck of radicalism in labor and corporate insanity."[56] In exchange for employment, housing, credit at the company store, and a gradually expanding variety of recreational and social welfare programs, employers expected deference from all workers, but especially from blacks.

Under the energetic editorship of M. T. Whittico, the paternalistic theme was a recurring feature of the *McDowell Times*. Describing the miners as "children" and the operators as "parents," the *Times* sometimes took the paternalistic theme to extremes. A *Times* columnist describing R. D. Patterson, general manager of the Weyanoke Coal Company, declared, "He is a father to every man, woman and child on his work—a kind but not overly indulgent one. He gets results because his men believe in him." Moreover, the columnist concluded, Patterson's personality, ideas, and way of doing things permeated the entire fabric of coal camp life. "If you will stop to watch him a little, you will see Patterson reflected in everything on that works. . . . Chamelion-like, he has caused everything about him to become Pattersonized." "On the Winding Gulf," another columnist exclaimed, "the men say that Mr. Tams," a company official, "is the working man's 'daddy.'"[57] Such language helped to perpetuate notions of racial subordination and superordination, suggesting critical limits to the benefits to coal miners of their alliance with black elites. Yet black editors, columnists, and other community leaders no doubt exaggerated managerial benevolence as a means of eliciting, as well as describing, the desired corporate behavior.

At times, elite leadership was a good deal more assertive. Under the leadership of the McDowell County Colored Republican Organization (MCCRO), during World War I and its aftermath African-Americans escalated their demands for representation in the state bureaucracy. Dominated by the region's small black elite, the civil rights struggle gave rise to a more urgent articulation of black demands, with greater attention to the needs of the black proletariat at work and at home, that is, in the larger community life of coal-mining towns.

In their efforts to move up in the bituminous coal industry, black miners perceived a great deal of value in the growing political alliance between black workers and black elites. It not only promised jobs for highly trained black miners in the state bureaucracy but also offered hope for the future training of black workers in the changing bituminous coal industry. Thus, in 1927, for example, the State Department of Mines appointed a black miner to the position of safety director. A former fire boss in the mines of McDowell County and a graduate of West Virginia State College, the new black appointee, Osborne Black, was responsible for instructing black miners in mine safety procedures. Mining experts soon came to regard Black as an effective official.[58]

Upon Black's death nearly two years later, the MCCRO passed a resolution "Paying a tribute of respect" to the miner, who was also an active member of the strongest black political organization in the region. The MCCRO also urged the State Department of Mines to replace the deceased safety director with another African-American miner, which it did. Upon John Patterson's appointment to the post, a contemporary student of black miners noted that "so far as is known, he is the only Negro safety director in the world." Patterson had prepared for the position by taking correspondence courses from Pennsylvania State University. Moreover, before passing his state mine safety examination and receiving appointment to the state job, Patterson had also worked for several years as "a practical miner" and a mine foreman in Raleigh County.[59]

Between World War I and the Great Depression, black coal miners in southern West Virginia developed a variety of responses to racial inequality in the workplace: high productivity in the face of white worker competition; solidarity with white workers in the face of capitalist exploitation; and, most importantly, a growing alliance with black elites in the face of persistent patterns of racial discrimination. Yet, although racial discrimination undercut the black miners' position in southern West Virginia, compared to black miners further north and south, black miners in the Mountain State secured a firm position in the bituminous coal industry. Black coal miners in the North remained few in number and highly dispersed, as employers recruited south, central, and eastern European immigrants. Their small numbers also made it impossible for them to wage the socioeconomic and political struggles that blacks waged in southern West Virginia.[60]

White workers also developed strong labor unions in the northern fields, a development that reinforced the exclusion of blacks from mines in the region. In order to resist the demands of white workers for higher pay and better working conditions, northern coal operators gradually employed black workers (some as strikebreakers). Paradoxically, however, given their precarious position within a union stronghold, black miners in the northern region soon joined white workers and spearheaded a vigorous tradition of interracial unionism. Indeed, black leaders from these northern fields later aided the UMWA's campaign to organize black and white miners in southern West Virginia.

If blacks were largely excluded from northern mines, they dominated the labor force in the Birmingham district of Alabama. Yet a variety of forces weakened their position in the Deep South and made them more vulnerable to the exploitative dimensions of industrial capitalism than their counterparts in southern West Virginia. They faced the abusive contract and convict labor systems, a program of political disfranchisement (reinforced by a vicious pattern of racial violence, including lynchings and race riots), and a racial wage scale, which placed black earnings distinctly below those of whites for the same work. These conditions helped to drive many Alabama miners to southern West Virginia. Although they occupied the lowest position in the bituminous labor force, in the Mountain State black miners gained comparatively greater opportunities than their counterparts further north and south. They gained a solid footing in the coal-mining labor force, received equal pay for equal work, were allowed to vote, confronted fewer lynchings and incidents of mob violence, and waged a vigorous and largely successful political struggle for recognition of their human and civil rights.

Notes

1. See Kenneth L. Kusmer, "The Black Urban Experience in American History," in *The State of Afro-American History: Past, Present, and Future*, ed. Darlene Clark Hine (Baton Rouge: Louisiana State Univ., 1986), 91–122; Joe William Trotter, Jr., "Afro-American Urban History: A Critique of the Literature," in Trotter, *Black Milwaukee: The Making of an Industrial Proletariat, 1915–45* (Urbana: Univ. of Illinois Press, 1985), 264–82.
2. Ronald L. Lewis, "Migration of Southern Blacks to the Central Appalachian Coalfields: The Transition from Peasant to Proletarian," *Journal of Southern History* 55:1 (Feb. 1989): 77–102; Robert P. Stuckert, "Black Population of the Southern Appalachian Mountains," *Phylon* 48:2 (Summer 1987): 141–51; Joe W. Trotter, "Black Migration in Historical Perspective: A Review of the Literature," *The Great Migration in Historical Perspective: New Dimensions of Race and Class in Industrial America*, ed. Trotter (Bloomington: Indiana Univ. Press, forthcoming, 1991).
3. Joe W. Trotter, *Coal, Class, and Color: Blacks in Southern West Virginia, 1915–1932* (Urbana: Univ. of Illinois Press, 1990), chs. 3, 4.
4. Ibid.
5. "Exceptional Opportunities . . . At Olga Shaft, Coalwood, W. Va.," *McDowell Times*, 8 Sept. 1916; Price V. Fishback, "Employment Conditions in the Coal Industry" (Ph.D. diss., Univ. of Washington, 1983), 284–85.
6. West Virginia Bureau of Negro Welfare and Statistics (WVBNWS), *Biennial Reports,* 1921–22, 58–59 and 1927–28, 15-17; newspaper clipping, *Welch Daily News*, 21 Sept. 1926, in U. G. Carter Papers (West Virginia Collection, West Virginia Univ.).
7. James T. Laing, "The Negro Miner in West Virginia" (Ph.D. diss., Ohio State Univ., 1933), 182–83, 213; "Exceptional Opportunities . . . At Olga Shaft, Coalwood, W. Va.," *McDowell Times*, 8 Sept. 1916.
8. Homer L. Morris, *The Plight of the Bituminous Coal Miner* (Philadelphia: Univ. of Pennsylvania Press, 1934), 297–8; Fishback, "Employment Conditions," 308–9; West Virginia State College Mining Extension Service, *Annual Report*, 1942–43, in U. G. Carter Papers.
9. WVBNWS, *Biennial Reports*, 1921–22, 86–87, and 1923–24, 36–37.
10. C. F. Fuetter, "Mixed Labor in Coal Mining," *Coal Age* 10 (July 22, 1916): 137, quoted in Ronald L. Lewis, *Black Coal Miners in America: Race, Class, and Community Conflict, 1780–1980* (Lexington: Univ. Press of Kentucky, 1987), 144–45; interview with Pink Henderson, 15 July 1983. Unless

otherwise stated, all interviews were conducted by the author and are in his possession.

11. "Memorandum, Willie Parker," Straight Numerical Files, No. 182363, U.S. Department of Justice Records, RG 60, National Archives, Washington, D.C.; interviews with Pink Henderson, 15 July 1983, and Charles T. Harris, 18 July 1983; Laing, "The Negro Miner," 242.

12. "Memorandum, Willie Parker," SNF 182363, RG 60, National Archives; interviews with Leonard Davis, 28 July 1983, and Roy Todd, 18 July 1983.

13. Fishback, "Employment Conditions," 284–85; Laing, "The Negro Miner," 191, 242, 249–50.

14. Laing, "The Negro Miner," 234–36.

15. "Looking Back with Columbus Avery," *Goldenseal* 8:1 (Spring 1982): 32–40.

16. Interview with Leonard Davis, 28 July 1983; Laing, "The Negro Miner," 225–28.

17. Interviews with Walter E. Moorman and Margaret Moorman, 14 July 1983, and Roy Todd, 18 July 1983.

18. Interviews with Andrew Campbell, 19 July 1983, Pink Henderson, 15 July 1983, and Henry L. Phillips and Ellen Phillips, 20 July 1983.

19. Interviews with North Dickerson, 28 July 1983, and Lawrence Boling, 18 July 1983.

20. Interview with Leonard Davis, 28 July 1983; Laing, "The Negro Miner," 189; Matt Witt and Earl Dolter, "Before I'd Be a Slave," in *In Our Blood: Four Coal Mining Families*, ed. Matt Witt, (New Market, TN: Highlander Research Center, 1979), 23–47.

21. Laing, "The Negro Miner," 225–28.

22. Ibid., 225–28, 474.

23. Trotter, *Coal, Class, and Color*, chs. 3, 4.

24. Laing, "The Negro Miner," 222–24; Fishback, "Employment Conditions," 169.

25. For the debate on the role of race and class in the coalfields, see Herbert Hill, "Myth-Making as Labor History: Herbert Gutman and the United Mine Workers of America," *International Journal of Politics, Culture and Society* 2, no. 2 (Winter 1988): 132–200, and Stephen Brier, "In Defense of Gutman: The Union's Case," *International Journal of Politics, Culture and Society* 2, no. 3 (Spring 1989): 383–95

26. Interviews with Roy Todd, 18 July 1983, and Charles T. Harris, 18 July 1983; Lewis, *Black Coal Miners in America*, 179–80, citing *Color: A Tip Top World Magazine*, 4 (Feb. 1948): 13; "Among Our Colored People," *The New River Company Employees' Magazine* (April 1928): 8 (West Virginia Collection, West Virginia Univ.)

27. Interview with Lawrence Boling, 18 July 1983.

28. Interview with Charles T. Harris, 18 July 1983.

29. Interviews with William M. Beasley, 26 July 1983, and Roy Todd, 18 July 1983; Laing, "The Negro Miner," 264–65.

30. Interview with Roy Todd, 18 July 1983; "First Aid Contest at Gary," 4 June 1915, and "Working Hard to Stop Accidents," 4 Aug. 1916, both in *McDowell Times*; "Pocahontas Wins Safety Meet . . . New River Pocahontas Consolidated Teams of Berwind Jones First Place Among Colored Division," *McDowell Recorder*, 22 Aug. 1929.

31. Interview with Charles T. Harris, 18 July 1983; "Looking Back with Columbus Avery," 32–40; Reginald Millner, "Conversations with the 'Ole Man': The Life and Times of a Black Appalachian Coal Miner," *Goldenseal* 5:1 (Jan.–Mar. 1979): 58–64.

32. Interview with Charles T. Harris, 18 July 1983; interviews with North E. Dickerson, 28 July 1983, and William M. Beasley, 26 July 1983.

33. Interviews with Walter E. Moorman and Margaret Moorman, 14 July 1983, and Charles T. Harris, 18 July 1983.

34. Interview with Roy Todd, 18 July 1983.

35. Interviews with Charles T. Harris, 18 July 1983, Roy Todd, 18 July 1983, Pink Henderson, 15 July 1983, North Dickerson, 28 July 1983, and Lawrence Boling, 18 July 1983.

36. For membership statistics on UMWA districts 17 and 29, see David A. Corbin, *Life, Work, and Rebellion in the Coal Fields: The Southern West Virginia Miners, 1889–1922* (Urbana: Univ. of Illinois Press, 1981), 76–77, 184. "Delegate [Frank] Ingham," in *Proceedings of the 28th Consecutive and 5th Biennial Convention of the United Mine Workers of America, Indianapolis, Indiana, 20 Sept. to 5 Oct. 1921. Vol. 1* (Indianapolis: Bookwalter-Ball-Greathouse, 1921), 538–39; and "Roll Call," in *Proceedings of the Re-Convened 28th Consecutive and 5th Biennial Convention of the United Mine Workers of America, Indianapolis, Indiana. 14 Feb. 1922* (Indianapolis: Bookwalter-Ball-Greathouse, 1922), 173; Records of Districts 17 and 29, UMWA Papers, UMWA Archives, Washington, D.C.

37. T. Edward Hill, "The Coal Strike and Negro Miners in West Virginia," ca. 1922, in "Early Surveys . . .," Series 6, Box 89, National Urban League Papers, Library of Congress; WVBNWS, *Biennial Reports, 1923–24*, 22–24; 1925–26, 131. For insight into black and white occupancy of the UMWA tent colonies of striking miners, see Box 2, Folders 9, 10, Van Amberg Bittner Papers, West Virginia Collection, West Virginia University.

38. "From Iowa: A Word to the West Virginia Miners," *United Mine Workers Journal (UMWJ)*, 1 June 1916; G. H. Edmunds, "West Virginia on Tap," 11 April 1917; "District 29 Holds a Splendid Special Convention," 1 Feb. 1919; and "Assignment of Speakers for 1921 Labor Day," 1 Sept. 1921, all in ibid.

39. Daniel P. Jordan, "The Mingo War: Labor Violence in the Southern West Virginia Coal Fields, 1919–1922," in *Essays in Southern Labor History*, ed. Gary M. Fink and Merl E. Reed (Westport: Greenwood Press, 1977), 102–43;

Corbin, *Life, Work, and Rebellion in the Coal Fields*, 195–224; Hill, "The Coal Strike and Negro Miners in West Virginia," *The Charleston Gazette*, 1 Sept. 1921, and "Confessed Murderer of John Gore is Given Life Sentence," *Logan Banner*, 19 Oct. 1923; Witt and Dolter, "Before I'd Be a Slave," 23–47. Heber Blankenhorn, "Marching Through West Virginia," *Nation* 113 (Sept. 1921): 289, estimates 2,000 blacks among the 8,000 marchers.

40. See *Charleston Gazette*, 1 Sept. 1921, and "Confessed Murderer of John Gore is Given Life Sentence," *Logan Banner*, 19 Oct. 1923. "From Silush, W. Va.," *UMWJ*, 1 Sept. 1921.

41. Testimony of Frank Ingham, *West Virginia Coal Fields: Hearings Before the Committee on Education, U.S. Senate, Vol. 1* (Washington: GPO, 1921), 26–38.

42. Ibid.

43. Ibid.

44. Testimonies of George Echols and J. H. Reed, both in *West Virginia Coal Fields*, 469–82.

45. Ibid.

46. "Agreement Between Carbon Fuel Company and Its Employees," 1923–25, in "Kanawha/Coal River," Mining Community Schedule-A, Box 28, U.S. Coal Commission Records, Record Group 68, National Archives.

47. Ibid.

48. "Easy," UMWJ, 15 Jan. 1925.

49. "Agreement Between Carbon Fuel Company and Its Employees," 1923–25, in "Kanawha/Coal River," Mining Community Schedule-A, Box 28, U.S. Coal Commission Records.

50. WVBNWS, Bienniel Report, 1921–22, 54–60; "The Coal Strike and Negro Miners in West Virginia," ca. 1922, in "Early Surveys . . . ," Series 6, Box 89, National Urban League Papers.

51. WVBNWS, Bienniel Report, 1921–22, 54–60; "The Coal Strike and Negro Miners in West Virginia."

52. Ibid.

53. "Discrimination Against the Negro," *Bluefield Daily Telegraph*, 20 June 1920.

54. "Negro Tricked into Logan County . . .," *UMWJ*, 15 June 1921, includes extensive excerpts from the operators' pamphlet directed toward black workers; testimony of Langdon Bell, director of the Red Jacket Consolidated Coal Company, *Conditions in the Coal Fields of Pennsylvania, West Virginia, and Ohio: Hearings Before the Committee on Interstate Commerce* (Washington: GPO, 1928), 1838–41.

55. W. H. Harris, "Exceptional Opportunities . . .," *McDowell Times*, 8 Sept. 1916. See also Agricultural Extension Service, *Annual Report, 1922* (Morgantown, WV), 40–47; Agricultural Extension Service, *Annual Report, 1923* (Morgantown, WV), 98–110.

56. S. R. Anderson, "News of Colored People," *Bluefield Daily Telegraph*, 2, 9, 22, and 23 Sept. 1920, 15 Nov. 1924, and 1 Jan. 1925.

57. Ralph W. White, "Weyanoke: The Eldorado of the Coal Fields in its Section of State," 13 July 1917; "Lynwin Coal Company: Offering Great Extra Inducements," 11 May 1917; "Lynwin Coal Company: Offering Great Opportunities for Money," 4 May 1917; "Sycamore C. Company: Located in Mingo County, W. Va.: Doing Good Work," 23 July 1915; "The Coal Miners Provided For," 26 Feb. 1915; Lawson Blenkinsopp, "The Colored Miner 'Don'ts' for Safety First," 15 Jan. 1915; "Improved Conditions in the Winding Gulf Fields," 17 Sept. 1917, all in *McDowell Times*. See also S. R. Anderson, "News of Colored People," *Bluefield Daily Telegraph*, 23 Sept. 1920, and Yvonne S. Farley, "Homecoming," *Goldenseal* 5:4 (Oct.–Dec. 1979): 7–16.

58. U. G. Carter, "Public Address" and "Speech to New River Colored Mining Institute, Fayette County," in Box 1, Folder 8, Carter Papers; "McDowell County Colored Republican Organization," *McDowell Recorder*, 23 Oct. 1920; Fishback, "Employment Conditions," 231, n. 9; Lewis, *Black Coal Miners in America*, 223, n. 18; and Laing, "The Negro Miners," 180–82.

59. Carter, "Public Address" and "Speech," Box 1, Folder 8, Carter Papers; *McDowell Recorder*, 23 Oct. 1929; Fishback, "Employment Conditions," 231, n. 9; Lewis, *Black Coal Miners in America*, 223, n. 18; Laing, "The Negro Miners," 180–82.

60. For documentation of the following comparative discussion, see Trotter, *Coal, Class, and Color*, ch. 11.

4. Heroines and Girl Strikers

Gender Issues and Organized Labor in the Twentieth-Century American South

Mary E. Frederickson

Southern women's labor history has focused on two primary sets of women: individuals who performed exceptional work for the labor movement, and groups of women workers who protested collectively within a public arena. These two powerful gender-based stereotypes have dominated twentieth-century perspectives of southern women workers. They have framed historians' discourse about southern women and organized labor, and have overshadowed the myriad of complex and subtle roles that southern women have played within the labor movement. While these images have portrayed two important aspects of women's labor involvement, they have obscured the efforts of rank-and-file women workers to enter unions as equal participants with their male counterparts. It is important to examine the prototypes of heroines and "girl strikers," to analyze their usefulness to organized labor and their role in labor militancy among women. It is essential to understand the reasons these stereotypes have resonated so profoundly in southern culture and to contrast these near-mythical images with the reality of women's work in southern unions. In doing so, it is possible to transcend the stereotypes themselves and to expand our understanding of the full spectrum of southern women's involvement in organized labor.

Women heroines have been recurrent figures in southern labor history. When Mary Harris "Mother" Jones traveled into the coal-mining areas of the American South in the 1910s and early 1920s she was hailed as a heroine and revered as the miners' "angel." Men who would not let a woman enter the mines for fear of bad luck willingly allowed Mother Jones to lead them into the union. Ella May Wiggins, songstress and martyr of the Gastonia strike in 1929, worked against enormous odds to organize North Carolina textile workers. Her efforts ended in her own violent death, but she lived on as a legendary heroine in southern labor history. Lucy Randolph Mason of the Congress of Industrial Organizations (CIO), worked unflaggingly from the late 1930s through the postwar years to realize the vision of industrial unionism in the South. She preached the social gospel of industrial democracy and believed southerners of all classes were ripe for conversion. Hailed by workers and union leaders alike, Lucy Mason became "the CIO's No. 1 trouble-shooter."[1]

As workers and unionists have recognized and respected heroines like Jones, Wiggins, and Mason, and historians have documented their lives, the collective actions of women workers have also remained in the forefront of contemporary and historical documentation of the labor movement. Referred to by journalists as "girl strikers," regardless of age, women workers consistently played crucial roles and received substantial publicity in southern labor struggles. The strikes and lockouts in three dozen North Carolina cotton factories in the last months of 1900, the walkouts of the pre–World War I era, the wave of strikes in southern textiles from 1927 through 1934, labor battles in the post–World War II period, and union fights in the civil rights decades of the 1960s and 1970s, all involved women workers. In a number of cases women led hundreds of male and female workers out of factories; in many instances women walked in the front ranks of strike parades, or filled conspicuous posts on picket lines. Without question, the actions of women workers have been crucial to labor's struggles in the South throughout the twentieth century.[2] In this context the girl striker was constantly in the limelight of the southern labor scene, and in literally thousands of situations over the past ninety years, unions organizing in the South have promoted this image.

Heroines within the southern labor movement have included individuals as different as Mother Jones, Ella May Wiggins, and Lucy Randolph Mason. Clearly, these three women encompass the spectrum of southern women labor heroines. But despite differences in age, class, and occupation, these women shared specific personal qualities, beliefs, ways of interacting, and methods of organizing. First, they were all "motherly" women. Second, they worked with groups of women and men. Third, they were the heroines, not of women only, but of women *and* men. Fourth, they dealt with men in ways that allowed males to save face. Fifth, they each took the labor movement's ideology of justice and equality literally, and insisted that it be applied to all laboring people, men and women, black and white.

Mary Harris Jones made a career of being a "mother." She had borne four children and raised them until they, and their father, died in a yellow fever epidemic in Memphis in 1867. At age thirty-seven she found herself a childless widow. Jones left Tennessee for Chicago where she supported herself as a seamstress and opened a dressmaking shop. The 1871 Chicago fire destroyed her shop, leaving Jones and 90,000 others homeless and adrift. Soon after this second tragedy, Jones joined the Knights of Labor. Welcomed as a woman, a worker, and the widow of a fervent unionist, Jones cast her lot with the labor movement. She claimed to make her home "wherever there is a fight"; she adopted America's workers, and encouraged them to call her "Mother."

Jones first entered the southern coalfields in 1891, when she answered a request from strikers in the Dietz mines. Over the next three decades she considered West Virginia, along with Colorado, to be her "stepdaughter of misery." She traveled South often, organizing workers in diverse industries. But she returned repeatedly to what she termed the "medieval" southern coalfields where "cruel is the life of the miners with the weight of the world upon their backs. . . . and their wives and little children in dire want."[3]

Ella May Wiggins was born in 1900 in the mountains of western North Carolina, near the town of Bryson City. Sent to work in a nearby spinning mill to help support the family, Ella May Mays met and married a fellow millworker named Johnny Wiggins. Together they left the mountains, migrating to the burgeoning industrial region of Gaston County, North Carolina, and settling in Bessemer City, where they took jobs in the American Mill sometime during 1919. A decade passed during which Ella May worked as a spinner, bore seven children, and was deserted by her husband. At age 29 she worked on the night shift in order to stay with her children by day. Money and food were scarce. Two of the children died. When employees at the Loray Mill in Gastonia went out on strike in April 1929, workers at the American Mill staged a spontaneous walkout to show their support, and also joined the National Textile Workers Union (NTWU). Wiggins emerged as a strong leader of the strike, frequently leading the singing among workers attending mass meetings at Loray. She recorded the events of the strike in the new lyrics she put to old ballads that folklorist Margaret Larkin claimed in 1929 were "better than a hundred speeches." On September 14, 1929, on the way to a National Textile Workers Union protest rally, the truck in which Ella May was riding was stopped by vigilantes who opened fire, killing Ella May and wounding two other strikers. Buried in an unmarked grave in Bessemer City's public cemetery, Wiggins, the "songstress of the mill workers," was declared a martyr by the NTWU, and in the years since 1929, she has endured as a heroine of the southern labor movement.[4]

Lucy Randolph Mason was born in 1882 in Alexandria, Virginia, into a family that traced its lineage to Virginia's early political leaders, including George Mason, author of the Virginia Bill of Rights. Mason's father was an Episcopal minister. Her mother was "a born social worker," especially involved in prison reform. In the Richmond home to which the family moved in 1891, she ran a halfway house for recently released convicts. Mr. Mason's church income was so limited that Mason and her younger sister left high school to work as stenographers in order to help support the family.

Working as a secretary throughout her twenties, Mason began teaching Sunday School classes to groups of industrial workers, predominantly young women, ages fourteen to twenty-five. She grew concerned about the effects of ten-hour days and meager wages on Richmond's women workers. Mason became convinced that neither the church, nor the efforts of well-meaning individuals, could change conditions for these workers. When she began to advocate protective legislation, she found her strongest allies in the labor movement. During the next decade, Mason worked with the industrial department of the YWCA, eventually becoming the general secretary of the Richmond Branch. In 1932 Mason moved out of the South for the first time, to become the general secretary of the National Consumers League (NCL), a position that brought her to Washington as a lobbyist for New Deal labor legislation. Failure of the League's efforts to get protective legislation passed, especially in the South, made Mason reconsider the League's effectiveness, and the wisdom of focusing on protective legislation as a way to change conditions for workers. In the middle 1930s, she turned her attention to those pushing for industrial organization through the labor movement.

In the spring of 1937 Mason was hired by John L. Lewis to work for the CIO in the South as a "publicist and public relations representative." Mason, who often quipped that had she been a man she would have followed in her father's footsteps and become a minister, finally received her call from the CIO. Hiring a Virginia blue blood made sense to John L. Lewis. What he did not realize at the outset was that he was hiring a woman extremely adept at public policy and tactical organizing. As with Mother Jones and Ella May Wiggins, the labor movement got more than they expected when they welcomed Lucy Mason into the fold.[5]

Jones, Wiggins, and Mason participated in the labor movement in different ways. Jones worked with miners, Wiggins with textile workers, and Mason with a national labor federation, the CIO. But each woman became a labor movement heroine. Reporters, workers, and labor leaders alike described all three as "motherly" women, and as such Jones, Mason, and Wiggins were accorded special status.

Mother Jones's biographer Dale Fetherling has argued that Mother Jones was almost "like a biological mother to the miners," a mother who "goes through the shadow of death in order to endow her child with life." She also was the mother who gave birth to "the revolt which simmered within them."[6] Mother Jones worked with great effectiveness in the matriarchal culture of mining communities, where men's lives were continually threatened. She endorsed the miners' concept of ideal womanhood as "militance combined with motherhood," and believed strongly, as Priscilla Long has argued, "that a woman's work in the family gave her rights in the struggle."[7]

Lucy Mason, like Mother Jones, had (in the words of an admiring journalist) "white hair and a warm, motherly smile." Journalists portrayed her as a woman who would "do almost anything to protect her 'boys,'—the union organizers who are leading the struggle to organize the South."[8] Unlike Jones and Mason, who were viewed as mothers within the labor movement, Ella May Wiggins joined the movement as a real mother, seeing in the union struggle a better way to provide for her children. In a speech delivered shortly before her death she said, "If we don't stand up for our rights . . . we are fighting ourselves and fighting our children." Alluding to the children she had lost, Wiggins insisted that she "never could do anything for my children, not even to keep 'em alive. That's why I'm for the union" she told Margaret Larkin, "so's I can do better for them." For Wiggins it was "for our little children," that all workers needed to "have a union here."[9] When she died, she became a labor movement heroine because of her work with the union, and a cause célèbre among southern liberals, because of the sympathy people felt for a slain mother, killed while working to achieve a better life.[10]

For Jones, Mason, and Wiggins, being seen as a mother usually brought a positive response from unionists and the general public. But this motherly guise was also a shield against the oppressive dichotomy of being seen as either a good or bad woman. After the deaths of her husband and children in 1867, Mother Jones had lived on her own. The fact that she traveled alone and stayed overnight in private homes, hotels, and jails made some question Jones's personal life. Critics and enemies frequently attacked her moral character. Regularly accused of having been a prostitute and having run a house of prostitution, Jones was also charged, at various times, with having been arrested for "drunkenness and disorderly conduct." At one point, these allegations against Jones were read into the *Congressional Record*; in southern West Virginia they were printed onto broadsides and tossed from a railroad car.[11]

Jones's frequent use of rough, bawdy language reinforced her image as a coarse fighter, willing to lash out at coal operators, ministers, the press, and miners themselves. But she was always seen simultaneously as a "mild-looking motherly figure," albeit one "who was metamorphosed into a Joan of Arc when she mounted the platform." Frequently called "an American Joan of Arc," Jones was also compared to Louise Michel, the "Red Virgin of Montmartre," the revolutionary French socialist born the same year as Mother Jones. Michel fought in the 1871 Commune, and throughout her life as a radical condoned the use of violence.[12] Jones's impassioned actions were excused because she had "a mother's heart torn by the sufferings of the poor." Her motherly love made her go to any lengths to protect her "children." In the words spoken at her funeral: "Her faults were the excesses of her courage, her love of justice, the love in her mother's heart."[13]

Ella May Wiggins, too, especially as her life became more public during the Gastonia strike in 1929, had to deal with charges of immorality. Her husband, John Wiggins, had had a reputation as "a ladies' man." He deserted his family around 1925. Ella May had started living with Charley Shope, a man she referred to during the strike as her "cousin." He was the father of her youngest daughter, age thirteen months in 1929, and of the infant she was carrying when she was murdered.[14] The union tried to protect Ella May from adverse publicity, no doubt because such exposure would further damage the

NTWU's reputation in North Carolina. In the articles following her death, Wiggins' role as mother is constantly emphasized, although no mention was made of her being pregnant at the time she was shot. In mainstream newspapers she was portrayed as a "mother of five, separated from her husband." The *Charlotte Observer* said that "Mrs. Wiggins . . . had been going under her maiden name, Ella May Mays." "Under the name of Ella May," the paper continued, she had joined the strike, become a union member, gone to New York to raise funds for the strikers, and had been shot in an "anti-red demonstration." In this account, Ella May, or Ella May Mays, the independent, single (separated) woman, was the one who went astray. Mrs. Wiggins, the mother of five, was never associated directly with the union or referred to as the victim of murder. In the trial of the vigilantes accused of Wiggins's death, the defense attempted to blacken her reputation and thereby exonerate her assassins by presenting evidence that her children were born out of wedlock.[15]

Even Lucy Randolph Mason, whose life history was a model of religious devotion and dedicated social service, was not exempt from whispered questions about her personal life. It was rumored that Mason came into the CIO because she was in love with John L. Lewis. This story had no factual basis whatsoever but served as an explanation for why someone like Mason would come into the labor movement. Some argued that only a personal attachment, one that would make an otherwise sensible woman lose her good judgment, would have brought Mason into the CIO. Her seemingly irrational acts to promote the cause of unions and the workers had to be explained in such terms. Yet even Mason's rumored liaison with Lewis could be cast in a positive light by her supporters, since his status as the "father" of the CIO made her by implication the "mother" of the union. Her actions could then be explained in terms of protecting southern workers, the "children" of this personal and professional alliance.[16]

As "mothers" within the movement, these heroines were perceived as women endowed with "magical" qualities. Mother Jones was described as an "angel." Lucy Mason was frequently said to have magical powers. "What kind of magic did you use?" queried Mason's friend and colleague Francis P. Miller in 1937. Paul Kellogg of *The Survey* wrote about Mason in the same year: "Her name has magic below the Mason and Dixon line." Like fairy godmothers, these women "always appeared in time of need," bringing "a ray of hope" before leaving for the next place, as Clarence Darrow wrote in his 1925 introduction to Mother Jones's autobiography. They routinely circumvented the legal system by petitioning judges and shaming sheriffs. They subverted normal political channels, appealing directly to governors, senators, the president and first lady. They used extraordinary means to communicate labor's message to the public by composing songs, contacting editors, ministers, writers, professors, and even by appealing directly to employers. They amended union protocol, bringing in new members whenever and however possible. When told she couldn't initiate a group of miners because she didn't have the induction ritual, Mother Jones retorted, "The ritual, hell, I'll make one up!"[17]

These magical motherly, or grandmotherly, women "organized" workers in the broadest sense of the word. To Mother Jones, who wrote of West Virginia miners screaming "Organize us, Mother! Organize us! Organize us!," inducting workers into the union, was like a sacramental baptism. "Organizing" to Jones meant putting lives in order, feeding families, and protecting them from evil forces. To Ella May Wiggins organization meant "freedom for the working class," obtaining "something to want to live for," and the promise of "a better life." To Lucy Mason, organizing southern workers meant, as she wrote to a friend in 1940, opening "doors of opportunity to depressed and exploited wage earners," extending freedom and democracy to the "dispossessed and submerged," and "promoting a socially desirable program for the common good."[18]

As organizers, these women faced danger in the traditional heroic sense. They stood up to enemies larger than themselves. They traveled to places where union men could not gain entry. In 1902, Mother Jones went into Laurel Creek, West Virginia, after seven organizers had been shot, beaten up, and chased from town at gunpoint. She told the tale in her autobiography: "Mother," one union man warned, "you mustn't go up there. They've got gunmen patrolling the roads." She replied: "That means the miners up there are prisoners and need me." Ella May Wiggins was one of two women traveling with twenty-two unionists to a union meeting on September 14, 1929, when vigilantes blocked the road and fired point-blank into the back of the truck. Her daughter claimed later that her mother "knew she would get killed, but that she was not afraid." In 1941, the Amalgamated Clothing Workers asked Lucy Mason to go into Sparta, Georgia, a town CIO labor leader Buck

Borah described as "too hot to stay in" and "too dangerous for Ed Blair [CIO organizer] to return to." Union leaders believed that women, especially older women, were protected by southern chivalrousness. Therefore, they could safely take risks that for men would mean certain attack. As Mason herself quipped to journalist Lawrence Lader, "After all, who'd hurt a little, white-haired old woman?" But the reality of the southern labor movement meant that no organizer was immune from attack. Jones, Wiggins, and Mason each faced real danger. On many occasions, Jones served time in jail. Wiggins was fatally shot, and Mason knew well from the experiences of her colleagues that as a representative of the CIO she was subject to flagrant violations of her civil rights.[19]

Willing to face violence, Jones, Wiggins, and Mason became female heroines, but they were not the heroines of women alone. They were also, perhaps even especially, men's heroines. In their work with a male-dominated labor movement, each of these women dealt with male unionists and union leaders, and with bi-gendered groups. When dealing with rank-and-file unionists, or with editors, ministers, judges, or sheriffs, each of these women gave men respect and room to maneuver. Mother Jones, for example, coerced miners into joining the union and fighting for a new life, all the while expressing her admiration and giving them time to make their own decisions. She opposed prohibition because it denigrated the working man; she honored men as family providers, but at the same time she spoke to them as small children. "Now, boys, let Mother talk to you," she would say.[20]

Mason accorded men respect and treated them with a certain formality. When dealing with editors, manufacturers, politicians, labor leaders, and unionists, Mason acknowledged the contributions of each individual, positively reinforced good actions, and, after presenting her point of view, gave each man time to decide for himself. Mason was known for bringing, as University of North Carolina president Frank Graham put it, "a spirit of sweet reasonableness into situations too often dominated by unreason and violence." She believed in, as Mason herself described, "prodding . . . with keen and penetrating barbs," while displaying "sympathy rather than anger."[21] Wiggins, too, accorded male unionists and labor leaders, male and female, respect and attention. She looked to them for guidance and grew into a strong leader as they endorsed her songwriting, her public speaking, her traveling North to raise strike funds, and her work to bring black workers into the union. Each of these women heroines had her own agenda for unionization of the South, but they also worked well with male unionists and respected, even if they at times vigorously disagreed with, the male leadership of the movement.

In their work to organize the southern region, these women gave to the movement without thinking of themselves. Self-sacrifice is a quality that traditionally men have admired in women, especially in their mothers. These heroines never gave up. In fact, each became a martyr for the movement. Ella May Wiggins was literally a martyr, giving her life for the union. Mother Jones dedicated herself to the labor movement, traveling across the country for over 50 years and frequently coming South to stand by the miners. When she died in 1930 at age 100 she was buried, at her request, in Mt. Olive, Illinois, in the Miner's Cemetery, with the martyrs of the Virden Massacre of 1898. To Jones "those brave boys" epitomized the determination and sacrifice of labor's struggle. During her years with the CIO, Mason also lived the life of a martyr, giving all of her time and energy to the movement. When asked about Mason's retiring, CIO men replied, "She'll never retire. As long as there's a fight going on down here, Miss Lucy will be right in the middle of it." Self-sacrificing women, Mason, Jones, and Wiggins, each referred to as "labor's Joan of Arc," gave of themselves for a cause they believed would change the world. A stanza from the popular ballad, "The Death of Mother Jones," summarizes these qualities well:

> She was fearless of every danger,
> She hated that which was wrong;
> She never gave up fighting
> Until her breath was gone.[22]

In contrast to the maternal heroines of the southern labor movement, girl strikers have symbolized the daughters of the southern work force, young women or girls whose courageous, feisty, or "disorderly" behavior quite literally expressed the intense desire of women to define their lives as workers.[23] Symbolically, these actions by women workers came to represent the collective defiance of the region's entire workforce. Strikes by women workers have punctuated southern labor history throughout the century.

During southern strikes, unions themselves often encouraged and focused attention on the activities of women strikers. There were many reasons for this. First, women strikers often consciously captured the attention of their fellow strikers and the community by organizing parades, or by playing a prominent role on a picket line. Second, the labor movement was in the position of having to counteract strike coverage by mainstream newspapers that put a disproportionate focus on strike violence. Press releases and articles about "girl strikers" served to neutralize headlines about dynamitings and shootings that usually implicated union men. Third, for the unions, if the actions of women workers could be carefully controlled, women strikers provided excellent publicity. The public, both within and outside a local community, found it difficult to ignore the plight of women, especially young women who reminded them of their own daughters. In 1937 during a sit down strike in Tupelo, Mississippi, the union and management competed for the allegiance of the town's young female work force by appealing not to the workers, but to their parents. The local newspaper would not print the union's announcements, but management bought numerous advertisements addressed to "The Farmers of This Territory, If your daughters or any of your relatives work in the garment factories." Farmers were advised to "stick by the homefolks— . . . . Advise your daughters and relatives to stick to their jobs and beware of outsiders' counsel." While daughters should be protected from outsiders, the articles also stressed "keeping the virgin Southland free at the present from a communistic organization."[24]

Throughout the century, unions organizing southern women workers have repeatedly emphasized the presence of young women workers. In North Carolina in 1900, the American Federation of Labor (AFL) quietly organized local unions in textile mills across the state. Women made up about 20 percent of the membership of these locals, and yet when walkouts occurred, they were often triggered by the grievance of a young woman worker. Observed one journalist in 1901, female workers, ranging in age from ten to thirty, were placed in the limelight so frequently that managers in a number of communities perceived that the unions were "being made up largely of women and children."[25]

The younger the women workers involved in a strike, the better it was for the union. Mill managers had significant difficulty defending the practice of child labor, and paying "girls" pennies an hour for a fifty- to sixty-hour workweek conjured up the practice of hiring children to work in the mills. The younger the workers involved, the greater the sympathy that could be elicited from the community at large. At Elizabethton, although the women strikers ranged in age from fourteen to thirty-five, they were described as "very young girls." A labor reporter wrote that "an outstanding feature of this most unusual rebellion is that it was led by children, the little girls in the inspection rooms. They were not only the first to come out but among the most determined. Numbers of them addressed the mass meetings of strikers which were held every day, pleading, in their piping, childish voices for the 'grown folks' not to weaken."[26]

In the *American Federationist*, photographs of the Elizabethton "strike leaders" featured four young women; none of the male strike leaders were mentioned. Author Sherwood Anderson, covering the southern strikes in 1929 and 1930 for *The Nation*, wrote: "Girls everywhere. . . . And many of these mountain girls are lovely little creatures. They have, at least when excited, straight hard little bodies, delicately featured faces. I sat beside a child that couldn't have been over thirteen—no matter what her 'mill age'—and as I looked at her I thought how proud I would be to have been her father." Male paternalists like Anderson, as well as the mill owners, union officials, and community leaders had varied responses to female sexuality in the strike context. Journalists and union officials sought to provide protection; employers and community leaders attempted to reassert their control over mill daughters fighting for autonomy and decent wages.[27]

The CIO used the same tactic of consciously emphasizing the participation of women in confrontational situations. For example, in 1938, *The CIO News* ran a front-page headline above a photograph of six women ranging in age from twenty to forty, reading "Girls Jailed By New Orleans Cops." In a raid on CIO headquarters police had arrested eighty-four CIO union officials and members, the majority of whom were men. The six "girl workers at the CIO office" were among those jailed. Their arrest captured the headline.[28] A decade later, in 1948, when Bessie Hillman visited an Amalgamated Clothing Workers of America (ACWA) local in Atlanta, she reported that she "did not expect to receive such a thrill" when she met the "beautiful girls" who had "forged a union during the heat of the 1941 struggle to organize Cluett's [the Cluett Peabody plant]." As she met with workers who were opening a new union center, Hillman "witnessed the same enthusiasm, the same loyalty, devotion and love" that she had experienced "as a girl striker in Chicago in 1910."[29]

Thus the image of "girl strikers" was useful to organized labor and popular with women workers themselves. The preadolescent implication of the term strengthened their identification as "daughters" (albeit errant) of the community, which conferred some degree of protection during their periods of open defiance. Indeed, this image may have fostered the continuation of managerial paternalism in the face of persistent labor militancy throughout the South. This is suggested in a ballad written by Odel Corley in Gastonia in 1929: "Manville Jenckes was the millionaire's name, / He bought the law with his money and fame. . . . / Told Violet Jones if she'd go back to work, / He'd buy her a new Ford and pay her well for her work."[30] Likewise, in the 1937 Tupelo episode, after a sit-down strike in the spring involving 400 workers, management encouraged women workers to expel the union's organizers. A group of 150 women cooperated, escorting two women ILGWU organizers out of town. To show their appreciation management treated 375 women workers to a 75-cents-a-plate celebration dinner at the local hotel. "Girl Workers Given Dinner," read the headline in the *Memphis Press-Scimitar*.[31]

While the image of the girl striker proved pervasive and perennially useful, it was engendered by extraordinary circumstances that distorted the reality of southern working-class community life. Strikes occurred on a sporadic basis. Whether a walkout lasted two hours or two years, strike situations were not the norm. Yet in southern communities in the years before World War II, strikes occurred often enough to become ritualized affairs. Parades, picket lines, relief stations, speeches, rallies, and meetings lent to most strikes a sideshow atmosphere. Journalists, visitors, and observers from outside the community made it impossible for anyone in the community to ignore the strike. The presence of extra police or military personnel further transformed the regular routine of local community life, heightening underlying tensions between competing groups of citizens and often unleashing previously dormant hostilities. Celebration, excitement, fear, confusion, and violence occurred simultaneously, bringing intense feelings to the surface and leaving individuals exhilarated and drained at the same time. In these atypical situations women workers readily assumed the role of girl strikers, a role that did not reflect the long-term reality of their involvement with the labor movement.

Being viewed as a girl striker did not confer equal status within the union. After a strike ended, "girl strikers" often became just "girls" in the eyes of male union leaders who were unwilling to consider women as co-equals within the organization. Thus the girl-striker image made it more difficult for women to be taken seriously within the labor movement and to realize their full potential as union members. By the same token, the stereotypes of girl striker and heroine both have interfered with a comprehensive analysis of women's broader role in the history of organized labor in the South. These circumscribed views of women do not encompass women's involvement in the day-to-day maintenance work of the union or their contributions as auxiliary members. They also obscure women's struggles for leadership roles within their locals and preclude analysis of the important alliances with middle-class women that working-class women used to support and sustain a variety of union activities. As white stereotypes, of course, these images do not speak to the role of black women in southern labor organizing, a role that has been increasingly important in recent decades. Finally, we must look beyond these stereotypes to see how labor women attempted to incorporate their own political agenda into southern unions.

Southern labor women have often proposed that the union address a broad range of issues that women readily identified because of their particular social and familial concerns. Women unionists argued that "working conditions" included not only wage-and-hour issues but hours off for meals, maternity time for bearing and nursing children, and housing policies, especially in the years before 1940 when many workers lived in company-owned houses. These issues often brought women into conflict with union leadership, and women members frequently described themselves as being "in the minority on policies." This was especially true in the late 1930s and 1940s when women unionists were frequently accused of moving too quickly on certain issues, particularly racial integration. In the 1930s and 1940s, women unionists in some southern communities led the way in introducing proposals to integrate local unions. In one instance, women members of the Textile Workers' Union local in Roanoke, Virginia, introduced a proposal to the membership at a union meeting that the union should put into practice the official ideology of equality and justice for all workers by opening the union to black workers in the factory. Because of the large percentage of women members in the union, the issue passed, but the women, having taken union leaders completely by surprise, were harshly criticized for not working through proper channels.[32] Despite opposition from the male union hierarchy, a significant minority of white southern women continued to advocate a union agenda that transcended wage issues, addressed the needs of all union members, and included black workers.

The crucial role of black women in the southern labor force cannot be underestimated. Black women participating in the southern labor movement have been hailed neither as heroines nor as girl strikers. But southern black women have long been recognized as autonomous workers, having a strong history of individual resistance and militancy, and a tradition of locally based self-organization that stretches across the twentieth century. Because of generations of experience in the church and in civil rights organizing, black women have proven exceptionally adept as leaders within the labor movement. In the South, after 1965, the relationship between black and white women workers in textile, garment, and tobacco factories, became *the* critical factor in whether union elections were won or lost. Fully cognizant of this, organized labor concentrated on the difficult process of uniting black and white southern women within the union. As the number of black women in southern mills began to increase in the late 1960s and early 1970s, the number of successful union elections multiplied. Black women took the lead in contacting unions, getting cards signed, fighting legal obstacles, and participating in contract negotiations. A majority of black women workers within a plant could usually convince younger white women to join them in supporting the union, and with this interracial coalition, election victories were frequent.[33]

Opening ourselves to a view of women in the labor movement not confined by racially specific, gender-based stereotypes allows us to include the role of African-American women and also to see the importance of networks of women workers in local communities, which have developed out of family, neighborhood, and work relationships. These networks developed slowly, over time, beginning with the family, reaching into the neighborhood, extending to the shop floor, and expanding into community-wide organizations like churches, the YWCA Industrial Department, the National Women's Trade Union Leagues, the Southern Summer School for Women Workers in Industry, and the Coalition of Labor Union Women (CLUW). Unions themselves have at times responded to initiatives by their female membership to form subgroups within a local union and then participate in regional meetings with women unionists from across the South.

At certain times, as they were building local and regional networks, southern women workers looked to cross-class women's organizations for support. In the 1920s and 1930s, the YWCA, the National Women's Trade Union League, the Southern Summer School, and even the League of Women Voters fostered the work of women unionists by offering strike support, workers' education, and a commitment to industrial organizing. In the 1960s, middle- and working-class southern women joined forces again as they worked for women's equality through organizations like the National Organization of Women. But throughout the twentieth century, male unionists have always viewed gender-based alliances across class lines suspiciously. Seen as co-optation, these alliances have often created tensions within the labor movement itself.

In addition to the specific strategy of taking advantage of cross-class alliances, there is good evidence that women unionists have used a distinctive leadership style, fundamentally different from that adopted by male unionists. Karen Sachs has described this style in her study of union organizing at the Duke University Medical Center, where, she argues, "Women and men both took leadership, although in different ways." She discovered that while almost all the public speakers and confrontational negotiators were men, women were what she called "centers and sustainers of workplace networks—centerwoman or centerpersons—as well as the large majority of the union organizing committee." By equating leading with speaking, Sachs had initially overlooked women's key leadership role as "centerwomen."[34]

Both black and white southern women have been most active in union work when they are not heavily involved in child rearing. This means that the women activists within a union usually are clustered in two groups: one of eighteen- to twenty-five-year-olds; another of thirty-five- to fifty-five-year-olds. Active male unionists do not follow this pattern but enter the union when they enter the work force and rise within the ranks throughout their career, until they reach their late forties. Because of this bimodal age distribution, middle-aged women often have found themselves competing for leadership posts with men who are a decade younger but who have more experience as union activists, having held minor offices since they were in their early twenties. This lack of seniority within the labor movement, resulting from discontinuity in women's working lives, has hampered women who have sought leadership positions within the union.[35]

Women unionists in many locals have taken responsibility for the "invisible" work of the union. Behind-the-scenes work accomplished by women has included helping other workers on the shop floor, providing food for union-sponsored activities, working to provide relief during a strike, fund-raising for the union in the local community, and tending union children so young parents can attend union functions, as well as performing numerous clerical tasks. Women undertaking this type of work for the union frequently have held offices like recording secretary or shop steward, but on a sporadic basis. Usually, their work remains unrecognized and often unappreciated by the union hierarchy.

Many southern women have come into the labor movement through the women's auxiliaries of craft unions, in coal, in steel, and even in the textile and garment unions. Women's auxiliaries have a long history in the South. Despite the region's greater dependence on women's wages and lower wages for male employees, southern unionists in the skilled trades have encouraged their members' wives to organize auxiliaries throughout the twentieth century. The Machinists' Union, founded in the South in 1888, encouraged members' wives to form local groups to support the membership and dozens of these groups thrived in communities throughout the region.[36] Southern women's auxiliaries also existed in the building trades, as well as in the railroad unions and the coal industry. In tightly knit industrial communities, women's auxiliaries merely formalize existing informal networks of women whose husbands or fathers work for a particular company. In larger, urban communities, auxiliaries have brought together women who have little in common except their husbands' union.

After 1938, the CIO was responsible for organizing women's auxiliaries to support workers in auto, steel, rubber, coal, and even in textiles. Auxiliaries grew in the postwar period, but as more women entered the work force in the fifties and sixties, the number of active auxiliary members again declined. In the seventies, as women moved into nontraditional jobs, especially in coal mining, women who would have joined the auxiliary, joined the union instead. As layoffs forced women out of mining in the 1980s, former women miners once again joined auxiliaries.

Auxiliaries have often provided women an avenue for participation, but auxiliaries have been limiting, too. Women do not join a union auxiliary and thereby become full-fledged union members. They are the "wives" of the movement. Women auxiliary members are viewed by the labor movement as supporters. As such, these women often have played crucial roles as ambassadors for the union within the community, as relief workers during strikes, as mothers rearing their children in the traditions of unionism. The work these women do for the union, within their households and within the labor force, has been viewed within the context of a properly functioning union family, with a male unionist as the head. Union auxiliaries were recognized as effective organizations in expanding the influence of the union; but the female auxiliary member has never been recognized as having autonomy, as being an equal within the movement or within the southern wage-economy.[37]

Actually, organized labor's view of women's participation in auxiliaries quite accurately reflected the attitude of many union leaders toward all women workers, regardless of the depth of their involvement in or commitment to the union. Even in the face of overwhelming evidence to the contrary, unions have continued to look at women workers as "temporary" members of the work force, or as workers who could not, for one reason or another, become a permanent part of the labor movement. The persistence of occupational segregation by gender has reinforced the idea that women workers are different from men. The greatest difference has been that women have been concentrated in low-wage jobs in the textile, garment, food, and service industries. These industries, in contrast to highly paid positions in steel, auto, rubber, and the building trades, have had consistently low levels of unionization.

Union membership always has reflected major shifts in the work force; in the last two decades, this has meant that as manufacturing jobs have been eliminated, male union membership has declined. The number of female union members in the South has increased, but the relative gains for the labor movement have been minimal because of the loss of highly paid union jobs in manufacturing. Consistent gains in female membership aside, the predominately negative view of women in organized labor has changed little over the course of the century.[38]

Because of negative experiences in unions, women workers often have viewed them as male-dominated organizations in which they had little control, sporadic access to top-level leaders, and constant battles on the grass-roots level to express their ideas. All unions are not the same, of course, but examples abound of women unionists running headlong into conflicts with union leaders. In the 1920s and 1930s as the National Women's Trade Union League, the YWCA, and the Southern Summer School for Women Workers sought to reach out to southern women workers and bring them into the labor movement, each group faced opposition from organized labor itself. AFL leaders feared that the NWTUL's organizing work would lead to a dual union structure for women that would undermine AFL supremacy. The Southern Summer School was accused of promoting "dual unionism" as former students from the school formed local networks of women workers in dozens of communities across the region. In Mobile, in 1935, a group of five women garment workers found themselves branded "radicals and agitators" by the union leadership. They appealed to the Regional Labor Boards in Atlanta and New Orleans claiming that their situation was "just another case of the industrialist trying to crunch the workers and in so doing, being protected by an old conservative international."[39] Louise Leonard McLaren, director of the Southern School, wrote to George L. Googe of the AFL about the case, explaining that she was "interested in this case . . . almost as much for the other locals in the south as for the one in Mobile. The one in Macon [Georgia], for instance, has excellent leadership and could become a powerful local if it were not held back by the New York leaders."[40]

In 1942, Molly Dowd, a longtime labor activist in Alabama, wrote to Margaret Dreier Robins of the NWTUL that her work with the State Labor Department under the progressive Gov. Bibb Graves "gave [her] a chance to be of some help to the workers in [the] state, especially the women who are always so neglected." She added, "The men in the Labor movement are paying a little more attention down here than they once did because its a matter of self-defense, but sad to say the only part they let women play is the paying of dues. They are not interested in developing any sort of leadership among their women."[41]

Unions organizing in the South have consistently paid women organizers lower salaries, often left them to work in complete isolation, and ignored their requests for assistance. In addition, union administrators often took the work of women organizers for granted. In 1938 ACWA's president Sidney Hillman admitted that "this is a man's world. It appears even in an organization that represents so many women." He then apologized for having "failed to mention the women" when discussing the leadership of the southern organizing campaign.[42] Many women have argued that their unions didn't "accept the idea of girls being active," and a lot of union women would sympathize with Virginia unionist Jennie Spencer who described the first year of her life in the union as "a period in which my spirits had been broken, all except a single thread."[43]

In its failure to recognize, accommodate, and legitimate women's various roles in the movement, organized labor has failed to live up to its own ideology of universal equality and justice. For many women this was a particularly bitter pill to swallow, for this very ideology had drawn them into union participation as members, activists, strikers, auxiliary members, and supporters. An ideology that has universal application, unionism is non-gender-based. From the beginning of the twentieth century as unions have campaigned for new members, the language of equality and justice has permeated their rhetoric. Labor slogans crafted by generations of unionists encapsulate this sentiment: "All for One and One for All"; "Labor Omnia Vincit"; "Workers Unite!"; "In Unity There is Strength"; "Solidarity Forever." This language has been particularly appealing to women, and at times unions have explicitly articulated their ideology of unity and fair treatment as a way to recruit women workers into the labor movement.[44]

The inclusive, democratic ideology of the labor movement has offered individual southern women an alternative to prevailing norms regarding female behavior. No doubt this accounts to some degree for the enthusiasm with which southern women have responded to the labor movement. Women who have joined unions signed on as individuals, in their own names. As unionists they acted independently of their fathers or husbands, and of the company. For women who grew up in a culture that taught women to be subservient to God and man, this independent status has had the positive attraction of underwriting their autonomy; it also has had the threatening potential of reordering gender relationships in the workplace and the home.

This is precisely what has happened throughout the South as female union membership has increased during periods of rapid economic change: in 1900, in the early and late 1920s, during the 1940s, and when the economy surged in the late 1950s and 1960s. For southern working-class men, union membership has meant assuming an adversarial stance vis-à-vis an employer, a risky undertaking in a culture based on adherence to a rigid social and economic hierarchy. The risks multiplied for southern women as they joined unions to improve their conditions as workers and as they became part of an organization independent of both the private and public spheres in which they normally lived and worked. Over many decades then, while women workers, black and white, have sought to claim unions as their own, to establish themselves as participants and leaders, the relationship between women workers and organized labor, in reality, has been one plagued by discontent and unhappiness, feelings never reflected in the static images of heroines and girl strikers.

Why then have heroines and girl strikers been so important within the context of the southern labor movement? First, because these models of women's behavior and roles reflect the limitations put on women by the labor movement. A woman, usually a younger woman, could be a striker, acting alone, as an individual, or with a group of her own. They were viewed as daughters, young and impetuous, as wild and disconnected from normal society. But if they were older, or dead, they could become heroines, larger than life motherly or grandmotherly figures, beyond the reach of the average worker. Auxiliary members have been the "wives" of the movement, but extra, auxiliary, not central to union life. Unlike unions, auxiliaries are not gender neutral; they are gender specific, specifically female.

The second reason that these stereotypes have been so persistent and have resonated so perfectly in southern unions is that they reflect southern cultural views of women so precisely. Traditionally, southern men have loved, adored, and revered their mothers, and they are well known for worshiping their daughters. But southern men rarely have been acculturated to treat women as equals, and many have had tremendous difficulty in doing so. Nowhere is this more clearly reflected than in southern country music where mothers are idolized and daughters are adored. On the other hand, the wife, the partner or co-equal, is more frequently the source of trouble and woe.[45] Within the labor movement this cultural standard has held: women can be motherlike heroines or daughterlike activists, but when women unionists have asked for, demanded, or expected equality within the union (often emboldened by the democratic rhetoric of the union itself), they have faced an uphill struggle.[46]

In the 1980s, many of the labor movement advances made in the previous two decades were eroded by a deep recession in the South's basic industries—textiles, tobacco, furniture, and steel. Efforts to organize southern workers during the Reagan years paralleled earlier organizing attempts in a region plagued by high unemployment rates, low wages, powerful manufacturers, and compliant state and local governments. In the final year of the decade, the strike against the Pittston Corporation once again drew national attention to employer intransigence and the determination of southern workers to fight for their benefits and rights. Following in a long tradition, women played a crucial role in the Pittston struggle. The ladies auxiliary of the district United Mine Workers of America (UMWA) locals renamed themselves "The Daughters of Mother Jones." In keeping with a strong heritage of female militancy and union loyalty, they fed 3,000 strikers and their families, as well as thousands of union supporters who visited the strike area; they walked the picket lines for over eight months, served time in jail, traveled North to raise money, and chronicled the strike in song. They participated in the union struggle exactly as southern women have done since the nineteenth century. Their decision to declare themselves "The Daughters of Mother Jones" confirmed their understanding of southern labor history. They appreciated the power that mother and daughter images hold for the labor movement, and in uniting these two symbols they forged a new and more powerful role for themselves, which the UMWA has acknowledged by assigning an organizer to this group of women activists.[47]

Symbolic representations of idealized figures were frequently used by the labor movement and other political and economic organizations as Americans entered the twentieth century. The Mariana figure on the cover of a 1900 edition of *The American Federationist* is a splendid example, incorporating aspects of both labor heroines and girl strikers.[48] She is huge and strong looking, she is young and beautiful. She holds olive branches in both hands and from the branches flow streamers printed with the motto "A Bond of Silk, Stronger Than Brass or Steel." This figure, so like the liberty figures used in political engravings of the same era, is clearly heroic in every sense of the word. She is protecting the two male workers, trade tools in their hands, who sit at her feet. She appears to be marching, leading the way, eyes straight ahead, arms outstretched, waist-length hair flowing. Her most outstanding feature though is her wings. They arch above her head, forming a halo within which a star is suspended. Then they spread in a wide white perfect arc to the ground. Guardian angel, virgin mother, heroine, and girl striker in one, this woman embodies a presence that has shadowed the labor movement throughout the century.

This angel of the labor movement embodied the protective characteristics of labor's female heroines and the boldness and bravery of the girl strikers. The engraving appeared on the cover of the *American Federationist* in both 1900 and 1901. Courtesy of The George Meany Memorial Archives.

This article is dedicated to Judith L. Catlett, Associate Professor, Center for Labor Education and Research, University of Alabama at Birmingham, whose perceptive understanding of southern women in the labor movement, and willingness to share what she knows, has immeasurably enhanced my efforts to decipher the past. I would also like to thank Clint Joiner, Susan Levine, Elliott Gorn, Curt Ellison, Cosby Totten, and Robert Zieger for their assistance and critiques.

Notes

1. *Autobiography of Mother Jones*, ed. Mary Field Parton (Chicago: Kerr, 1925; reprint ed., 1969); Dale Fetherling, *Mother Jones: The Miners' Angel: A Portrait* (Carbondale: Southern Illinois Univ. Press, 1974), ch. 1; Priscilla Long, *Where the Sun Never Shines: A History of America's Bloody Coal Industry* (New York: Paragon House, 1989), 272–89; *The Correspondence of Mother Jones*, ed. Edward M. Steel (Pittsburgh: Univ. of Pittsburgh Press, 1985). On Wiggins, see Margaret Larkin, "The Story of Ella May," *New Masses* 5:6 (Nov. 1929): 3–4; Larkin, "Tragedy in North Carolina," *The North American Review* 208 (1929): 686–90; Larkin, "Ella May's Songs," *The Nation* 129 (Oct. 9, 1929): 382–83; Jacquelyn Dowd Hall et al., *Like a Family: The Making of a Southern Cotton Mill World* (Chapel Hill: Univ. of North Carolina Press, 1987), 226–27. On Mason, see John A. Salmon, *Miss Lucy of the CIO: The Life and Times of Lucy Randolph Mason, 1882–1959* (Athens: Univ. of Georgia Press, 1988); Lucy Randolph Mason, "I Turned to Social Action Right at Home," in *Labor's Relation to Church and Community*, ed. Liston Pope (New York: Harper, 1947), 145–55.

2. For accounts of southern strikes involving women workers see: Merl E. Reed, "The Augusta Textile Mills and the Strike of 1886," *Labor History* 14:2 (Spring 1973): 228–46; Jerome Dowd, "Strikes and Lockouts in North Carolina," *Gunton's Magazine* (Feb. 1901): 136–41; Jacquelyn Dowd Hall, "Disorderly Women: Gender and Labor Militancy in the Appalachian South," *The Journal of American History* 73:2 (Sept. 1986): 354–82. The 1929 southern textile strikes are documented in Tom Tippett, *When Southern Labor Stirs* (New York: Cape & Smith, 1931); F. Ray Marshall, *Labor in the South* (Cambridge, MA: Harvard Univ. Press, 1967); Philip S. Foner, *Women and the American Labor Movement from World War I to the Present* (New York: Free Press, 1980), 225–43. For an overview of women's labor militancy in the South, see Mary Frederickson, "'I Know Which Side I'm On': Southern Women in the Labor Movement in the Twentieth Century," in *Women, Work and Protest: A Century of U.S. Women's Labor History*, ed. Ruth Milkman (London: Routledge & Kegan Paul, 1985), 156–80.

3. Jones, *Autobiography*, 58, 232.

4. Eugene Feldman, "Ella Mae [sic] Wiggins, North Carolina Mother Who Gave Her Life to Build a Union," *Southern Newsletter* 2 (March–April 1957): 15–17; Eugene Feldman, "Ella May Wiggins and the Gastonia Strike of 1929," *Southern Newsletter* 4 (Aug.–Sept. 1956): 8–11; Vera Buch Weisbord, *A Radical Life* (Bloomington: Indiana Univ. Press, 1977), 217–19; 258–60; quotations from Larkin, "Ella May's Songs," 382, and Weisbord, 288.

5. Salmon, *Miss Lucy of the CIO*, 73–74.

6. Fetherling, *Mother Jones,* 166–68.

7. Long, *Sun,*156–57.

8. Lawrence Lader, "The Lady and the Sheriff," *New Republic*, Jan. 5, 1948, 17–19.

9. Larkin, "Ella May's Songs," 382–83.

10. Frank Graham of the University of North Carolina at Chapel Hill was one of many North Carolina liberals shocked by Wiggins's murder. Wrote Graham of Wiggins's death, "100% Americanism was somewhere deep in the heart of this mother who went riding in a truck toward what to her was the promise of a better day for her children. . . . She willed to ride on a dangerous road and her courage shines out in death amid our complacency." (Graham to Nell Battle Lewis, Sept. 23, 1929, Frank Graham Papers, Southern Historical Collection, University of North Carolina).

11. Fetherling, *Mother Jones,* 134–36; see also Long, *Sun,* 233, 370.

12. Fetherling, *Mother Jones,* 138.

13. Ibid., 209.

14. Ella May Wiggins's daughter, seven years old in 1929, reported that her mother was about seven months pregnant at the time of her death. Telephone interview by author with Wiggins's daughter, Mrs. Merritt Wandell of Waverly, New York, Sept. 1979.

15. *Charlotte Observer*, Sept. 16, 1929, 10; Weisbord, 288.

16. Author's conversation with Brownie Lee Jones, April 20, 1976.

17. Fetherling, *Mother Jones*; Francis P. Miller to Lucy R. Mason, May 18, 1937, Lucy Randolph Mason Papers, Manuscript Department, William R. Perkins Library, Duke University; Paul Kellogg to Sidney Hillman, June 14, 1937, copy of original letter in Mason Papers; Jones, *Autobiography*, 8, 155.

18. Jones, *Autobiography*, 155; Larkin, "Ella May's Songs," 382; Feldman, "Ella May Wiggins," 10; Mason, "I Turned to Social Action," 150; Lucy R. Mason to Dr. Walker, March 24, 1940, Mason Papers.

19. Jones, *Autobiography*, 65; *Charlotte Observer*, Sept. 15, 1929, 1; Wandell interview, Sept. 1979; Bernard Borah, southern director, ACWA, to Gladys Dickason, June 12, 1941, Mason Papers; Lader, "The Lady and the Sheriff," 1.

20. UMW *Proceedings*, 1916, 230–34, quoted in Fetherling, *Mother Jones*, 166.

21. Frank Graham to Lucy R. Mason, June 25, 1937, Graham Papers; Lucy R. Mason to Jonathan Daniels, Sept. 17, 1938, Mason Papers.

22. Fetherling, *Mother Jones,* 207–9; Lader, "Lady and the Sheriff" 19; the text and tune of "The Death of Mother Jones" is analyzed in Archie Green, *Only a Miner: Studies in Recorded Coal-Mining Songs* (Urbana: Univ. of Illinois Press), 251–52.

23. No work better describes this phenomenon than Hall's study of Elizabethton, "Disorderly Women." See also Carroll Smith Rosenberg, *Disorderly Conduct: Visions of Gender in Victorian America* (New York: Knopf, 1985).

24. Typescript of quotations from Willson Whitman, *God's Valley* (New York: Viking Press, 1939), Highlander Research and Education Center Papers, Mss 265, State Historical Society of Wisconsin, Madison.

25. Jerome Dowd, "Strikes and Lockouts in North Carolina," *Gunton's Magazine* (Feb. 1901): 138–41.

26. Quoted in Philip Foner, *Women and the American Labor Movement,* 228.

27. Sherwood Anderson, "Elizabethton, Tennessee," *The Nation,* May 1, 1930, 527.

28. *The CIO News,* July 2, 1938, 1.

29. Bessie Hillman, *The Advance,* March 15, 1948, 6.

30. Margaret Larkin, "Ella May's Songs," 382–83.

31. Typewritten copy of article in *Memphis Press-Scimitar,* June 22, 1937, Highlander Papers.

32. Jennie Spencer, "My Transition," autobiography written at Highlander Folk School, 1937, Highlander Papers.

33. In the recession of 1979–1983, more black workers than white were laid off, so that some workforces that were predominantly black in the 1970s once again have a majority of white workers. Leadership positions within some unions started by black workers have passed to white women, who have been less successful in uniting the work force across racial lines. In 1982, in a south Alabama mill, for example, soon after a white slate of officers took office, the plant's six-year-old union was voted out. Black workers felt betrayed by white officers who, they argued, did not fight hard enough to keep the union. A further drain on the black leadership of biracial locals has been the mobility of black women activists. As these women worked within the union they sharpened their organizing abilities and developed new skills that put them into competition for better jobs. But occupational mobility has often meant leaving the union behind, and workers remaining in newly organized locals have suffered from the absence of well-qualified leaders. On the Alabama mill election see Paula McLendon, "Sarah Boykin: I'm Still Here," *Facing South* (Chapel Hill: Institute of Southern Studies, 1980), and Frederickson, "'I Know Which Side I'm On,'" 173–75. For an overview of black women in the southern labor movement in the period after 1965, see Frederickson, "Four Decades of Change: Black Workers in Southern Textiles, 1941–1981," in *Workers' Struggles, Past and Present,* ed. James Green (Philadelphia: Temple Univ. Press, 1983), esp. 77–80; Paul Giddings, *When and Where I Enter* (New York: Morrow, 1984), 154–55.

34. Karen Sacks, *Caring by the Hour: Women, Work and Organizing at Duke Medical Center* (Urbana: Univ. of Illinois Press, 1988), 120–21.
35. This bimodal pattern of active union participation is not followed during times of crisis, such as a strike, when all workers, male and female, young and old, become involved to whatever extent possible, regardless of personal concerns. See Sacks, *Caring by the Hour*, ch. 5, and Linda Frankel, "Women, Paternalism, and Protest in a Southern Textile Community: Henderson, North Carolina, 1900–1960," Ph.D. dissertation, Harvard Univ., 1986, 188–90.
36. Marshall, *Labor in the South*, 34. I am grateful to Susan Levine for sharing her knowledge about southern women's auxiliaries.
37. For an excellent discussion of auxiliaries, see Marjorie Penn Lasky, "'Where I Was a Person': The Ladies' Auxiliary in the 1934 Minneapolis Teamsters' Strikes," in Milkman, *Women, Work and Protest*, 181–205.
38. Interview with Judith Catlett, January 1990.
39. Minutes of the Central Committee, Southern Summer School, Arden, N. C., Aug. 15–16, 1931, American Labor Education Service Papers, Catherwood Library, Cornell University.
40. Louise Leonard McLaren to George Googe, April 16, 1935. Copy of letter in Mary Barker Papers, Emory University, Woodruff Library Special Collections, Box 6, Folder 3.
41. Mollie Dowd to Mrs. Robins, [Jan.?] 1942, Margaret Dreier Robins Papers, Papers of the Women's Trade Union League and Its Principal Leaders, Reel 1, Frame 47; Louise L. McLaren to George L. Googe, April 16, 1935, Mary Barker Papers, Emory University, Box 6, Folder 3.
42. Evidence for CIO treatment of women organizers in "Operation Dixie: The CIO Organizing Committee Papers, 1946–1953," New York, Microfilming Corporation of America, 1980, Series 4, Reel 55, 1150–92. See also Frederickson, "'I Know Which Side I'm On,'" 173. Hillman quotation in *Documentary History, ACWA: 1936–1938*, "Report of the General Executive Board and Proceedings of the Twelfth Biennial Convention, May 9–17, 1938" (New York: Herald-Nathan Press, Inc., 1938?), 413.
43. Spencer, "My Transition," Highlander Papers.
44. The AFL announced a campaign to organize women workers in 1914 with Samuel Gompers declaring that "women do not want charity or patronage any more than men do. They want justice." See the *American Federationist*, 20:8 (March 1914): 234. William Green similarly condemned discrimination against women in 1934. See Alice Kessler-Harris, *Out to Work: A History of Wage-Earning Women in the United States* (New York: Oxford Univ. Press, 1982), 268. The TWUA-CIO also targeted women workers in a post–World War II organizing campaign promising that "women get whatever men get." See Textile Workers Union of America Pamphlet, "What Every Woman Should Know" (New York, 1946).
45. See Dorothy Horstman, *Sing Your Heart Out, Country Boy* (Nashville: Country Music Foundation Press, 1975), for the lyrics of numerous songs with

these themes. The prototype of traditional southern songs praising mothers is the powerful "Can the Circle Be Unbroken" recorded by the Carter family in 1935. The ballad laments the death of the mother who bound the family together (Horstman, 40). Other important mother songs include the 1922 gospel tune "If I Could Hear My Mother Pray Again," by James Rowe and J. W. Vaughn (Horstman, 49); Bob Miller's creations composed during the 1920s and 1930s, including "My Mother's Tears," "Story of a Dear Old Lady," and "Rockin' Alone in an Old Rockin' Chair" (Horstman, 49, 245); and Hoyt Bryant and Jimmie Rodgers's "Mother, the Queen of My Heart" (Horstman, 392). Songs about daughters are not as numerous as those written to mothers but they are uniformly loving ballads. Examples include Bill Monroe's "I Hear a Sweet Voice Calling" and his "The Little Girl and the Dreadful Snake." These ballads are discussed in Robert Cantwell, *Bluegrass Breakdown: The Making of the Old Southern Sound* (Urbana: Univ. of Illinois Press, 1984), 213–31. A more recent rendition of the same genre can be found in Merle Haggard's "If We Make It through December" (Horstman, 303). In sharp contrast, southern songs written to wives are frequently about strife and trouble, duplicity and broken promises. This theme abounds in the 1940s when singing openly about illicit love and infidelity became more accepted. Examples include "Address Unknown" by Vaughn Horton, Gene Autry, and Denver Darling (Horstman, 149), "Cold, Cold Heart" by Hank Williams, and "San Antonio Rose" by Bob Wills (Horstman, 183). In contrast to songs about unrequited love or rejection, those written to celebrate successful romance often portray women as daughters, using lyrics such as "my pretty little girl," or as mothers, with words like "a saint in a dress made of gingham."

46. Rosabeth Moss Kanter has argued that when "a woman is alone, or virtually alone in a group of men, there is pressure on her to adopt one of four stereotypical roles: mother, sex object, pet, or 'iron maiden.'" Kanter acknowledges that some women may choose to adopt these roles for the security they provide, while others struggle against the limitations the stereotypes impose. She contends that all of these roles provide ways of resolving the issues of sexuality, competence, and control that arise when a woman enters a group of men. These roles help men confine a woman to a limited place where she will not be able to compete with them, and at the same time limit the exercise of a woman's competence. Kanter's model for contemporary women entering male-dominated workplaces reinforces my argument that the stereotypical roles open to women in the southern labor movement have been limited to heroine and girl striker. Heroines are both mothers and "iron maidens"; girl strikers are both sex objects and pets, and at times "iron maidens." Union wives would not be included here for they remain safely outside the confines of the male-dominated union. See Rosabeth Moss Kanter "Women in Organizations: Sex Roles, Group Dynamics, and Change Strategies," in *Beyond Sex Roles*, ed. Alice G. Sargent (New York: West

Publishing Co., 1977), 371–86. Thanks to Judith Catlett for drawing my attention to Kanter's article.

47. Telephone interview by author with Cosby Totten, Jan. 26, 1990. See Denise Giardina, "The Pittston Strike: Solidarity in Appalachia," *The Nation*, July 3, 1989, 12–14.

48. *American Federationist*, 7:6 (June 1900), front cover. This figure reappeared on the May 1901 cover.

5. The 1922 Railroad Shopmen's Strike in the Southeast

A Study of Success and Failure

Colin J. Davis

On July 1, 1922, 400,000 railroad shopmen nationwide laid down their tools, instigating an industrial conflict that threatened the country's economic and social lifeline. The striking workers were nonoperating craftsmen, notably machinists, boilermakers, blacksmiths, sheet-metal workers, electricians, and carmen. The shopcrafts strike raised key questions about the nature of labor relations on the railroads, the impact of federal involvement, and relationships between union bureaucracies and the rank and file.

National in scope, the strike had an important southern component, for among the major affected lines were the two key roads serving the coastal South, the Atlantic Coast Line and the Seaboard Air Line. In the 1920s, journalists, academic observers, and others familiar with the labor movement regarded southern workers as distinctive if not aberrant. However, on the whole, the experience of these southern men in the 1922 shopcrafts strike mirrored that of their counterparts elsewhere. As in other sections of the country, variations in local strike organization and conduct, along with differences in the intransigence of the companies, were the primary variables in explaining the course of the strike. Thus the partial victory of the Seaboard strikers, as well as devastating defeat of their Coast Line counterparts, owed primarily to divergent local circumstances, not to some distinctive southern component.

The Atlantic Coast Line (Coast Line) and the Seaboard Air Line (Seaboard) were two of the major railroads in the Southeast. They ran parallel through Florida, Alabama, Georgia, South Carolina, North Carolina, and Virginia. The Coast Line Railroad stretched 4,900 miles, while the Seaboard was 3,600 miles long.[1]

In the 1920s, shopcrafts workers constituted an important segment of the industrial labor force of the South Atlantic states. About 12,500 were employed in repairing and maintaining the region's rolling stock, constituting over 20 percent of its total number of iron and steel workers. The ACL and the Seaboard employed, respectively, 5,600 and 4,000 shopmen, among whom the shopcraft unions had established a relatively strong foothold. The national and religious divisions that often undercut worker solidarity in the North and Midwest were largely absent, as southern railroad shops employed hardly any immigrant workers. At the same time, however, racial divisions loomed large since well over one-third of the shopcrafts workers were African-Americans. Blacks were concentrated in the unskilled occupations but in many cases African-American "helpers" and general laborers in fact were quite highly skilled and were kept out of higher classifications by virtue of racial restrictions rather than by lack of ability or knowledge. All of the shopcraft unions discriminated against or, more usually, entirely excluded black workers.[2]

By the 1920s, the nation's shopmen had achieved a sort of quasi-industrial form of organization. On each road, the six nonoperating unions were grouped into an umbrella body, called a "system federation." Overseeing these railroad system federations was a national AFL structure called the Railway Employees' Department (RED) and led by Bert Jewell.[3] The unwillingness of these unions to recruit black workers, however, compromised this cross-crafts unity.

The 1922 strike severely tested the shopcrafts' federated organizations, nowhere more so than on the southern coastal roads. The shopmen on the Coast Line, the Seaboard, and others throughout the country went on strike for numerous reasons. In 1920, the Esch-Cummins (or Transportation) Act established a federal agency to oversee the wages and working conditions of over two million railroad workers. Railroad workers did not completely trust this body, the Railroad Labor Board (RLB).[4] In 1921 this mistrust intensified when the RLB issued rulings that cut wages and abolished time-and-a-half payments for overtime.[5] In addition, railroad managements initiated "open-shop" drives on their roads. Management refused to recognize trade union representation rights, closed down railroad shops, and subcontracted work.[6] The railroads, supported by key members of the Railroad Labor Board, were determined to return to the prewar conditions of unfettered, union-free relations. By the spring of 1922, railroad workers were ready for industrial action.

An RLB decision to cut wages again ignited the conflict.[7] Prior to this ruling on June 5, the local union officials on the Seaboard and the Coast Line, in common with their counterparts throughout the country, had made it clear that under no circumstances would they accept another wage cut. RED president Jewell warned that "the gang [i.e., the shopcraft workers] is mad so mad that they are through with protesting and are preparing to act."[8] It was this rank-and-file pressure, which had built up in response to the railroads' policies on subcontracting and piece rates, that forced the RED to submit a strike vote to the membership.

The results of this nationwide ballot were staggering: 98 percent voted to strike.[9] The resulting walkout, which began on July 1, brought out the two roads' 9,400 shopmen, who thus joined nearly 400,000 of their counterparts throughout the nation. On July 1, on all Seaboard points from Richmond through Raleigh, to Columbia, South Carolina, Savannah, Birmingham, and Jacksonville, all the mechanics and helpers came out.[10] On the Coast Line the shopmen left in droves, the major strike centers being Rocky Mount (which counted 1,100 strikers) and Wilmington, North Carolina; Waycross, Georgia (1,800); Florence, South Carolina; and Sanford and Port Tampa City, Florida.[11] The bulk of those who remained were foremen.[12]

The strikers on both lines immediately set up pickets and arranged daily meetings to keep the membership informed of events. However, though the early strike response was similar on both lines, the organizational strategies differed. The Coast Line strikers divided the road into six divisions, based upon state lines, and the president of the system federation, Geoff Rosser, stayed in Rocky Mount.[13] On the Seaboard, the president of the system federation, Henry Fallon, and the system secretary, who was also the general chairman of the International Brotherhood of Railway Carmen, stayed in Jacksonville, Florida. The other five chairmen were situated in Portsmouth, Virginia, and Savannah. The justification for this concentration was provided by system secretary Jim Wilds, who explained that Portsmouth was the "largest shop point on the system" and that Savannah was the "other important point." Thus by concentrating their organizational resources at these three most important points, the Seaboard leadership believed, as Wilds pointed out, that they would be better able to assist the "strike by keeping these points in line."[14] As it turned out, the Seaboard union leaders were able to better organize and run the strike in the major centers along its line, while the Coast Line leaders were scattered and at times unreceptive to their members' calls for information and support.

More important than the differing strategies of the two sets of railroad workers were their strike experiences. From the beginning, Coast Line strikers encountered fierce resistance from management, while their Seaboard counterparts faced less intransigent opposition. Throughout the bitter strike, the degree of management hostility was a critical variable in shaping the results for the two groups of workers.

From the start, the Coast Line resorted to court injunctions, employed armed guards, and hired strikebreakers. On July 6, the Coast Line management released a statement exhorting their men to return to work within four days and threatened that those shopmen who refused to go back to work "will have lost all rights and can enter service thereafter only as new employes."[15] The Coast Line strikers ignored this threat and on July 10 violence broke out when hired guards from St. Petersburg pistol-whipped pickets on duty in Rocky Mount.[16] Nor were shopmen the only victims, for on July 18, reported a newsman, a guard shot and killed Coast Line engineer H. J. Southwell, because "Southwell half jokingly" had called him a "scab."[17]

White and black strikebreakers presented further difficulties for the Coast Line strikers. In Savannah, for example, the local union secretary explained that the railroad was "importing a good many white boys off the farm." Just as troubling, the Coast Line's recruitment of black strikebreakers exacerbated the strikers' difficulties and exposed the self-imposed vulnerability that white workers had courted through their discriminatory practices. As the Savannah secretary further pointed out, management had "been able to secure all the negro labor they can use."[18] The shopcrafts had long histories of racial exclusivism. Just five years earlier, for example, a Georgia unionist had boasted that a "colored man" would never be given a "seat in our lodge rooms," because if that happened, he declared, the union would be "stocked with a class of people that has no self-respect, no honor, no refinement, no culture, and no character."[19] Even when Coast Line strikers did court black support, it was all too clear to the recipients of their sudden solicitude that the newfound acceptance was purely opportunistic. Thus, declared a North Carolina unionist, African-American helpers "could easily fill our places," while also being "a great help to us as pickets."[20]

Local and state authorities also impeded the fighting ability of the

Coast Line strikers. Numerous injunctions made it difficult to continue effective action. For example, one court order issued in Augusta, Georgia, allowed for only one picket. The local union lodge, concerned that the sole picket would be intimidated by railway guards, dismantled their defensive line.[21] In another case, strikers were involved in criminal law suits. Commenting on the large number of these suits, one strike leader noted that his men had been "accused of everything but starting the World War."[22]

Just as menacing to the Coast Line strikers was the threat of state troops being sent to both Waycross and Rocky Mount. On July 17, when two shop foremen in Waycross attempted to hire two nonunion men, the sheriff, H. J. Sweet, appealed to Gov. Thomas Hardwick for troops. The following day, the *New York Times* reported that "three companies of National Guardsmen and a machine gun unit arrived" in the city.[23] The presence of troops in Waycross had a stultifying effect on the Coast Line strikers and their supporters. Authorities even closed down "three union barber shops" whose owners had refused "to serve non-union workers of the Atlantic Coast Line shops."[24] In North Carolina, troops protected returning shopmen. In Rocky Mount, for example, two companies of National Guardsmen protected the movement of 100 black laborers into the local railroad shops.[25] Strategically supporting the troops was an abundance of U.S. Marshals. So eager was Attorney General Harry M. Daugherty to support local authorities in their strikebreaking efforts that by July 17 he had appointed over 2,200 marshals nationwide for duty in strike areas. By July 26, the Department of Justice had sent 25 to North Carolina, 40 to Florida, 13 to South Carolina, and 58 to Virginia.[26]

One other major stumbling block for the Coast Line strikers was a breakdown in communication between the rank and file and their local leaders. Internal communications between the Coast Line strikers and their own system federation officers was uneven. Thus, local strikers in Florence, South Carolina, complained to the national headquarters in Chicago that they had had no information from their general chairman even though they had wired him twice.[27] This deterioration in communication became one of the main stumbling blocks in building an efficient and strong strike organization on the Coast Line.

The situation, however, was not entirely bleak for the Coast Line strikers. Some local communities provided a great deal of support. For example, after a series of clashes between strikers and gun-toting guards in Charleston, Mayor L. M. Grace informed the superintendent of the Coast Line that he would "use the utmost diligence against the transgressions of the company."[28] Local newspapers also offered their support. Thus the *Jacksonville Journal* lambasted not only the Coast Line management but railroad managements throughout the United States in remarking, "For fifty years America has known no class of men to equal railroad directors for unmitigated gall."[29] But outside support could not compensate for the inability of the Coast Line strikers to mobilize their own families. True, other labor groups came to the rescue, with the ladies auxiliaries of the Brotherhood of Railroad Trainmen particularly notable in their efforts in behalf of the Coast Line shopcraft strikers.[30] Reliance on women's auxiliaries from other unions, however, underscored the Coast Line strikers' lack of foresight and resourcefulness. By not directly involving their wives and lovers in the struggle, they left themselves vulnerable. Not only would active support on the part of wives and other women have bolstered the strikers on the picket line, but failure to involve the women heightened the likelihood that ill-informed and uninvolved family members might be a source of anti-strike pressure. Shopmen throughout the rest of the nation (such as the machinists and carmen) either had supportive female organizations or established them once the conflict began.[31] In contrast, the Coast Line men never did tap this potentially powerful source of strength.

In this aspect of strike conduct, as well as other areas, the Seaboard Airline strikers fared much better than their brothers on the Coast Line. The Seaboard men were better organized and management was not as obstructionist. Until July 20, nearly three weeks into the strike, the Seaboard management, unlike that of the Coast Line, refrained from employing strikebreakers or guards. In a July 13 meeting the vice-president and the superintendent of motive power of the railroad tried to convince the shopcrafts to stop their strike action. As H. M. Fallon, a general chairman of the shopcrafts, explained, management wanted "to come to some understanding regarding a settlement before they would employ other men." The managerial group also promised that they would accept the shopmen's definition of the rules and would be willing to discuss the wage cut. On Jewell's order, however, the unions ended these negotiations following the shopcrafts' decision to settle the strike on a national rather than an individual basis.[32]

The RED's insistence on a national settlement was the key to the shopmen's strike strategy. Before the conflict a vigorous debate raged within the RED regarding the scale of battle. The leadership and the rank and file had agreed that localized strikes were doomed to failure. A nationwide strike required a nationwide settlement. Only through unified mass action could the shopcrafts counter the railroads' use of strikebreakers. Agreements with individual roads, on the other hand, would pit worker against worker and wreck the RED's nationwide bargaining structure. According to David Williams, vice-president of the International Association of Machinists (IAM), one of the affected shopcraft unions, the signing of individual agreements, leaving large numbers of shopmen on strike, "would be one of the worst debacles in industrial history."[33]

In the end, however, the accommodationist actions of the officials of the Seaboard Airline Railroad played a major role in shaping the strike settlement. The fifty-nine-year-old president of the Seaboard, Solomon Davies Warfield, had long been an exponent of equitable relations with his employees. Warfield had been deeply influenced by government control of the railroads during World War I. He was particularly impressed by the actions of Daniel Willard (president of the Baltimore and Ohio Railroad) who as chairman of the War Industries Board had achieved the swift movement of freight during the war.[34] Warfield's attitude toward railroad labor was benign. Not only did he recognize the collective bargaining rights of his workers, he also argued that one-third of "excess earnings" should be handed over to employees. Profit sharing, Warfield believed, was "a reward for faithful and efficient service and would furnish a constant factor to assure loyalty and fidelity."[35]

After the strikers ignored Warfield's entreaties, the Seaboard undertook actions similar to those that the Coastline had earlier implemented. The Seaboard advertised for workers to replace those on strike, offering new employees higher wages than those previously paid to the striking shopmen as well as "board and lodging on the railway property or in cars furnished if desired."[36] The company recruited armed guards, showing little concern as to the character or reputations of the men it selected for this duty. Thus the Duval County, Florida, sheriff described those sent to Jacksonville as "thugs" from nearby rural Baker County. Indeed on August 19 a full-scale gunfight took place in Jacksonville. Remarkably, no one was seriously injured, but city authorities, prodded by pro-union mayor J. W. Martin, arrested and jailed five guards.[37]

The Seaboard strikers were better prepared than their Coast Line fellows to meet the anti-union onslaught. In Savannah, for example, the strike committee organized boat rides.[38] Unlike their Coast Line brothers, they formed their own women's auxiliary to represent the six shopcrafts. This newly formed organization provided invaluable support by raising money through events such as whist drives, picnics, and street collections. These women also distributed food to the more needy strikers' families.[39]

The superior fighting spirit of the Seaboard strikers attracted attention both from unionists and management. As one local officer explained, the Coast Line strikers in his city "were sitting steady in the boat[.] it was like pulling teeth to get them fellows to picket their own shops." But, he added, "it was different with the Seaboard [men, who were] all willing to do their little bit." This militancy paid off in terms of greater strike effectiveness but it also put the Seaboard strikers in jeopardy. "[R]ight here in Jacksonville," this local leader noted, "the Seaboard gang were the only ones that were placed in jail for first one cause then another."[40]

Throughout the South, the strike cut into railroad traffic. On the Seaboard line in particular, it sharply curtailed the number of trains in service. On July 14 the Seaboard "discontinued" four Georgia trains, and on July 19 it canceled two more trains serving South Carolina.[41] In a one-week period between September 1 and September 9, the railroad was forced to discontinue thirty-two passenger trains, eight express trains, and fourteen freight trains.[42] Even the Seaboard's prestige train the "Shu-Fly" was canceled.[43] The major reason for the scratching of these trains was the breakdown of both locomotives and cars. Even though the Seaboard did have scab labor in its shops, the new hires, declared one union leader, were "totally inexperienced in mechanical skill and are doing us more good than harm."[44]

Because of the unreliable nature of scab labor, the management of the Seaboard decided to contract out repairs of locomotives and cars. Many southeastern repair works, including large facilities in Columbus, Georgia, Charleston, Tampa, and Savannah, responded to the Seaboard's call for help.[45] These companies, however, were not entirely capable of handling large batches of work. One local union official described Columbus's Pekor Iron Works as "a one horse affair . . . [that] cannot do any repairs other than small scale."[46] Other companies might handle the heavy work but, as strike leaders in one city believed, "the majority if not all their men would quit."[47] Thus inadequate facilities and union solidarity blunted the subcontracting strategy of the railroads.

The Seaboard thus experienced real difficulties keeping its rolling stock active. Train cancellations, striker solidarity, the poor quality of scab labor, the dearth of alternative repair shops alongside their railroad, and, finally, the absence of troops disrupting picket lines, all combined to make the strike effective. For Seaboard strikers, strong organization and effective mobilization paid dividends even when the employer began using strong-arm tactics.

The Atlantic Coast Line was also experiencing difficulties. The Herceleaf Powder Company of Brunswick, Georgia, for example, was unable to acquire enough cars to transport lumber to its refinery. The Cotton Mills Company in Atlanta had to take the drastic step of having its product transported in open cars.[48] In Montgomery, Alabama, the Coast Line's shortage of operating coal and gondola cars cut coal movements drastically and forced the road to resort to "the wasteful and cumbersome use of flat cars."[49]

But Coast Line strikers never obtained a clear picture of the precise state of the road's difficulties. Just as some rank-and-file unionists on the ACL proved less steadfast, their leaders failed to establish strong networks of intelligence and communication. In contrast to the frequent reports from Seaboard strike centers, little accurate information was sent to the national headquarters. In September, a Seaboard activist reported that "conditions [for the company] on the ACL are not as bad as [on] the Seaboard."[50] Thus the strike leaders on the Coast Line were not taking a commanding or guiding role. Clearly, the strike was more effective on the Seaboard than on the Coast Line. The breakdown in communications between system chairmen and local leaders on the Coast Line did much to spread the mood of isolation and abandonment. Moreover, Coast Line strikers did not always maintain vigilant picket lines, too often permitting scabs to return to the line's shops. Of course the return to work of a few men would not necessarily jeopardize the overall strike, but with foremen performing strikers' work and instructing the scabs, the ACL was able to meet at least minimal repair and maintenance schedules in key locations.

More important than the breakdown in local leadership, however, was the presence of troops in Waycross and other points on the Coast Line. These troops and U.S. Marshals guaranteed the unfettered movement of strikebreakers to the railroad shops. Thus the railroad was able to obtain large numbers of replacements that could at least engage in car repair.

For the first two months, the course of the two strikes was determined to a large extent by local conditions, but by the end of August federal authorities transformed the fortunes of the respective strikers. In late August, after conferences between President Warren Harding, the presidents of the "Big 4" Operating Brotherhoods (who acted as go-betweens for the shopmen), and the Association of Railway Executives (ARE, the railroad owners' organization), Harding offered to place the wage dispute back in the hands of the Railroad Labor Board and to have the shopmen agree to return to work with seniority rights unimpaired. The shopmen's leaders accepted this offer but the ARE turned it down. Instead, the association proposed that the shopmen could return to work but without a guarantee of their seniority rights. Tantamount to a stipulation of surrender, this proposal was unacceptable to the shopmen's leaders, who now broke off negotiations.[51]

Late in August, however, just as the momentum for a settlement seemed to have dissipated, moderate railroad executives proposed a tempting compromise. Led by Daniel Willard of the Baltimore & Ohio Railroad and Warfield of the Seaboard Air Line, the maverick group offered the shopcrafts a separate agreement. Although the proposal would have preserved seniority rights of workers on these roads, Bert Jewell rejected this offer saying, "We cannot give consent to make individual settlement at this time."[52]

Soon, however, RED resistance to signing individual agreements broke down. Precipitating its abrupt reversal was a sweeping injunction, issued on September 1 by Federal Judge James H. Wilkerson. After prodding from Attorney General Harry Daugherty, Judge Wilkerson enjoined both the leadership and membership from issuing instructions and finances and from discussing the strike either in the mail or on the phone.[53] As one later observer stated, the purpose of this injunction was "to prevent the continuance of the strike by prohibiting every possible means of carrying it out."[54] Because of this injunction, the RED lost no time in reopening negotiations with Willard and Warfield.

Coast Line strikers regarded these negotiations as traitorous. Strikers in Florence, for example, made it clear that the conflict was a national one and that the "separate agreement now about to be consummated . . . will be detrimental to all men on strike . . . we uphold settlement on a national basis and consider all persons traitors who agree to separate agreement."[55] Other strikers around the country joined the Coast Line men in condemning separate negotiations. The strike leader of the Santa Fe Railroad pointed out he was "receiving all kinds of protests against separate agreement . . . some of our men have already returned to work and others are threatening to do so immediately if separate agreements are entered into."[56] Even some Seaboard strikers opposed individual settlements. The chairman of Local 45 of the Carmen's Union in Atlanta, for example, pointed out that the strike was becoming more effective every day and if the leadership held out, he said, "we will get better conditions . . . advise you that we don't want separate peace."[57]

National RED leaders, however, had already decided. On September 13, they signed an agreement with the Baltimore and Ohio. Eventually one-third of the nation's railroads, including the Seaboard, signed agreements with unions representing 125,000 shopmen. The accords recognized seniority rights and established a commission to look into wages and working conditions. In addition, those roads that signed this agreement promised not to repair railroad equipment of those roads that were not signatories.[58] The Coast Line Railroad refused to accept the agreement. The stubbornness displayed by the Coast Line management in refusing even to have a conference led Jewell to later describe them as "probably the most vicious of any railroad officials in the southeast."[59]

The B&O agreement received a mixed reaction from Seaboard strikers. Some refused to go back to work altogether, and others refused to work with the foremen who had remained in the shops during the strike. In Portsmouth, Savannah, and Jacksonville, returning strikers even went as far as escorting foremen and other workers to the gates. Within a couple of weeks, however, the Seaboard shops settled down and on September 26 a local union official reported that there were no longer "any new men remaining on the System" and that "things should go along nicely" from then on.[60]

In sharp contrast, Coast Line strikers were angry and resentful. The secretary-treasurer of the Coast Line Federation reported that the men were "very despondent."[61] Another report pointed out that the men were "discouraged" over the B&O plan and that they felt they had been deserted to "fight it out alone."[62] Also feeling betrayed were the shopmen of the Santa Fe, Wabash, Burlington, and Southern Pacific railroads.[63]

The Coast Line management, on the other hand, was delighted with this new turn of events and stepped up its campaign to break the ranks of the strikers. In an effort to persuade strikers to return to work, managers sent railway clerks, or as one local striker labeled them, "a duly authorized propaganda squad," to visit workers' homes.[64] Management also sought to intimidate strikers by pressuring local merchants to cut off credit. In Wilmington, these tactics nearly worked when 60 strikers seemed about to return to work. Only after the swift intervention of local union representatives did these strikers hold their ranks. On September 16, these same union officials appealed to the RED to send a field force down to go over the railroad and instill a fighting spirit once more.[65] The national leadership, however, did not contact the strikers until November when they informed the System Federation chairman, O. R. Otterberg, that two grand lodge officers from the IAM and the International Brotherhood of Boilermakers were being sent down to help. Jewell also issued strictures on how to continue the strike. He urged local officials to keep track of the strikers and called upon them to organize local fund-raising events, generate publicity, appeal to local merchants and clergy to persuade Coast Line officials to settle, and keep the RED fully informed on a weekly basis.[66]

But the local leadership disdained this advice. They wanted meetings with the Coast Line management and greater financial help from the RED. But, reported a local leader, the Coast Line management "flatly" refused to "grant a conference."[67] On the issue of finances, Jewell informed the strikers that the RED and "the International Organizations have practically exhausted the funds that were available" and that "the local men must do everything they can do to assist themselves."[68] Another important problem that the Coast Line strikers faced was that with the signing of the separate agreement, those strikebreakers who had been released from roads that had settled were pouring into their region. The Coast Line management could therefore carefully select the more competent among them for employment. And, just as threatening, striking shopmen from other railroads (such as the Pennsylvania and Norfolk & Western) were working on the Coast Line. Finally, on some sections of the Coast Line various crafts were buckling under the strain. Thus in Florence, one local official reported that "the carmen and blacksmiths are hopelessly beat."[69]

But the deterioration of equipment had also put the railroad in a tenuous position. As Arthur Bennet, an international representative for the International Brotherhood of Electrical Workers, reported in February 1923, "the rolling stock of the road in general is becoming a physical wreck."[70] But in the protracted war of attrition that followed the RED decision to seek separate agreements, the situation became steadily more favorable toward the railroad.

The strikers' dwindling numbers, combined with energetic recruitment of defectors, strategic deliveries of new and rebuilt locomotives, and lax enforcement of federal safety regulations enabled the Coast Line to persevere. As the strike continued, more striking shopmen obtained jobs to supplement their income, sometimes many miles from home, leaving fewer and older men to engage directly in strike activity. Moreover, some men went back to work on the Coast Line. Although by April 1923, returnees still numbered only about 15 percent of the total originally on strike, these men were used as "instructors," according to Carmen's president J. F. McCreery. The railroad employed these experienced men to train "specialists out of auto mechanics and handymen." Each instructor broke in a half dozen or so of these so-called learners, each of whom was given some particular job to do.[71]

New locomotives and cooperative federal inspectors also strengthened the Coast Line's hand. Between February and May 1923, the Baldwin Locomotive Works furnished twenty-five locomotives and private shops overhauled several others. As an IAM national officer reported in May 1923, "if it had not been for these new engines and those overhauled by outside shops the A.C.L. would have been compelled to settle up long ago."[72] Additionally, the Coast Line was able to transport passengers and goods with substandard equipment. It could do so because of the paucity of federal inspectors, a mere fifty of whom were available for covering the nation's major 4,600 repair facilities.[73] When train wrecks occurred, mainly due to the lack of inspection, railroad managements were generally given time to adjust the situation to their advantage.[74]

Finally, the breakdown in the organization of the strike itself benefited the Coast Line. By June 1923 the system secretary of the ACL Federation had left the area and the general chairman had opened up an automobile agency. The strikers were thus left without a centralized leadership. Strikers continued to battle the road in Waycross, Georgia, and Wilmington, North Carolina. The men at these points battled on bravely and implored Jewell not to cancel the strike but rather to "just stand back and see one of the damndest bear fights you ever saw."[75] But Jewell and various international presidents were tiring. The failure of the governors of Georgia and North Carolina to settle the strike in the southeast led to a general questioning of the conflict. The governors had asked the Coast Line management to settle the walkout with their employees, but management insisted they would take the men back on a case-by-case basis and without recognition of their seniority rights.[76]

Also contributing to Jewell's frustration was the belief that the Coast Line men had not done enough during the struggle. As Jewell said in October 1923, "there has never, in my judgment, . . . been any real, honest-to-God campaign conducted on the Coast Line R. R. to win the strike." Jewell pointed out that one of the major reasons for this supposed lack of commitment was that "the average American railway employee has craft pride. He is proud of his skill, of the strata of society in which he travels. . . but great numbers of them are unwilling, as you know, to suffer the humiliation and make the sacrifices which are required."[77] These comments caused a great deal of anger among the strikers in Waycross. It even encouraged Gertrude West, a secretary for the strikers who had been arrested three times for allegedly carrying a concealed pistol, to accuse Jewell of wanting to call the strike off for the purposes of organizing the "scabs" then working in the shops. Gertrude West placed the blame on those local leaders who had deserted the strikers and argued that "THE RANK AND FILE have virtually had to fight on the A.C.L. without leaders from the first."[78] One local IAM leader lashed out at Jewell and the international presidents, charging that they were "not satisfied unless they are a straddle of our backs beating us in the head with a Black Jack or giving us hell in some other way." Facing, along with fellow strikers, a cheerless holiday, he offered Jewell a bitter greeting for Christmas 1923: "Hoping you will have turkey for Christmas, while most of us will have the underside of a hog."[79]

On December 26, 1923, the RED called the Coast Line strike off. Jewell urged the Coast Line strikers to get their jobs back, get control of the company union, and thereafter reinstate the unions on their road.[80] For most strikers, however, these pious admonitions offered cold comfort. Strikers faced the destruction of bona fide unionism on the ACL and, in some cases, the loss of their jobs.

The course and results of the strikes on these two southern railroads differed for a number of reasons. Harding's sweeping federal injunction had in fact precipitated the separate agreement and left the Coast Line men to fight on alone. However, a major factor contributing to the differing results was the contrasting managerial strategies of the Coast Line and Seaboard railroads. President S. D. Warfield of the Seaboard, like Daniel Willard of the B&O Railroad, was more amenable to discussing a settlement with his workers. As early as two weeks into the strike, Warfield was looking for a settlement and this interest was repeated again both in late August and September 1922. To some degree, this effort to come to terms was based on the strike's effectiveness, but this was not the sole reason. The Seaboard was not out to smash the unions on its road; it had indeed developed a working relationship with its unions. The Coast Line, on the other hand, was determined to break the shopcrafts' organization on its road.

But perhaps the most significant factor determining the divergent paths the strike took on these two roads was the overall level of active involvement of the strikers themselves. The Coast Line men were hampered early in the strike by injunctions and state troops protecting railroad shops. Also, the Coast Line men were at odds not only with the railroad company but also with their own local and national leadership. The internal conflict left the strikers isolated and weakened their resolve to fight. In addition to this already unstable situation, the union's lack of organized support from women's auxiliaries made its cause difficult indeed.

The ability to fight an effective strike determined both the pattern and result of these conflicts. Lacking strong local leadership the Coast Line men quickly drifted into a state of lethargy, leaving only a few men and women to fight on. On the other hand, the local leadership on the Seaboard were not faced with restrictive state action, and they were also better organized and committed to winning the strike. The factors of state power (both local and national), organization, and commitment determined the differing outcomes on these two southeastern railroads.

The southern struggle did, however, contain some unique features. The refusal to organize African-American helpers and female auxiliaries diminished the effect of the strike, particularly on the Atlantic Coast Line Railroad. Nonetheless, the battle on the two railroads indicates the presence of a southern labor force far closer to national norms of working-class behavior than many observers have recognized.

Notes

1. For the development of the Atlantic Coast Line and the Seaboard Airline Railroads, see John F. Stover, *The Railroads of the South: A Study in Finance and Control* (Chapel, Hill: Univ. of North Carolina Press, 1955); United States District Court: for the Northern District of Illinois, in Equity No. 2943, U.S. v. Railway Employees' Department, Final Hearing (1923), 125–26, 150.

2. U.S. Department of Commerce, Census Bureau, *Census of the Population, 1920* (Washington, 1923), 60–122, 874–1032. For an examination of the organizational development of the nation's shopmen, see Colin J. Davis, "Bitter Storm: The 1922 National Railroad Shopmen's Strike" (Ph.D. diss., SUNY Binghamton, 1989), 41–118. See also Robert H. Zieger, *Republicans and Labor, 1919–1929* (Lexington: Univ. of Kentucky Press, 1969), 117–22, 129–40. "[M]y father," writes historian William H. Harris, "who knew as much about fixing locomotives as anyone in town [Fitzgerald, Georgia], always remained a machinist's helper while younger whites, who learned their work from him, became machinists." William H. Harris, *The Harder We Run: Black Workers since the Civil War* (New York and Oxford: Oxford Univ. Press, 1982), vii.

3. Davis, "Bitter Storm"; Albert T. Helbing, *The Departments of the American Federation of Labor* (Baltimore: Johns Hopkins Univ. Press, 1931), 69–85.

4. Harry D. Wolf, *Railroad Labor Board* (Chicago: Univ. of Chicago Press, 1927), 379. During the legislative stage of the 1920 Transportation Act, the shopcraft unions and others attacked specifically the tripartite structure of the Railroad Labor Board. The board was to have nine members, of whom three represented labor; three, employers; and three, the public. The shopcrafts argued prophetically that the public members would combine with the employer group against them. "Resolution Unanimously Adopted by the Standard Recognized Railroad Organizations," *Proceedings, Railway Employees' Department, 1920*, 104–5. For a useful survey of federal railroad labor legislation, see Lawrence Scott Zakson, "Railway Labor Legislation 1888–1930: A Legal History of Congressional Railway Labor Policy," *Rutgers Law Journal* 20:2 (Winter 1989): 327–91.

5. "Decision No. 147—N.Y. Central Railroad et al. v. Brotherhood of Railway & Steamship Clerks, Freight Handlers, Express & Station Employees et al., June 1, 1921," *Decisions of the United States Railroad Labor Board with Addenda and Interpretations, 1921* (Washington, DC: GPO, 1922), 133–51; "Decision No. 222—Chicago & North Western Railway Company et al. v. Railway Employees' Department, A.F. of L. (Federated Shop Crafts), August 11, 1921," ibid., 224–35; Wolf, *Railroad Labor Board*, 154, 202.

6. See Railway Employees' Department, *The Case of the Railway Shopmen* (Washington, D.C.: The Department, 1922), 1–12. Selig Perlman and Philip Taft, *History of Labor in the United States* (New York: Macmillan, 1935),

517, and James Green, *The World of the Worker: Labor in the Twentieth Century* (New York: Hill and Wang, 1980), 119–20.

7. "Decision No. 1036—Alabama & Vicksburg Railway Company et al. v. Railway Employees Department, A.F. of L. (Federated Shop Crafts), et al., June 5, 1922," *Decisions of the United States Railroad Labor Board, 1922* (Washington, DC: GPO, 1923), 423–55.

8. Letter from Bert Jewell to John Scott, secretary of the RED, June 12, 1922, in *Railway Employees' Department Files*, Martin Catherwood Library, New York State School of Industrial and Labor Relations, Cornell University, Box 90 (hereafter cited as *REDF*).

9. *REDF*, Box 97, Folder 21.

10. Report from Seaboard Air Line System Federation, July 6, 1922. *REDF*, Box 108, Folder 10. The *Atlanta Constitution* (July 2, 1922, pp. 1–2) reported that from 500–750 Seaboard shopmen left the shops in Portsmouth, VA; 50–100 in Americus, GA; and 50 in Greensboro, NC.

11. Letter to RED from Geoff Rosser, president of the ACL Federation, July 16, 1922, *REDF*, Box 102, Folder 11; *Atlanta Constitution*, July 2, 1922, pp. 1–2.

12. Strike report from the ACL System Federation, July 7, 1922, *REDF*, Box 108, Folder 10.

13. Strike report from ACL System Federation, July 2, 1922, *REDF*, Box 102, Folder 11.

14. Report from J. S. Wilds, secretary-treasurer of the SAL System Federation, Aug. 14, 1922, *REDF*, Box 108, Folder 10.

15. "Atlantic Coast Line Railroad Company Statement," July 6, 1922, *REDF*, Box 102, Folder 11.

16. Report from Rocky Mount, NC, July 10, 1922, ibid.

17. *New York Times*, July 19, 1922, p. 2; *San Francisco Chronicle*, July 19, 1922, p. 1.

18. Report from Savannah, July 22, 1922, *REDF*, Box 102, Folder 11.

19. "The Negro Question," *The Boilermakers Journal* 29 (Aug. 1917), 609. The shopcrafts that barred African-Americans were boilermakers, machinists, and carmen. Philip Foner, *Organized Labor and the Black Worker, 1619–1981* (New York: International Publishers, 1981), 64–101.

20. C. P. Chipman, chairman of the executive strike committee, Wilmington, NC, to Bert Jewell, July 6, 1922, *REDF*, Box 102, Folder 11.

21. Report from Savannah, GA, July 31, 1922, ibid. The potential for violence and intimidation on the picket line was real. Two shopmen in Lakeland, FL, were reported shot and wounded on July 22 (*San Francisco Chronicle*, July 23, 1922, p. 1). Striking shopmen of the Georgia Railroad were also victims of picket-line violence. On Aug. 5, the *New York Times* (Aug. 6, 1922, p. 2) reported, "F. A. Smith, a union shop picket, was shot and seriously wounded in an encounter at the Georgia Railroad shops here [Atlanta] today with a number of negro employees. . . ."

22. Report to the RED from the ACL System Federation, July 31, 1922, *REDF*, Box 102, Folder 11.
23. *New York Times*, July 18, 1922, p. 2; ibid., July 19, 1922, p. 2. The *Times* reported that "Eight hundred shopmen . . . adopted resolutions condemning violence in connection with their strike and communicated to Governor Hardwick an expression of their desire to conduct the walkout without the necessity of military control."
24. Ibid., Aug. 6, 1922, p. 2.
25. Ibid., July 22, 1922, p. 2.
26. "Digest of Strike Situation to July 26, 1922, Office of U.S. Attorney-General, H. M. Daugherty," *Warren Harding Papers*, Box 464, Reel 149. Daugherty regarded the strike as communist-inspired: "Here indeed was a conspiracy worthy of Lenin and Zinoviev." Harry M. Daugherty, *The Inside Story of the Harding Tragedy* (New York: Churchill Co., 1932), 127. Other states where troops were mobilized included Missouri, Texas, Indiana, Illinois, Kansas, California, and New Hampshire. *New York Times*, July 26, 1922, p. 2; *Chicago Tribune*, July 11, 1922, p. 4; ibid., July 15, 1922, p. 2; *San Francisco Chronicle*, July 12, 1922, p. 2.
27. Telegram to Bert Jewell from G. W. Gifford, local chairman at Florence, SC, July 5, 1922, *REDF*, Box 102, Folder 11.
28. *The Charleston American*, July 10, 1922, p. 8.
29. *The Jacksonville Journal*, July 26, 1922.
30. Report from M. Cohen, secretary of the local federation at Florence, SC, July 9, 1922, *REDF*, Box 102, Folder 11.
31. *New York Times*, July 6, 1922, p. 2.
32. Letter to Bert Jewell from general chairman H. M. Fallon of Raleigh, NC, July 9, 1922, *REDF*, Box 102, Folder 11. Other railroads engaged in settlement talks were the Northern Pacific and the Baltimore and Ohio. *New York Times*, July 16, 1922, p. 2; "Strike Circular—Baltimore and Ohio System Federation, July 20, 1922," *REDF*, Box 103, Folder 5.
33. *New York Times*, July 7, 1922, p. 3.
34. Discussing Daniel Willard's role during the war, Warfield described him thus: "In this work, Mr. Willard has signal ability." S. D. Warfield, *Address of S. D. Warfield on the Occasion of the Dinner Given in His Honor, Waldorf, Astoria* (New York: N.p., 1920). See also Edward Hungerford, *Daniel Willard Rides the Line: The Story of a Great Railroad Man* (New York: G. P. Putnam, 1938), 199–225; Walker Hines, *War History of American Railroads* (New Haven, CT:Yale Univ. Press), 12, 244, 295.
35. U.S. Congress, House of Representatives, Committee on Interstate and Foreign Commerce, *Testimony of S. Davies Warfield*, 66th Cong., 1st sess., Aug. 29, 1919; correspondence between Mr. J. P. Harris, vice-president of the Citizens Savings and Trust Company, and Mr. S. D. Warfield, president of the National Association of Owners of Railroad Securities, in *The Return of the Railroads to Private Ownership* (N.p., 1919).

36. *The Charleston American*, July 10, 1922, p. 8.
37. Report from Jacksonville, FL, July 28, 1922, *REDF*, Box 108, Folder 10.
38. Report from Savannah Local Federation, Sept. 2, 1922, ibid.
39. Ibid. Throughout the country, and particularly in the Northeast, women took an even greater role in the strike. Women not only stood on the picket line but also organized picket duties. Women pickets were in evidence in Buffalo, Cleveland, Toledo, and Easton, PA., *New York Times*, July 13, 1922, p. 2; July 14, 1922, p. 2; July 27, 1922, p. 2; July 28, 1922, p. 2; Buffalo Strike Circular, New York Central System Federation, July 13, 1922, *REDF*, Box 99, Folder 14.
40. Letter to Bert Jewell from "Irish" of Jacksonville, Oct. 22, 1922. This same writer also mentioned that the strikers were also "giving scab foremen the silent treatment . . . no human being can stand that long as their conscience will beat them out." *REDF*, Box 108, Folder 10.
41. *Atlanta Constitution*, July 15, 1922, p. 1; ibid., July 20, 1922, p. 1.
42. Report from A. E. Courtenay of Waycross, GA, Sept. 9, 1922, *REDF*, Box 108, Folder 10.
43. *Columbia Enquirer Sun*, July 15, 1922.
44. Report to Bert Jewell from J. S. Wilds, Aug. 28, 1922, *REDF*, Box 108, Folder 10.
45. Report from G. H. Ray, secretary Columbus, GA, federation, July 16, 1922, ibid.; report from Charleston, SC, July 9; report from general chairman H. M. Fallon, Aug. 10, 1922, ibid. A. W. R. Bonswall, who was an official of the Seaboard Airline, was also a stockholder of this company. Ibid; *Atlanta Constitution*, July 29, 1922, p. 5.
46. Report from Columbus, GA, July 16, 1922, *REDF*, Box 108, Folder 10.
47. Ibid.
48. Report from Waycross, GA, Sept. 11, 1922, *REDF*, Box 102, Folder 11.
49. Report from Montgomery, AL, Aug. 11, 1922, ibid. This report also mentioned that 2,670 carloads were side-tracked because there was "no motive power to move them with."
50. Report from Waycross, GA, Sept. 9, 1922, *REDF*, Box 108, Folder 10..
51. Letter to President Warren Harding from executive council of the Railway Employees' Department, Aug. 11, 1922, *REDF*, Box 90; Zieger, *Republicans and Labor*, 134; Perlman and Taft, *History of Labor in the United States*, 520–21; Wolf, *Railroad Labor Board*, 246–47.
52. Telegram from Bert Jewell to Warren S. Stone, Sept. 1, 1922, *REDF*, Box 198, Folder 11.
53. United States District Court: for the Northern District of Illinois, in Equity No. 2943, U.S. v. Railway Employees' Department (1922), 1–10; James N. Giglio, *H. M. Daugherty and the Politics of Expediency* (Kent, OH: Kent State Univ. Press,1978) 148–51; Zakson, "Railway Labor Legislation," 257–358.
54. Edward Berman, *Labor and the Sherman Act* (New York: Russell and

Russell, 1930), 142. The attorney representing the shopmen, Donald Rich-berg, wrote in his autobiography, *My Hero, the Indiscreet Memoirs of an Eventful but Unheroic Life* (New York: Putnam Press, 1954), that the injunction "was an injunction to prevent the settlement of a strike. There is no doubt in my mind whatsoever that it was engineered by those railroads which were determined to crush the labor unions once and for all and who were certainly out of sympathy with President Willard and his associates in their effort to arrive at a peace treaty," p. 117.

55. Telegram to Bert Jewell from Geoff Gifford, chairman of Florence, SC, federation, Sept. 10, 1922, *REDF*, Box 102, Folder 11.

56. Report from T. L Personette, general chairman of the Santa Fe System Federation, Sept. 16, 1922, *REDF*, Box 102, Folder 1.

57. Report from A. L. Flynn, recording secretary of Georgia Lodge No. 45, Brotherhood Railway Carmen of America, Sept. 9, 1922, *REDF*, Box 108, Folder 10.

58. "Special Circular–R.E.D.," Oct. 2, 1922, *REDF*, Box 90; Interstate Commerce Commission, *Statistics of Railways in the United States* (Washington, DC: GPO, 1924), x.

59. Letter from Bert Jewell to J. W. Kline, president of the International Brotherhood of Blacksmiths, Drop Forgers & Helpers of America, Aug. 16, 1923, *REDF*, Box 102, Folder 11.

60. Reports from H. M. Fallon, general chairman, Jacksonville, FL, Sept. 26, 1922, and J. S. Wilds, secretary-treasurer, Norfolk, VA, Sept. 18, *REDF*, Box 108, Folder 10.

61. Report from C. B. Otterburg, Rocky Mount, NC, Sept. 10, 1922, *REDF*, Box 102, Folder 11.

62. Report from G. F. Mounts, general vice president of the Brotherhood of Railway Carmen of America, Sept. 16, 1922, ibid.

63. Clarke Cary, a local strike leader on the Chicago, Burlington, and Quincy Railroad, remarked that "all the men on strike are not in favor of any separate agreement but still stand by the old slogan one for all and all for one." Cary telegram to Jewell, Sept. 10, 1922, *REDF*, Box 8, Folder 9. A report from the general chairman of the Southern Pacific System Federation stated that "the rank and file have been considerably discouraged when it became known that there was talk of other than a national settlement." Letter from Walter Nash, general chairman, Southern Pacific System Federation, to L. G. Valentine, secretary-treasurer, Southern Pacific System Federation, Sept. 10, 1922, *REDF*, Box 107, Folder 1.

64. Report from C. B. Otterburg, secretary-treasurer of the ACL Federation, Rocky Mount, NC, Sept. 10, 1922, *REDF*, Box 102, Folder 11.

65. Report from G. F. Mounts, general vice president of the Brotherhood of Railway Carmen of America, Wilmington, NC, Sept. 16, 1922. Mounts also urged the national leadership "to get out a letter of information and instructions to the membership on the roads where no settlement has yet been reached." *REDF*, Box 107, Folder 11.

66. Letter from Bert Jewell to system chairman C. R. Otterburg, Nov. 10, 1922. Jewell also reminded Otterburg that "this is a federated strike and there will be a federated settlement and each General Chairman, regardless of the craft he represents, should get out and work . . . the interests of all crafts involved in the strike." *REDF*, Box 102, Folder 11.
67. Telegram to Bert Jewell from C. R. Otterburg, Sept. 29, 1922, ibid.
68. Letter to C. R. Otterburg from Bert Jewell, Nov. 10, 1922, ibid.
69. Report from M. E. Cohen, local strike secretary at Florence, SC, to William Johnston, president of the International Association of Machinists, Nov. 8, 1922. This local secretary did point out that with winter approaching, the northern scabs would have a hard time acclimatizing: "We are praying for a cold winter for strange as it may seem these men can not stand our winters as they are not protected as we are and they will quit and go home." Ibid.
70. Report to President E. J. Evans of the International Brotherhood of Electrical Workers (IBEW), from Arthur Bennet, Cumberland, MD, Feb. 12, 1923. Bennet toured the whole line and he found that even though there had been some desertions, the major points of strength were Rocky Mount, NC, Waycross, GA, Jacksonville, FL, and Port Tampa, FL. The major weak points were Montgomery, AL, and Savannah, GA; at this latter point Bennet reported that the strikers, mainly carmen, were set on going back to work. Because of this, Bennet lambasted the men: "I spared them not, for I felt that they had no sympathy coming to them. In my mind they had only damnation and I gave it to them." Ibid.
71. Report to Martin Ryan, general president of the Brotherhood of Railway Carmen of America (BRCA), from General Vice-President J. F. McCreery, BRCA, April 28, 1923, Savannah, GA, ibid. McCreery pointed out that another major problem was the lack of finances: "The system federation of officers have been handicapped since the beginning of the strike due to a depleted treasury."
72. Report to Bert Jewell from George Marshall, Grand Lodge Representative (IAM), May 26, 1923, ibid. By March 1923 the Atlantic Coast Line had only one serviceable locomotive in reserve. (United States District Court for the Northern District of Illinois, in Equity No. 2943, U.S. v. Railway Employees Dept, in Equity No. 2943, Final Hearing, [1923], p. 129.)
73. U. S. Interstate Commerce Commission, *Thirty-Sixth Annual Report of the Interstate Commerce Commission* (Washington, DC: 1922), 22.
74. Following a train wreck resulting in three deaths, company officer O. A. White, the master mechanic of the Coast Line, ordered other supervisory personnel to have their inspection reports in order. White justified this action by explaining that "in all probability quite a number of Government Locomotive Inspectors will . . . investigate this accident." The closing sentence of his instructions stated, "This information is sent to you for your specific and personal information and after you have read this letter carefully, I want you to destroy the same." Memo from O. A. White, master mechanic, Waycross, GA, March 16, 1923, *REDF*, Box 102, Folder 11.

75. Letter to Bert Jewell from J. Q. Williams, secretary to District Lodge No. 35, IAM, Rocky Mount, NC, Oct. 12, 1923, ibid.

76. Report to Bert Jewell from G. W. Marshal, Grand Lodge representative for the IAM, Jacksonville, FL, Oct. 5, 1923. This report also mentioned the unlikelihood of ever coming to terms with the ACL: "It is my opinion that under the present circumstances we cannot hope to secure a conference with the officials, nor any kind of agreement, nor any kind of direct assurance of anything, except that the company is entirely satisfied with conditions as they are." Ibid.

77. Letter to H. M. Rowling, president of District No. 35, from Bert Jewell, Oct. 15, 1923; letter to J. Q. Williams, secretary, Local Crafts, Rocky Mount, NC, from Jewell, Oct. 16, 1923, ibid.

78. Letter to Bert Jewell from Gertrude Perry West, Waycross, GA, Oct. 25, 1923. This same woman started her letter with these words: "Hoping that you will excuse the presumption I am taking in writing you,—being only a woman who has fought like a tiger, if you will excuse the expression, for the winning of the A.C.L. strike since July 1, 1922." Ibid.

79. Letter to Bert Jewell from H. M. Rowling, president of District No. 35, Dec. 18, 1923, ibid. Rowling went on to say, "We have lost our homes, our jobs, our seniority and lots of good time, but we have not lost this strike and we not going to lose it, but we are going to Win it just as Cane killed Able."

80. Letter of instructions from Bert Jewell to H. M. Rowling and R. F. Milligan, both of Waycross, GA, Dec. 26, 1923, ibid.

6. Industrial Unionism
and Racial Justice in Memphis

Michael Honey

When Dr. Martin Luther King, Jr.. came to Memphis to support striking black sanitation workers in 1968, the situation confirmed his belief
in the need for a "poor people's" campaign for "radical reconstruction" of American society. Although the civil rights movement had
achieved great victories, poverty, unemployment, low wages, limited
educational opportunities, racism, and police repression still stalked
black America. When the sanitation workers rose up against these
conditions, Memphis authorities responded first with paternalism, then
with tear gas, billy clubs, shootings, and court injunctions. Only the
murder of Dr. King on April 4 brought the city to the bargaining table.[1]

Civil rights, Dr. King had insisted, remained hollow without economic justice. Since his death, effective movements linking labor
rights, civil rights, and economic justice remain few and far between.
One of the most significant examples of such a movement arose some
thirty years prior to Dr. King's entry into Memphis. In the late 1930s
and early 1940s, war, industrialization, and unionization promised to
bring about a dramatic change for southern workers under the banners
of the Congress of Industrial Organizations (CIO). The CIO had an
especially powerful effect on African-American workers, who utilized
picket lines, mass meetings, and union organization to overcome conditions and attitudes even worse than those facing the sanitation workers in 1968. They did this in cooperation with white workers, whose
racial attitudes for a time seemed to be shifting away from the intolerance and bigotry characteristic of the segregation era. By the end of
World War II, Memphis had produced one of the largest industrial
union movements in the South and the first significant biracial organization of the city's workers in the twentieth century. A new day seemed
to be dawning.

But by 1968 the CIO's interracial presence seemed to have evaporated. The historian asks why. To understand the achievements and the failures of the southern CIO, it is first necessary to consider what it had to overcome. The southern racial system, intertwined as it was with economics, politics, and class relations, played an overarching role in keeping Memphis industrial workers unorganized. First slavery and then segregation had rigidly divided working people socially and occupationally along lines of color and caste. Efforts to overcome the color cleavage between potential allies had thwarted the Knights of Labor, Populists, and every other movement for labor reform. In the name of white supremacy, the state adopted a poll tax, which continued to accumulate every year it was not paid, leading to widespread disfranchisement of poor whites and most blacks. And yet many if not most whites remained convinced that they stood to gain from white supremacy and participated in race riots, lynchings, and the daily forms of coercion required to keep blacks oppressed.[2]

Employers, the news media, and politicians generally viewed the caste system as necessary for business prosperity. In the 1930s, the city's economic base rested heavily on the wholesaling and distribution of cotton and other agricultural goods, and on industries related either to agriculture, the area's lumber resources, or transportation. Black labor, which became a caste apart from white labor, played a critical role in these enterprises. Employers kept black labor cheap by using the plentiful supply of rural workers, refugees from the surrounding sharecropping and tenant-farming system, to break up unionization and depress wage levels. The historic social division of southern workers by color also undercut organizing efforts, thereby perpetuating low wages, terrible job conditions, bad housing, and high mortality rates for white as well as black industrial workers. For all but a handful of white craftsmen, wages remained half the depressed northern rates in the 1930s, and many white as well as black industrial workers in Memphis made as little as ten cents an hour.[3]

Labor organization provided the only possible means for industrial workers to improve their conditions, yet any effective campaign would require breaching the walls of segregation. Forty percent of the city's population of 300,000 consisted of African-Americans, and they made up the majority of the work force in cotton compressing and cottonseed oil companies, in woodworking industries, and on the riverfront. Blacks also constituted a significant portion of the work force at the city's handful of mass production industries—one-third of the work force at Firestone Tire, half or more at Fisher Body, and a small fraction of the work force at Ford auto. Industrial workers for the most part could not be organized until whites became willing to join with blacks in the same unions, the very thing that employers and politicians counted on them not doing.

Racial divisions rested not just on the attitudes of white workers, however, but also on a repressive social order adopted over the years to enforce segregation and cheap wages. This repressive order originated in the pre–Civil War era, when citizens could be run out of town on a rail or worse merely for speaking against slavery. In the "progressive" era, entrepreneur and power broker E. H. Crump put a new face on old forms of intolerance. Crump improved municipal services, kept the streets clean, maintained strict segregation, and obtained practically unanimous support from the business classes. He also built a political machine unsurpassed in the South. Crump almost single-handedly controlled Tennessee's most populous voting district and thus wielded enormous power at the state and even the federal level. During the Democratic party's heyday in the 1930s, he became increasingly arbitrary and brutal in using his power, driving political opponents and civil rights organizations underground. He also guaranteed the open shop to industry, pledging that, unlike Chicago or New York, Memphis would tolerate no CIO "nigger unionism" in Memphis.[4]

Crump accepted the business unionism of the American Federation of Labor as long as the craft unions did not try to organize mass production. In return, he gave craft unionists municipal jobs and positions on all the city's licensing boards, rewarded AFL labor leaders with judgeships, and placed union men in elected local and state offices. For the most part, white craft unionists faithfully supported the Crump regime, espoused a philosophy of labor-management cooperation, and succeeded in monopolizing a handful of high-wage occupations in the building trades and printing industries. In common with their craft-union counterparts throughout the country, they did this by using unions to exclude blacks from skilled labor markets and by limiting employment in the building trades to relatives and friends. The white "brotherhoods" of railroad workers went so far as to assassinate blacks in order to eliminate them as brakemen and firemen. Clearly, the existing craft unions provided a major barrier to interracial organizing, and therefore to industrial labor organizing as well.[5]

The national CIO recognized that the color line helped to confer unchallenged power on employers and Democratic party politicians at the expense of the majority of the southern population and resolved to oppose racial discrimination, lynching, and the poll tax. The CIO also recognized that racial division had helped to destroy organizing drives in packinghouse, steel, and other major industries in the North. Hence CIO unions adopted an interracial organizing strategy, hired black organizers and radical interracialists of the Communist Party, and in numerous organizing drives made alliances with civil rights groups. This strategy of building bridges between the black community and white workers proved more successful in the North—where blacks exercised some degree of political and economic power—than in Dixie, however.[6]

Hence, during the 1930s, in places such as Memphis, the long-standing social barriers to industrial unionism seemed overwhelming. Conservative forces within the AFL's Labor Council engulfed the earliest efforts of progressive trade unionists to organize among white workers, and AFL unions ignored blacks when they attempted to organize following the 1935 passage of the Wagner Act. White women in a few garment shops gained bargaining rights, but no breakthroughs occurred such as those in the North during the CIO sit-down strikes. Only the Southern Tenant Farmers Union, headquartered in Memphis, demonstrated that blacks and whites could join together effectively in unions. By 1936, however, plantation bosses and their political allies had used savage repression to decimate this initiative. And when the United Auto Workers union (CIO) sent Norman Smith to Memphis in 1937 to organize the Ford auto plant, paid thugs, possibly employed by the Crump machine, beat him nearly to death on two separate occasions. Thus, at the very time the northern CIO achieved its greatest victories in 1936 and 1937, police and mob violence turned back industrial union organizers in Memphis, as they did in community after community in the South.[7]

Not until the spring of 1939 did any hope for industrial or interracial organizing appear in Memphis. An unusual alliance of black stevedores in the AFL's International Longshoreman's Association (ILA) and white riverboat men in the CIO's Inland Boatmen's union, which later became a division of the National Maritime Union (NMU), nourished CIO hopes. Some 4,000 black and white workers shared power in a cross-federation alliance called the Joint Council of River Workers, and together they shut down traffic on the Mississippi from St. Louis to New Orleans for over a month. The strike not only closed the city's commercial lifeline; in addition, it defied racial customs and challenged the AFL's determination to keep the CIO out of Memphis. Company supervisors, hired thugs, and local police attempted to intimidate strikers, and the AFL's Memphis Labor Council leader Lev Loring even brought in scabs to break the strike. Under the fiery leadership of black longshoreman Thomas Watkins, however, Memphis ILA workers defeated efforts to use Memphis as a port for strike-breaking. The strikers eventually gained recognition, bargaining rights, and a contract, sending a signal of hope to workers in other industries and establishing a beach head for the CIO.[8]

None of this would have been possible, labor activists recognized, without the cooperation and unity of black and white workers. However, the dangerousness of adhering to this principle remained clear to everyone, most of all to blacks. Only days after the success of the riverfront strike, Memphis police arrested Watkins and took him down to the river to kill him. Watkins barely escaped Memphis with his life, never to return. Other black longshore leaders, one of whom was spotted floating face down in the Mississippi, disappeared in subsequent months, and thugs used lead pipes to attack a black community activist who had worked with Watkins to open up the building trades to blacks. Crump's town lacked middle-class support for workers' rights or civil liberties, leaving organizers and especially blacks vulnerable to such attacks.[9]

When the CIO's United Rubber Workers union launched a 1940 effort to organize the city's largest factory, the Firestone Rubber Company, the city's overt use of racism and anti-union terrorism revealed the barriers still confronting the CIO. Supervisors brutally beat a white worker in the plant who supported the union, E. H. Crump issued a vitriolic attack on the CIO, and Firestone thugs constantly threatened URW organizer George Bass. In one incident, they trapped him in an overturned car and tried to set it on fire and in another clubbed him so brutally that he required thirty-seven stitches to close head and face wounds. For their part, the police arrested a number of white CIO members as "fifth columnists," made intimidating visits to black workers in their homes, and brought the city to the verge of a race riot, shaking down blacks on the streets and ruining the businesses of several black Republican leaders. The national NAACP and the Southern Conference for Human Welfare both called this campaign of harsh harassment, accurately, a "reign of terror" against anyone who spoke for change in Memphis.[10]

The Firestone campaign also revealed the continuing racial split within the working class. Blacks, constituting 800 of Firestone's 3,000 workers, supported the CIO almost to a man, in part because Bass clearly upheld the principle of interracialism. In order to defeat the organizing drive, the Crump regime backed an all-white AFL local, which baited the URW as the "nigger-loving Communist union." In a labor board election in December, blacks voted massively for the CIO while white workers voted overwhelmingly to elect the AFL, which subsequently provided only a facade of unionization. Thus, in the period before the outbreak of World War II, a combination of racial hysteria and police state tactics blocked meaningful organization at Firestone, the jewel crowning the city's efforts to attract big companies to Memphis.[11]

When other CIO organizers came into Memphis, they drew conflicting conclusions about the meaning of the defeat at Firestone. Forrest Dickenson, who came in after Bass to organize the rubber and wood industries, concluded that his predecessor had made a basic tactical mistake by accepting black support before winning a large white following. In subsequent organizing drives, it became a standard CIO strategy to win whites before blacks, in hopes that the "nigger unionism" label would be less damaging. Leaders of the CIO's all-white local of the American Newspaper Guild, part of an industry where blacks played only a menial role, made this strategy into a principle, concluding that unionists should avoid racial issues at all costs.[12]

A different conception of the union's role on race questions emerged among leftists, who entered Memphis via the NMU and the United Cannery, Agricultural, Packing, and Allied Workers Union (UCAPAWA). Following the 1939 river strike, a handful of unionists associated with UCAPAWA and the NMU secretly formed the first functional Communist Party branch (the police had successfully suppressed CP organizing earlier in the 1930s). They began holding interracial meetings in the old working-class neighborhood of Fort Pickering, where many industrial workers lived or worked. This secret group of Communists and their associates became a nucleus for trade-union activism and provided a core of support for the national CIO principle of interracialism. Although the circle of leftists remained small, in the early years of the Memphis CIO they exercised decisive influence because they organized blacks, and blacks and whites together where possible, without reservation. At the very time the CIO lost its campaign in the Firestone plant, the Communist-led UCAPAWA achieved its earliest organizing victories among some of the city's lowest-paid workers in the cotton and food processing industries. UCAPAWA also aided the organization of the International Woodworkers of America (IWA) in sawmills and woodworking factories.[13]

Blacks predominated in these locally owned industries, and they took hold of the CIO movement with a fervor that stunned some white observers. Lucy Randolph Mason, southern publicist for the CIO, felt moved to tears by the powerful prayers and speeches of the half-literate blacks wearing overalls at union meetings. Ed McCrea, Tennessee district organizer for the Communist Party (and later a UCA-PAWA organizer), spoke at one of these gatherings, and later observed that "you didn't have any trouble explaining unionism to blacks, with the kinds of oppression and conditions they had. It was a question of freedom." Black cotton worker Hattie Walls made the connection between the traditions of the black freedom struggle and the union movement explicit during a 1940 Memphis UCAPAWA school, turning "Old Ship of Zion," the black hymn about spiritual deliverance, into "Union Train." Pete Seeger and Woody Guthrie later carried this organizing anthem to CIO unions across the country.[14]

The spiritual intensity of the black working class indicated that something more than mere trade unionism was at stake in the movement to build the CIO. At a time when civil rights organizations remained almost nonexistent in Memphis and the Mississippi Delta, the CIO provided an equal-rights philosophy combined with a specific means to change social conditions. It offered blacks, in Mason's words, "the acknowledgement of themselves as persons entitled to democratic respect," a status relative to whites found nowhere else in the South. Industrial unionism also provided a means to alter one of the most constant sources of oppression in the daily lives of black workers, their relationship to their bosses. The CIO provided an avenue, legally recognized by the federal government, to improve wages and working conditions and to resist arbitrary and dictatorial white rule at work. Black workers seized this opportunity, and became the backbone for the new union movement. Based largely on black support, UCAPAWA became the CIO's fastest-growing Memphis local in 1940–1941, and its membership elected John Mack Dyson as the CIO's first black local president.[15]

UCAPAWA, NMU, the Newspaper Guild, and a few other locals built the ground floor for the Memphis CIO, but World War II played the decisive role in precipitating and legalizing unionization. The economic growth caused by the war dramatically expanded the city's manufacturing base in cotton, woodworking, and rubber, and added new munitions, chemical, and aircraft industries. As a result, between 1940 and 1943, Memphis manufacturing employment doubled to a total of some 40,000 workers. The number of women industrial workers tripled, making them 31 percent of the industrial work force in 1943, while blacks remained at about one-third of the industrial work force. The massive influx of new workers coincided with a return to economic prosperity and a labor shortage that put labor in a vastly more advantageous position than during the 1930s.[16]

As the national climate increasingly stressed the need for unity and production, and the War Labor Board and other federal agencies demanded that local employers recognize and bargain with unions in order to get federal contracts, the city government muted its antagonism to the CIO. The mayor even welcomed the 1942 meeting of the Tennessee State Industrial Union Council, held in Memphis. Disillusioned with the AFL, whites at Firestone now voted in the CIO, and the Crump machine could do little to stop them. By 1943 about half of the 40,000 industrial workers in Memphis belonged to the CIO, with the rubber workers' local being the largest, followed by UCAPAWA, and then the smaller steel, woodworking, furniture, packinghouse, and other locals. As the sit-down strikes had been a turning point for the CIO in the North, the war proved decisive in the South, with Memphis one of the CIO's largest southern centers.[17]

The antagonism of most white industrial workers to the CIO collapsed in the face of this unprecedented opportunity to unionize. "By that time," the first president of the CIO local at Firestone recalled, "we didn't give a damn about black or white. We didn't care if they were polka-dot. We were tired of the sweatshop conditions." Once organized, white workers experienced the fact that, far from degrading them, biracial unionism improved wages and working conditions, caused foremen and bosses to treat them with greater respect, and offered the possibility of more dramatic improvements in the postwar era. It also remained clear that without biracial industrial organization the unions could again break down into competing units organized by color or craft.[18]

Racial politics played an increasingly significant role in the CIO, but they also raised new questions about the organization's future. Organizers could for a time concentrate simply on bringing people into unions and finesse racial issues by appealing to the simple principle of biracialism as a necessary means to a larger end. But what was the larger end? Eventually the implications of *how* unions organized became evident, and here the various tendencies in the labor movement diverged. UCAPAWA Local 19, Firestone Local 186, and the city's official CIO leaders each adopted distinctive ways of handling racial questions. At the same time, housing shortages, a seven-day work-week, and a no-strike pledge led to increasing tensions, and, inevitably, to racial conflicts.

UCAPAWA Local 19 represented one pole in the configuration of CIO racial politics. With a black president, a strong core of black and white shop stewards and committeemen, some 4,000 members, a third or more of them white, Local 19 provided a model of success for interracial unionism. The implications of this success became most evident among the local's black members, who wanted more than the recognition and the resulting contracts that they achieved with the help of War Labor Board policies. At Buckeye Cottonseed Oil, black union members initiated repeated walkouts protesting racial wage differentials, separate job bidding and seniority lines, and occupational classifications for whites and blacks, until the management finally abolished the discriminatory practices. Blacks began representing UCAPAWA in negotiations and UCAPAWA's president John Mack Dyson challenged black exclusion from politics by becoming active in the CIO's political action committee. As Dyson, Earl Fisher, and a number of other black UCAPAWA members became increasingly skilled in using union procedures, they also gained increasing recognition in the African-American community as advocates of equal rights. Local 19 held integrated union meetings and social gatherings and developed a reliable interracial leadership. No other union's activities so clearly represented the aspirations of black workers for equal rights or so sharply contrasted to the discriminatory treatment of blacks in other unions.[19]

United Rubber Workers Local 186's experimentation with biracialism produced more ambiguous results. During the war, the union's membership at the Firestone plant expanded from 3,000 to 7,000 (about one-third of them women and one-third of them black). Compared to the situation in 1940, the local now achieved at least a modicum of cooperation between whites and blacks. Although, unlike the situation in Local 19, blacks and whites sat separately in union meetings, organizers considered it a victory that they met together at all. And though whites controlled the top four officer positions, the union at least ensured that blacks always held one or more of the eleven executive board positions, as well as shop steward and committeeman positions. Blacks and whites did not mingle socially, and the local lacked the infusion of civil-rights-minded and leftist business agents that stimulated the integrationist sentiments in Local 19. Nonetheless, the rubber union implemented the CIO's biracial principles on at least a minimal level and effected important changes. Although few white rubber workers accepted blacks as social equals, most understood the necessity to cooperate with them in union affairs.[20]

The extent of the changes made in the racial thinking of white rubber workers is problematic, but clearly the CIO experience significantly impacted some white workers. Richard Routon, from a typically rural and racially prejudiced family background, had been among the workers who voted for the AFL in 1940 in order to keep the CIO "nigger union" out. During the war, however, he gained prominence as the result of a speech he made that helped to break up a racial conflict at the plant. In that speech he urged workers to recognize that they would never improve their conditions unless blacks and whites worked together. They elected him first president of the CIO local, and, bit by bit, Routon abandoned his racial prejudices. In the course of a long trip to a union convention in Washington, he became increasingly outraged at the humiliations imposed on a fellow black unionist by the Jim Crow system. Finally, he and other white unionists walked out of a Washington restaurant that refused to seat their black companion. Routon came to see discrimination as divisive and harmful. His conversion to this point of view was not unique. Routon, along with many CIO local leaders, attended Highlander Folk School, which, he felt, moved most of them to a more liberal position on race.[21]

Despite its achievements in bringing blacks and whites together, however, the rubber workers local lacked a program for dealing with the deeper schisms between workers enforced by the segregation system. The Firestone factory maintained segregated cafeterias, restrooms, parking lots, and even time clocks. The company kept blacks in separate departments, with uniformly lower pay scales even when they did highly skilled work, and assigned them to the hottest and dirtiest jobs. The company classified skilled blacks as "helpers" and forced them to teach their skills to whites, who then made higher pay rates than the blacks who taught them. Union seniority provisions, which operated on a departmental rather than plantwide basis, locked blacks into this system of segregated occupations, and white union leaders did little to challenge white supremacy on the job. Although union members met together, and voted together in the CIO, the color line still pervaded every aspect of shop floor and union life. During the war, the U.S. Employment Service and management made the situation worse by channeling blacks away from training programs that would qualify them for better-paid work, and from factory employment generally. The influx of previously non-unionized white workers, the heavy wartime production schedules, and the War Labor Board's restrictive wage policies heightened tensions, leading to racial altercations and walkouts by both white and blacks. The Rubber Workers leadership offered no program to deal with these problems.[22]

If UCAPAWA Local 19 and the Rubber Worker's Local 186 offered different visions of change, the official leadership of the city CIO offered no vision at all. In 1942 national CIO leaders placed Newspaper Guild member William A. Copeland in charge of the Memphis CIO, to take advantage of his writing and administrative skills during a period of rapid expansion—and also to limit the influence of UCAPAWA and NMU Communists. Copeland opposed all but the most minimal challenges to the South's racial system and regarded integration and communism as related and pernicious evils. Copeland condemned UCAPAWA representatives for holding interracial parties, hiring a black office secretary, using black representatives in negotiations, and "allowing" John Mack Dyson to be involved in politics. He criticized Highlander staffer Mary Elkuss for addressing blacks as "Mr." and "Mrs.," contrary to white racial conventions, and, on account of her liberal racial attitudes, accused her of being a Communist. Copeland and CIO publicity director Pete Swim (also from the Newspaper Guild) demanded a "completely economical" approach to trade unionism and flatly refused to follow national CIO fair employment practice guidelines. Initiating challenges to segregation, wrote Swim, "would be cutting our own throats." Hence, CIO officials continued to practice Jim Crow, even enforcing segregation in the CIO union hall.[23]

Unfortunately for blacks, by the end of the war most of the South's CIO regional and local directors (all of them white) adhered to this "completely economical" approach to unionism. When Highlander proposed to "integrate" the CIO's training school by bringing in one black, for example, white CIO staff members almost unanimously opposed even this tokenism as too dangerous. And in Memphis, the domination of white males over the decision-making positions in most CIO unions made it extremely difficult to change Copeland's segregationist policies. Even where blacks made up a majority of the membership, as in the Woodworkers union, whites filled the top positions and blacks held only secondary offices. The South's racial etiquette remained firmly in place in most CIO unions, with blacks in subordinate positions and expected to remain deferential to whites. Union racial composition also had shifted away from the early CIO days, when blacks made up a majority of union memberships. Increased white employment during the war dramatically weakened the numerical influence of black workers, and of racially egalitarian leftist unions, within the Memphis CIO.[24]

However, most blacks, and some whites, held views directly contrary to those of Copeland and other CIO staffers. Returning GIs had fought against fascism overseas, and in light of that experience black GIs especially found segregation intolerable. The national CIO's struggle to maintain federal fair employment practices after the war further encouraged opposition to Jim Crow by black unionists. It appeared to be a ripe time to challenge segregation, and blacks increasingly did challenge it. Black Firestone workers initiated a major altercation with supervisors and the police by refusing to sit in the back of buses at the factory gates when they quit work, and repeatedly engaged in wildcat strikes over racial incidents at the plant. Blacks in a number of industries also began during the war to challenge racially discriminatory hiring, promotion, job classification, and wage practices.[25]

Black workers had many grievances, and despite the quiescence of most white CIO leaders, stepped up their opposition to Jim Crow in the postwar labor movement. The hypocrisy of CIO unions which officially protested discrimination while openly practicing it on the local level especially aggravated black CIO stalwarts. Josh Tools, a black committeeman at Firestone, later complained that white union leaders failed to initiate educational programs or take steps to eliminate segregation in the factory, despite the international's constitutional provisions against discrimination. "Black workers always supported the union," he angrily recalled, "but it never made a concerted effort to eliminate discrimination."[26]

Racial divisions remained a potent source of conflict, controversy, and weakness in CIO unions. Workers might have had a better chance of resolving the issues involved had it not been for the external pressures of the Cold War. The national upsurge of anti-communism following World War II made it easy for segregationists to don the mantle of patriotism while attacking all advocates of unionization and racial change as Communists. During the CIO's postwar "Operation Dixie" campaign, the red scare encouraged vicious attacks against organizers and in small textile towns the South began to look like the 1930s all over again. In 1947 when the Republican-dominated 80th Congress crippled major provisions of the Wagner Act with the Taft-Hartley law, southern legislatures drastically curtailed the right to organize and banned the union shop. In 1948 segregationists formed the Dixiecrat party and initiated all-out war against what they saw as the interrelated evils of integration, unionism, and "communism."[27]

The World War II aberration of federal support and local acceptance of unions gave way in the postwar years to sharply escalating violence against anyone organizing unions or demanding social change in the South. The CIO had previously weathered similar storms, but the red scare now became more damaging as CIO top leadership united in support of American foreign policy and attacked the fellow unionists who opposed it. Under the pressure of federal loyalty oaths, anti-communist legislation, and inquisitorial Congressional committees, both CIO and Communist party leaders used increasingly strident language to attack their opponents. The party launched a divisive internal purge of "white chauvinists" that some felt only weakened it in the South, and, at a time when they needed allies the most, became increasingly isolated within the labor movement.[28]

The collapse of CIO unity in the postwar years had a powerful ripple effect throughout the South. The Operation Dixie campaign set the tone, as director Van Bittner cut the CIO's ties to the integrationist Southern Conference Education Fund (SCEF) and excluded some of the most effective leftist organizers from his staff in favor of racial conservatives and implacable anti-communists. Similarly, Memphis director Copeland attacked leftists and civil rights activists, holding meetings to alert his fellow unionists to Communist activity and leading the charge to amend CIO bylaws to prohibit Communists from serving as delegates to the CIO Council. Copeland's attacks focused especially on Local 19 activists, who not only won a string of organizing successes and wage increases after the war but conducted integrated picketing, tried to organize a chapter of the National Negro Labor Council, passed world peace resolutions, and demanded an end to segregated seating in CIO meetings. Local press accounts magnified these activities into a "communist threat" within the labor movement and encouraged the banning of Local 19 and certain NMU members from meetings of the Industrial Union Council.[29]

By 1947 the CIO's southern organizing drive had clearly failed in the textile industry and a massive propaganda campaign equating unionism with integration and communism had taken its toll in the South. In response to this onslaught, Operation Dixie organizers emphasized their "Americanism," and, following passage of the Taft-Hartley Act, many of them spent more time raiding the membership of left-wing unions (denied federal labor board protections because their leaders would not sign the act's anti-communist oath) than organizing new ones. Similarly in Memphis, as the CIO's efforts at expansion bogged down, Copeland accelerated his efforts to root out "communism," promoting a deadly atmosphere of political conformity. At his instigation, the state CIO investigated Highlander Folk School because it refused to ban left-wing unions from its premises. These unions, according to Highlander director Myles Horton, were doing the most to bring blacks and whites together; Highlander would not exclude them because it was trying to do everything it could at that point to promote integration. Ultimately, the national CIO withdrew its support from Highlander, citing its refusal to ban the leftist unions.[30]

The political conflicts in the CIO had disastrous consequences in the South, not only in weakening Operation Dixie, but in further polarizing industrial unions along racial lines. During the Henry Wallace presidential campaign of 1948, the divisiveness, which had definite racial overtones, intensified. At the national level, the CIO executive council first opposed and then reluctantly endorsed Truman for president, while a number of left-led CIO unions opted to support third-party candidate Wallace. In the South, Wallace drew his support from SCEF and the leftist CIO unions. He made his southern tour a crusade against segregation, speaking before integrated audiences, supporting blacks running for office, and featuring black performing artist Paul Robeson. In Memphis, Local 19 turned out 2,000 people for an integrated rally with Robeson and backed an interracial slate of candidates for state office. Most significantly, the Food, Tobacco, and Agricultural Workers (as the UCAPAWA had been renamed) Local 19 mobilized the African-American community to join the rest of the Memphis CIO in voting against the Crump candidate for the U.S. Senate. Unionized workers could now afford to pay the poll tax and their overwhelming vote for Estes Kefauver handed Crump his first major political defeat since World War I.[31]

However, mob violence against Wallace supporters in other parts of the South and Wallace's dismal showing in the election overshadowed this bright spot in Tennessee. So did the aftermath of the Wallace campaign. The CIO executive board followed Truman's reelection by expelling eleven of its left-wing unions containing nearly one-fifth of the CIO's membership for supposedly following Communist Party directives on foreign policy issues. Although not the result intended by the national CIO, which continued to uphold interracialism in principle, the purge's effect in the southern CIO was to remove the remaining restraints on racial conservatives. In Winston-Salem, North Carolina, CIO organizers cooperated with the House Un-American Activities Committee (HUAC), the news media, and city authorities to destroy FTA Local 22, the largest black-led union local in the South. In Bessemer, Alabama, CIO Steelworkers' union members beat up Mine, Mill and Smelter Workers' union officer Maurice Travis (he lost one eye as a result), while Ku Klux night riders and local police terrorized black union supporters, leading to the destruction of the area's most integrated union.[32]

In Memphis, Copeland and Steelworker administrator Earl Crowder led the city's anti-communist inquisition. In the summer of 1949 Copeland helped to undermine a critical strike by 800 black women in the United Furniture Workers Union by setting up a committee to investigate communism in that union and in Local 19. In September, with the strike in ruins, the CIO council passed a resolution calling on all constituent unions to set up special committees to root out "traitorous agents of a foreign government," and sent a special letter to Furniture Worker members asking them to cleanse their ranks. Copeland also directed two raiding campaigns against Local 19 at its stronghold in the Buckeye factory, with the support of black Urban League ministers who visited black workers in their homes and appealed to them to desert FTA "for the good of family and country." But though whites dropped away from Local 19, blacks remained "sold on the union," according to one CIO staffer, and defeated the CIO in two separate NLRB elections.[33]

Other methods existed for destroying unions, however. As in Winston-Salem, the full weight of the federal government's inquisition against Communists now fell on FTA. In 1951 Copeland and Crowder appeared as star witnesses in red-hunting hearings in Memphis under the auspices of the Senate Internal Security Subcommittee (SISS), conducted by arch-segregationist James Eastland of Mississippi. SISS investigators confiscated the union's membership lists and the local press placed pictures, names, and addresses of Local 19 members on the front pages. After the hearings, many employers refused to bargain with the local. The union's business agent, Ed McCrea, was forced out of town, police and FBI agents constantly harassed black FTA leader Earl Fisher, and membership went into drastic decline. The NMU and the Furniture Workers unions likewise conducted purges which eliminated leftists from the ranks of Memphis unions.[34]

As CIO disunity reached its height, employers took the offensive. The Memphis Furniture Company destroyed the largest local of the CIO's furniture union in 1949 and the American Snuff Company in 1950 adopted a similar union-busting campaign against a major local of the Steelworkers union. In both cases, employers forced unionists into unwanted strikes in unfavorable conditions, and the Memphis police played the key role in destroying the locals by escorting bus loads of strikebreakers into the plants. The CIO gave only sporadic support to the black women at the Snuff Company. The strike failed and the union collapsed after 200 days of violent picket-line conflict reminiscent of the 1930s. Combined with the CIO's internal purge, the failed strikes signaled the end of industrial unionism's expansion in Memphis. According to CIO organizer George Dhuy, "the most vicious anti-union companies" still remained unorganized, and in some respects Memphis seemed "just like it was when the CIO first came to Memphis."[35]

This was not quite the case, however, for now CIO official leaders, like the AFL leaders before them, were integrated into the city's establishment. The 1950s was not a time when CIO leaders wanted to battle it out with a multitude of small, anti-union employers and city police.

By the time the CIO officially liquidated Operation Dixie in 1953, Memphis CIO leaders had settled into building new union halls and conducting legislative action. Harry Martin and Pete Swim of the Newspaper Guild moved on to jobs supporting American foreign policy abroad; Copeland received an "Americanism" award from the Veterans of Foreign Wars; and across the state of Tennessee, business and labor joined their forces in the anti-communist "Crusade for Freedom." When Boss Crump died in 1954, the CIO joined with Memphis businessmen to bring about a series of mild civic reforms, insuring its inclusion in political decision making. The unions made few subsequent moves to endanger this newfound respectability. The days of organizing the unorganized were over.[36]

During the postwar era, Communists first predicted a radical shift to the left, which never came, then concluded that fascism had arrived. These and other political shifts, plus extreme rhetoric, inability to disassociate themselves from Stalinism, opposition to the Marshall Plan, union polarization during the Wallace campaign, and the Taft-Hartley oath, all served to isolate Communists from "center" forces in the CIO. Ed McCrea and Karl Korstad, both of whom served as business agents for Local 19 in Memphis, felt that the CIO Left, particularly in its handling of the Taft-Hartley oath and the ill-fated Wallace campaign, set itself up for defeat. (McCrea resigned from the party in order to sign the oath and keep his position in the labor movement.) Neither, however, regretted his union's efforts to break down Jim Crow, and in the South this was one of the main reasons that Copeland and other CIO regional leaders targeted them for destruction. It seems unlikely that a change of strategy on other issues would have spared them from attack, for the Cold War merely rationalized what many racial conservatives felt from the beginning: that the CIO had to put a stop to leftist and civil rights agitation in order to become respectable.[37]

The red scare had very disturbing consequences in the South. The CIO's war against the left helped to destroy strong black leadership and integrationist forces almost wherever they existed. In numerous instances, the CIO collaborated with the very forces of racism and "anti-communism" that had sought to wreck union organizing. In the process, it helped to destroy a nascent civil rights movement within the black working class, a movement that had offered a promising avenue for change.

However, this setback for a labor and civil rights coalition did not simply result from the Cold War's polarization of the CIO during the red scare, but revealed long-standing inadequacies of the CIO on the race question. These inadequacies were especially apparent in a heavy industrial center such as Birmingham, but they were also obvious in Memphis. From the inception of the CIO, organizers had placed their emphasis on the economic benefits to be gained by organizing blacks and whites into biracial unions. In the 1940s they succeeded in convincing white workers to join with blacks in bargaining units in order to protect their own self-interests. However, the practical accommodation of whites to the necessity of biracial collective bargaining did not move them to accept black demands for an end to racial wage differentials, discriminatory departmental seniority systems, and segregated facilities. Yet these steps remained necessary in order for the labor movement to maintain a social vision, to build unity in the shops it had organized, and to provide a sound basis to expand into unorganized industries with large numbers of black workers. Without such changes, the city's labor force increasingly divided into an upper echelon of higher-paid white production workers and a subproletariat of blacks denied access to training and higher-paying factory jobs—essentially the situation King found in Memphis in 1968.[38]

The passage of years magnified the ramifications of the failure of the CIO in the 1940s to move further than it did on racial questions. During the 1950s, the economic achievements of industrial unionism remained significant for those who were organized, but as a social movement, the CIO stagnated. The segregation of Memphis union halls remained commonplace and the national CIO's anti-discrimination policy proved largely ineffectual in this context. Throughout the decade, resistance to desegregation intensified in many CIO locals. In the case of the UAW's Local 988, which had bargaining rights at the International Harvester plant, white resistance finally forced Walter Reuther to intervene personally. In support of Local 988's only black elected leader, George Holloway, Reuther had the Memphis UAW hall padlocked and placed the local into receivership for defying all directives to desegregate its facilities. White hostility to blacks who attempted to upgrade their jobs or break down discriminatory seniority practices and workplace segregation remained implacable at both International Harvester and Firestone.[39]

The 1955 merger of the AFL and CIO further undercut efforts to desegregate Memphis unions and workplaces. The merger produced a federation of some 42,000 members in Shelby County (which included Memphis) and brought conservative white craftsmen back into dominance in the labor movement. The lack of black faces at local and state conventions became even more noticeable, and the city's labor journal assiduously avoided the issue of race, even as the desegregation crisis descended on the South. At the national level, labor economist F. Ray Marshall has noted, the merger accelerated the unraveling of coalitions between the labor and civil rights movements, leaving most black leaders skeptical that George Meany and other AFL-CIO leaders were serious about implementing their rhetorical support for integration.[40]

By the 1960s, the distinctive interracial presence that the CIO once brought to the Memphis labor scene seemed to have vanished, leaving behind an ambiguous legacy. Even if tainted in many cases by white paternalism and domination, industrial unionism had for a time stimulated the growth of the freedom movement within the black working class, established new levels of organization and cooperation between white and black, and caused significant changes in the thinking of some whites about race relations. Improvements in race and labor relations stopped at this point, particularly as the unions halted efforts to alleviate the conditions of the poor and unorganized, such as the black sanitation workers. When the CIO purged the unions of leaders most interested in organizing such workers, it cut off promising possibilities for union expansion and left the city's working class prey to increasing stratification by race, gender, and occupational status.

Union inaction on the pressing need for organization and desegregation left both the unions and civil rights activists considerably weakened during the upheavals of the 1960s. During that era, African Americans gained civil rights support in the South not from the unions, but from their own institutions and a few integrated organizations of activists such as the Southern Conference and Highlander Folk School.[41] At this point, however, the existing interracial organizations did not have the base among working people, the majority of the South, that the unions had once established. When Dr. King came to Memphis in 1968, the struggle to unite labor and civil rights efforts begun in the era of the CIO still had not prevailed. These many years later, such a coalition still remains to be built, only now in the much more unfavorable climate of the deindustrialization and labor fragmentation of the late twentieth century.

Notes

1. David Garrow, *Bearing the Cross: Martin Luther King, Jr., and the Southern Christian Leadership Conference* (New York: William Morrow and Co., 1986), final chapter; Joan Turner Beifuss, *At the River I Stand: Memphis, the 1968 Strike, and Martin Luther King* (Memphis: B & W Books, 1985).
2. Michael Honey, "The Labor Movement and Racism in the South: An Historical Overview," in *Racism and the Denial of Human Rights, Beyond Ethnicity,* ed. Marvin J. Berlowitz and Ronald S. Edari (Minneapolis: MEP Press, 1984), 77–82, provides background and historiography on the South generally in the period prior to the CIO. See David M. Tucker, *Memphis since Crump: Bossism, Blacks, and Civic Reformers, 1948–1968* (Knoxville: Univ. of Tennessee Press, 1980), and Roger Biles, *Memphis in the Great Depression* (Knoxville: Univ. of Tennessee Press, 1982), introductory chapters in each, on specific conditions in Memphis.
3. Michael Honey, "Labor and Civil Rights in the South: The Industrial Labor Movement and Black Workers in Memphis, 1929–1945" (Ph.D. diss., Northern Illinois Univ., 1988), chs. 1–2.
4. Ibid.; Tucker, ch. 2, and Biles, ch. 2.
5. Honey, "Labor and Civil Rights," ch. 2, and personal interview with International Typographical Union leader Robert Tillman, Memphis, 26 Feb. 1983. See also Biles, ch. 6, and Kate Born, "Memphis Negro Workingmen and the NAACP," *West Tennessee Historical Society Papers* 28 (1974): 90–107.
6. Philip S. Foner, *Organized Labor and the Black Worker, 1619–1981* (New York: International Publishers, 1981, 2nd ed.), ch. 16; F. Ray Marshall, *The Negro and Organized Labor* (New York: Wiley, 1965), 34–37; and August Meier and Elliott Rudwick, *Black Detroit and the Rise of the UAW* (New York: Oxford Univ. Press, 1979).
7. For a brief account, see Roger Biles, "Ed Crump versus the Unions: The Labor Movement in Memphis during the 1930's," *Labor History* 25:4 (Fall 1984): 533–52. See also Honey, "Labor and Civil Rights," chs. 2–4. On the union civil rights struggle in the South, see Lucy Randolph Mason, *To Win These Rights: A Personal History of the CIO in the South* (1952; reprint, Westport, CT: Greenwood Press, 1970).
8. See ch. 6 in Honey, "Labor and Civil Rights." Research on the river strike is based on the Annual Reports and various files of the Inland Waterways Corporation, Maritime Records, in the files of the U.S. Department of Commerce, Record Group 91, National Archives and Records Administration (NARA), Washington, DC.
9. Ibid., and file numbers 144–72–0, and 16–208–1, Classified Subject Correspondence and Investigative Files, U.S. Attorney General, Criminal Division, Justice Dept., RG 60, NARA.
10. Honey, "Labor and Civil Rights," ch. 8. Material on the Bass incident is found in the Department of Justice records cited in note 9 above, and in the

Files of the Workers' Defense League, Archives of Labor and Urban Affairs, Wayne State University, Detroit (ALUAWSU).

11. Ibid.
12. Personal interview, Forrest Dickenson, Memphis, 20 Feb. 1983; Honey, "Labor and Civil Rights," ch. 9.
13. Personal interview, W. E. Davis, St. Louis, 26–28 Jan. 1983; Federal Bureau of Investigation documents obtained under the Freedom of Information Act, in author's possession; and *UCAPAWA News*, 1937–41.
14. Mason, *To Win These Rights*, 104–14; personal interview, Ed McCrea, Nashville, 17 Oct. 1982; Claude Williams to Harry Koger, n.d., Williams Collection, ALUAWSU. Pete Seeger confirmed the origins of "Union Train," personal interview, 19 Jan. 1986, Washington, DC.
15. Mason, *To Win These Rights*, 30.
16. U.S. Employment Service Records (USES), Memphis file, Div. of Negro Labor, U.S. Dept. of Labor, RG 183, NARA; and USES "Re-Survey of the Labor Market Situation in the Memphis, Tn., Area," 19 March 1943, and "Labor Market Development Report," 15 Oct. 1943, in "Labor, 1943" file of the Mayor's Papers, Memphis Public Library, Memphis.
17. Memphis *Press Scimitar*, 6 June 1942. *The Labor Journal,* August 1956, provides membership figures. W. A. Copeland to Paul Christopher, 9 Sept. 1945, Tennessee Organizing Committee, Operation Dixie Papers, Perkins Library Manuscript Department, Duke University (hereafter cited as Operation Dixie Papers).
18. Personal interview, Richard Routon, Memphis, 18 Feb. 1983.
19. On union membership, see William A. Copeland to Paul Christopher, 9 Sept. 1943, in Region 8 Papers, Southern Labor Archives, Georgia State University, Atlanta (hereafter cited as Region 8 Papers); on the Buckeye disputes, see the National Mediation and Conciliation files 196–8955, 209–6926, 301–574, 300–2855, 301–3446, 442–572, 442–2182, 482–1668-69, NARA, Suitland, MD; and personal interviews, Leroy Boyd, 6 Feb. 1983, George Isabell, 10 Feb. 1983, both in Memphis; Karl Korstad, Greensboro, NC, 20 May 1981, and Ed McCrea, Nashville, 6 March 1983 and 28 Oct. 1984.
20. Personal interviews, Richard Routon; F. M. Dickenson; Josh Tools, 3 March 1983; Matthew Davis, 30 Oct. 1984; George Clark, 30 Oct. 1984; Clarence Coe, 28 May 1989, all in Memphis.
21. Ibid.
22. Ibid.; Memphis files, Div. of Negro Labor, USES Records, NARA; and John Beecher correspondence, Tension files, Div. of Review and Analysis, Fair Employment Practices Committee, RG 228, NARA, both provide details on World War II discrimination against black workers in Memphis.
23. Memphis CIO staff meeting minutes, 19 Oct. 1944, Tennessee Organizing Committee, Operation Dixie Papers; personal interview, Mary Elkuss, St. Louis, 27 Jan. 1983; and Swim to James Carey, 26 May 1944, George Weaver files, CIO Secretary-Treasurer Papers, ALUAWSU.

24. A variety of letters to Paul Christopher in March 1945 reflect the controversy over the CIO school, Region 8 Papers. The Operation Dixie Papers indicate the overwhelmingly white control of CIO staff positions.

25. Personal interviews, Clarence Coe, and George Isabell, Memphis, on the struggles of black workers against work place segregation during World War II. See also Honey, "Labor and Civil Rights," ch. 9.

26. Phone interview, Josh Tools, 3 March 1983, Memphis.

27. *The Southern Patriot*, Wisconsin Historical Society, Madison, provides ample documentation of the postwar reaction, as does the material in Stetson Kennedy's files, at the Southern Labor Archives, Atlanta.

28. Personal interviews, Ed McCrea, 6 March 1983, Nashville, and Junius Scales, New York City, 14 Nov. 1987; and see Scales's book *Cause at Heart: A Former Communist Remembers* (Athens: Univ. of Georgia Press, 1987), 208–11, 222–24 ff. Bert Cochran *Labor and Communism, the Conflict That Shaped American Unions* (Princeton: Princeton Univ. Press, 1977), says the CIO purgers and the Communist Party leaders "deserved each other," p. 305; and see ch. 12. See also Harvey A. Levenstein, *Communism, Anti-Communism, and the CIO* (Westport, CT: Greenwood Press, 1981), 283–86.

29. Honey, "Operation Dixie, the CIO's Last Organizing Campaign," paper given at the 1982 Southern Labor Studies Conference, 2 Oct. 1982, Atlanta, in author's possession; Copeland staff notes, 19 Oct. 1944, in Tennessee Organizing Committee files, Operation Dixie Papers; McCrea interview.

30. On the effects of CIO raiding, generally and in the South, see Levenstein, *Communism, Anti-Communism* , ch. 14, and Barbara S. Griffith, *The Crisis of American Labor: Operation Dixie and the Defeat of the CIO* (Philadelphia: Temple Univ. Press, 1988), 140, 152–56. Personal interview with Myles Horton, 1 June 1983, New Market, TN, and Highlander Research and Educational Center archives file on Highlander relations with the CIO.

31. For detail on the postwar period, see Honey, "Labor, the Left, and Civil Rights in the South: Memphis during the CIO Era, 1937–1955," in *Anti-Communism, the Politics of Manipulation*, ed. Judith Joel and Gerald M. Erickson (Minneapolis: MEP, 1987). On the Wallace campaign, see Curtis MacDougall, *Gideon's Army*, 3 vols. (New York: Marzani and Munsell, 1965), and Patricia Ann Sullivan, "Gideon's Southern Soldiers: New Deal Politics and Civil Rights Reform, 1933–1948" (Ph.D. diss., Emory University, 1983).

32. Robert Korstad, "Daybreak of Freedom: Tobacco Workers and the CIO, Winston-Salem, North Carolina, 1943–50" (Ph.D. diss., University of North Carolina, Chapel Hill, 1987); and Horace Huntley, "Iron Ore Miners and Mine Mill in Alabama: 1933–1952" (Ph.D. diss., University of Pittsburgh, 1977).

33. "To All Officers of Local 282, United Furniture Workers," from B. R. Allen, Memphis CIO Council President, 16 Sept. 1949, enclosing CIO Council

resolution, District 9 file, United Furniture Workers files, Southern Labor Archives; Memphis CIO staff meeting notes, 24 Sept. 1951, Tennessee Organizing Committee, Operation Dixie Papers.

34. McCrea interview. Distributing, Processing and Office Workers of America, Subject Files of the Internal Security Subcommittee of the Senate Judiciary Committee, Records of the U.S. Senate, RG 46, NARA.

35. News clippings file on the American Snuff strike in the papers of Mayor Watkins Overton, Mississippi Valley Collection, Memphis State University. George Dhuy comments on the halt in CIO local organizing in the CIO's *Labor Journal,* July and Aug. 1953.

36. CIO *Labor Journal,* 1950–55.

37. McCrea interview; personal interview, Karl Korstad, Greensboro, NC, 20 May 1981. Also see Levenstein, *Communism, Anti-Communism,* 276–78 and ch. 15 on the party's self-defeating tactics.

38. See Hosea Hudson on CIO racism in Birmingham, in Nell I. Painter, *The Narrative of Hosea Hudson, His Life as a Negro Communist in the South* (Cambridge, MA: Harvard Univ. Press, 1979), ch. 19, and Robert J. Norrell, "Caste in Steel: Jim Crow Careers in Birmingham, Alabama," *Journal of American History* 73:3 (December 1986): 669–94. Conditions for black workers in 1960's Memphis are detailed by F. Ray Marshall and Arvil Van Adams, "Negro Employment in Memphis," *Industrial Relations* 93:3 (May 1970): 308–23.

39. Personal interviews, George Holloway, Baltimore, 23 March 1990, and Clarence Coe, Memphis.

40. CIO *Labor Journal,* 1956; Marshall, *The Negro and Organized Labor,* 53–85.

41. Aldon D. Morris, *The Origins of the Civil Rights Movement: Black Communities Organizing for Change* (New York: Free Press, 1984), notes the role of Highlander and the Southern Conference. See also the *Southern Patriot* in the files of the Wisconsin Historical Society, Madison.

7. Interracial Unionism in the Southwest

Fort Worth's Packinghouse Workers, 1937–1954

Rick Halpern

The largest southern outpost of the meatpacking industry, Fort Worth, Texas, was an important prize for organized labor in the early twentieth century. Armour and Swift, the nation's two leading packers, operated major plants in Fort Worth, and the sprawling stockyards complex shipped thousands of head of livestock each month to packinghouses in Omaha, Kansas City, St. Louis, and Chicago. Yet organization of Fort Worth's 3,000 packinghouse workers proved an elusive goal. In 1904, and again in 1922, campaigns directed by the AFL's Amalgamated Meat Cutters (AMC) ended in dismal failure as the packing companies effectively manipulated antagonisms among the deeply divided work force. The major cleavage ran along racial lines, with most black workers remaining aloof from the "white man's union."[1]

Only in the mid-1930s, when the CIO's Packinghouse Workers Organizing Committee (PWOC) brought a unique brand of militant, egalitarian unionism to Fort Worth, did black, white, and Hispanic Workers take their first steps toward interracial accommodation as well as solidarity. The nature of the coalition they formed changed dramatically over the course of the next two decades. Originally, a cautious response on the part of veteran white workers and a handful of black activists to the initiatives of outside organizers, the alliance developed in the early 1940s into an institutionalized power-sharing arrangement held together by the material benefits it brought to the rank and file.

In the late 1940s and early 1950s, the implementation of an aggressive civil rights program shattered the racial equilibrium prevailing in Fort Worth and starkly revealed the boundaries and limitations of the interracial movement there. Subject to severe stress and strain, the coalition ruptured, with white workers withdrawing from active participation in the union. In the highly charged southern atmosphere of the 1950s, black and Hispanic workers eagerly embraced the civil rights program of the international union, using it as a lever with which to redress longstanding racial grievances, even while recognizing that such advances were purchased at the cost of diminished white support.

Initial Organization, 1937–1939

In October 1937, after several years of restive rank-and-file activity in the major northern meatpacking centers, the CIO established the Packinghouse Workers Organizing Committee. Bringing together independent, regionally based unions that had been operating since the early thirties, the PWOC gave national direction and coherence to a previously scattered and decentralized movement. Following the strategy employed by the CIO in auto and steel, the new organization immediately announced a drive on the largest and most powerful corporation in the industry—Armour & Company, the meatpacking giant that operated twenty-nine plants in twenty-two states. Having inherited a foothold in the company's flagship Chicago plant, and with sizable organization in place in Omaha and Kansas City, the PWOC soon turned its attention to Armour's outlying facilities.[2]

Because of its size and its position in a major stockyard, the Fort Worth Armour plant was a high priority for the PWOC. Yet it also posed special problems; unlike the northern packing centers, it did not experience independent organizing initiatives in the early thirties. In Fort Worth, the PWOC could not build upon a preexisting core of activists as it was doing elsewhere but had to begin from scratch. Moreover, the PWOC could not count on assistance from a weak and AFL-dominated local labor movement. Finally, southern racial mores formed a potential obstacle to the kind of inclusive organization that the meatpacking industry necessitated. With black workers accounting for close to one-third of the Armour work force and heavily concentrated on the strategic animal-killing floors, successful unionization depended upon a high degree of interracial cooperation. The presence of large numbers of Hispanic workers, probably around 10 percent of the labor force, further complicated the project.[3]

In December 1937 the PWOC dispatched Joseph Barrett to Fort Worth. A veteran Chicago packinghouse worker, Barrett was no newcomer to union organizing. A member of the AFL's Amalgamated Meat Cutters during the 1917–22 campaign, he represented his fellow Swift workers before the company's Joint Conference Board in the 1920s, and later helped establish an independent organization in the plant in the mid-1930s. Early in 1938 Kermit Fry, a union founder at Armour's Kansas City plant, joined Barrett in Fort Worth. At a time when a majority of white workers in the packing industry were of Polish or Slavic origin, the selection of these two men as southern organizers was a shrewd and calculating move. Native white Protestants, they were able to move relatively freely among southern workers. Essentially conservative men, they possessed trade-union experience that allowed them to speak to the concerns and fears of skilled whites and to make tentative inroads among older butchers who had participated in the 1917–22 organizing drive.[4]

The most encouraging response to this PWOC initiative, however, came not from packinghouse workers but from the 200 livestock handlers employed by the Fort Worth Stockyards Company. A proud, tightly knit group who enjoyed great autonomy over their work, the handlers had played active roles in earlier organizing efforts. They had kept the union tradition alive, sustaining a small Amalgamated local through the 1920s, and now proved receptive to the appeal of the CIO. Since the handlers controlled the flow of livestock into the plants surrounding the yards, they exercised considerable power and formed a potentially important ally for the packinghouse workers. Led by C. B. McCafferty, a socialist-leaning weighmaster with family ties to the labor movement, and L. Y. Cockrill, a former Texas Ranger, the livestock handlers joined the PWOC en masse. From the start, these initial recruits were a decisive influence on packinghouse unionism in Fort Worth.[5]

Barrett and Fry immediately enlisted the support of the livestock handlers for their drive on the Armour plant. They employed K. H. Burson and J. L. Holley on a part-time basis and formed teams of volunteer organizers who called upon packinghouse workers at their homes. By the late spring of 1938, over 300 Armour workers had enrolled in the PWOC, and a smaller number of Swift employees had become involved in the organization. Yet these gains were limited to a narrow segment of the work force. The livestock handlers recruited among their friends and relatives but made little effort to reach the hundreds of black workers whose support was critical to the union's success.[6]

Black packinghouse workers had good reasons for distrusting the livestock handlers who appeared to dominate the local PWOC. The handlers maintained an iron grip on hiring practices in the yards and had never permitted a black man to work there. Moreover, many blacks laboring in the packinghouses in the late thirties first entered the industry during the 1921–22 strike and harbored vivid memories of the racial violence accompanying that conflict. Some of the livestock handlers were known racists, and a few were suspected of membership in the Ku Klux Klan. If the CIO was going to bring Fort Worth's black work force into the union fold, it needed emissaries other than livestock handlers.[7]

PWOC leaders realized this. The reports from Fort Worth that trickled back to the union's Chicago headquarters caused a certain degree of concern—the national drive against Armour had reached full swing and national leaders feared that Fort Worth might be a weak link in the chain. Accordingly, the national office moved to boost the Texas organizing campaign. In the fall of 1938, Don Harris, the PWOC's national director, traveled to Fort Worth to lend assistance. The new regional director, James Porter, soon followed him. Both men hailed from Iowa and were relative newcomers to the meatpacking industry. They were experienced organizers, though, having worked with the unemployed and with the Communist Party's Trade Union Unity League affiliates before being tapped by John L. Lewis for duty with the CIO. In Fort Worth, they injected new life into the packinghouse drive, holding mass meetings that attracted many new recruits and carrying news of encouraging developments in Chicago and Kansas City. An especially important addition to the Fort Worth campaign was Henry Johnson, the PWOC's black assistant national director. The son of a Wobbly from West Texas, Johnson was a Communist who had been on the Steelworkers payroll before his transfer to packing. Before that, he had spent a number of years organizing for the International Workers Order and was a founding member of the National Negro Congress. He provided an important bridge to the black work force and his legendary oratorical abilities and polished manner reassured many suspicious whites.[8]

Although only Porter remained on the scene for any extended period, the national office's intervention pushed the organizing campaign in a new direction. It helped build an awareness of insurgency elsewhere in the Armour chain, making Fort Worth's workers feel less isolated and more a part of the national effort. It also presented the PWOC as an interethnic and interracial alliance, something considerably different from the impression left by Kermit Fry and the livestock handlers. Moreover, the involvement of the Left gave the movement additional resources and organizational talent. Working behind the scenes, Harris and Johnson secured the active support of the Texas Communist Party and the services of seasoned organizers from the Oil Workers International Union. Perhaps the most important consequence of the Left's involvement was that the Communists' commitment to interracialism helped overcome the mistrust with which black workers had heretofore regarded the union. At their insistence, union meetings and social events were conducted on a nonsegregated basis, and teams of black volunteer organizers joined whites leafleting at the plant gates and canvassing workers. Johnson and Harris, who periodically stopped in Fort Worth during their tours of the Armour circuit, spoke of the strong alliance between blacks and whites developing in the larger packing centers and reported on the elimination of discriminatory practices in many northern plants.[9]

While unsettling to many conservative white workers, these overtures produced results. By the midsummer of 1939, the PWOC registered its first real gains inside the Armour plant. Black-dominated departments provided the union with its most reliable base of support. Joe Harris, a 50-year-old hog butcher who had been one of the few blacks to side with the union in 1921–22, emerged as the most important rank-and-file leader. He organized all of the 200 workers on the hog kill, as well as those in several adjacent departments. On the loading dock, black beef luggers George Thomas and Frank Wallace enrolled their work gangs, with only a few whites holding out. Organization proceeded more slowly in other areas of the plant with certain departments, especially the lily-white sliced-bacon room and the mechanical gangs, resisting bitterly. Nevertheless, union membership grew steadily, prompting the PWOC to petition for a Labor Board election in the fall.[10]

Yet the scheduled election never took place. Several factors combined to derail the Fort Worth campaign. Foremost among these was a shift in national PWOC policy that sparked a damaging factional fight.

By July 1939, the union had secured bargaining rights for 17 of Armour's 29 plants. A conference of rank-and-file delegates held in Chicago that month voted overwhelmingly to press for a national contract and, if necessary, to strike the entire Armour chain in December. Harris and Johnson, as well as Communist officials in the Chicago district, were the most vocal supporters of this approach. CIO-appointed PWOC chairman Van Bittner, however, viewed the course with alarm. In addition to harboring legitimate concerns about the union's ability to orchestrate a national strike, he feared that such a conflict might undermine his authority and greatly enhance the position of the Left within the organization. Meeting with Secretary of Labor Frances Perkins at the height of the crisis, he agreed to withdraw the demand for a national contract and to bargain instead on a plant-by-plant basis. Armour's giant flagship facility in Chicago became the union's first priority. The ongoing organizing drives in other areas, including Fort Worth, lapsed as the PWOC devoted its full attention to Chicago.[11]

Nationally and locally, the response was predictable. Packinghouse activists reacted angrily upon learning of Bittner's subterfuge, charging him with selling out Armour workers. They immediately began organizing to replace the "dictator maniac" with an elected packinghouse worker accountable to the membership. Bittner reacted defensively and further aggravated the situation by purging the leading Communists from the organization, including Don Harris and James Porter.[12] In Ft. Worth, workers felt abandoned and betrayed by the national office. Sensing an opportunity, Armour mounted a counteroffensive. Capitalizing on the factional fight brewing in the PWOC, local management distributed propaganda depicting the CIO as a Communist organization and directed supervisory personnel to visit workers' homes to dissuade them from supporting the union. Membership fell off sharply, and the dismissal of Porter left a vacuum that local leadership was unable to fill. Demoralized and uncertain of how to proceed, Kermit Fry called off the NLRB election days before it was to take place.[13]

The progress made by the Fort Worth PWOC between 1937 and 1939 was due almost entirely to the efforts of the national organization. As long as the Fort Worth Armour plant fit into its overall strategy, the PWOC devoted considerable energy to the Texas campaign. Their efforts yielded encouraging, if modest results. Particularly promising in light of past failures were the favorable response of black workers to the union and the tentative steps taken toward interracial solidarity. Not only did black and white workers join the same organization, they shared local leadership and conducted union business without regard to Jim Crow. These practices stood in marked contrast to those of the Amalgamated Meat Cutters and other AFL unions. Yet a true alliance had not been forged. Although the livestock handlers enthusiastically embraced the union, the mass of white workers held back. With few exceptions, Hispanic laborers withheld their support as well. On their own, without the weight of the national PWOC, Fort Worth's black workers could not sustain the organization, much less extend it beyond a committed core of activists.

Institutionalization and Racial Accommodation, 1942–1948

For nearly two full years, the PWOC, torn apart by internal factionalism and primarily concerned with securing contracts in the northern meatpacking centers, devoted little attention to its Fort Worth locals. Livestock handlers, who had won recognition in 1939, periodically contemplated launching a new organizing drive on the packinghouses. The national office, however, offered no support, cold-shouldering appeals from local unionists for organizational assistance and funds. Only in 1942, after the National Defense Mediation Board compelled Armour to surrender to the PWOC and sign a blanket agreement, did the union again turn its attention to Fort Worth's packinghouses.[14]

The arrival of A. J. Pittman in Fort Worth signaled the PWOC's renewed commitment to workers there. A recent addition to the union's payroll, Pittman had helped organize the Armour plant in St. Joseph, Missouri, where he had worked since 1928. He seemed to possess a natural talent for leadership and soon set about reviving the defunct Armour local. His first step was simple but dramatic: positioning himself at the plant gate, he distributed copies of the recently signed Master Agreement to workers as they changed shifts. The wage rates of the contract stood at as much as 25 cents an hour more than those paid to southern packinghouse workers. In addition, the document contained a strongly worded non-discrimination clause certain to impress black workers.[15]

In managing the Fort Worth campaign, Pittman drew upon his experience in St. Joseph. He placed a premium upon direct membership participation, encouraging workers to organize on the job and take advantage of their knowledge of the production process to exert power. "It takes Organizers inside the plant to Organize the plant. . . . You cannot wait for the National Organizer to do all the work," he admonished his constituents. "You people here can have a union, but you will have to work to build it." Pittman also realized that the most effective way to break down the fear holding workers back from the union was through direct action. By early 1943 a functioning steward system was in place in the Armour plant, and rank-and-file leaders began planning and orchestrating job actions designed to win the support of hesitant workers. In certain departments, repeated use of these actions resulted in de facto recognition of the union and the adjustment of grievances.[16]

The killing floors again emerged as centers of union strength. Stoppages here proved a particularly powerful weapon owing to the structure of the labor process and the perishable nature of the product. The constantly moving "disassembly" lines in these departments allowed small groups of workers to bring production to a halt. After 20 minutes, watchful government inspectors condemned carcasses left hanging on the "dead rail," costing the company hundreds or even thousands of dollars. Prolonged stoppages on the kill floors soon idled adjacent departments by depriving them of meat. Furthermore, management could not readily discharge these workers since many butchering operations—skinning cattle and splitting hogs, for example—required great dexterity, high levels of skill, and years of experience. Similarly, the loading dock occupied a strategic position in the production process. As Frank Wallace explained, "Regardless of what happened in the other departments, the product had to be shipped out of the loading dock. If it got blocked there, well, there was no use killing or processing the meat."[17]

The union's growth at Armour progressed at an encouraging rate. Although some departments continued to resist the PWOC's overtures, by February 1943 more than half of the plant's employees had signed cards. Shop-floor organization had pushed black and white workers to cooperate in unprecedented ways, and sections of the previously aloof Hispanic work force had come over as well. When James Dean, the new district director, visited Fort Worth he found "circumstances far more favorable than indicated by earlier reports." Even though local management continued to harass union activists and attempted to set white workers against the PWOC "by saying it is a nigro [sic] organization," Dean reported that "our people pay little mind to such tactics and can be counted on to stand fast." With an NLRB election scheduled for March, he confidently predicted victory by a ten-to-one margin.[18]

The situation across the yards at the Swift plant, however, was quite different. Long considered the most paternalistic of the large packers, Swift retained the loyalty of many employees. "They pat you on the back and make out you're just one of the family," remarked Mary Hammond, a veteran bacon slicer. "I used to think that Swifts was the cream." In the 1920s the company had developed an ambitious program of welfare capitalism. Aimed primarily at skilled workers in each of the company's eighteen plants, the program included medical care, recreational activities, vacations, and a limited pension plan. Its centerpiece was a system of employee representation in which departmental delegates met regularly with an equal number of appointed management representatives in a "joint conference" or "assembly." Although by the end of the decade Swift abandoned most of these programs, it resurrected its company unions in the mid-1930s in an effort to counter independent workers' organization. After the Wagner Act outlawed such strategies, the company helped establish the National Brotherhood of Packinghouse Workers (NBPW), an organization that cropped up in the Swift chain wherever the CIO seemed on the verge of winning bargaining rights.[19]

In Fort Worth, the National Brotherhood first appeared in October 1942, just as the CIO campaign gathered steam. Given permission to roam the plant and openly solicit workers, company unionists appealed to their sense of loyalty to Swift and to their intense localism. The depicted the Brotherhood as a "home organization" that had won many benefits for Swift workers in the past, and they portrayed the PWOC as outsiders: "Northern Dictators . . . here to collect as many dollars from us southerners as possible and take these dollars back north." A PWOC spy, who attended meetings between Brotherhood leaders and the plant superintendent, reported that the group discussed race-baiting—even going so far as contemplating the staging of violent incidents in the plant. Whether as a result of these tactics or not, in the spring of 1943 the PWOC's Swift drive clearly was faltering. The card count lagged well behind that in the Armour plant, and Swift's well-timed decision to distribute back pay for overtime work in excess of eight hours further sapped PWOC support. Especially damaging was a growing rift between white and black workers. Widened by the company's manipulation of preexisting tensions and exacerbated by offensive remarks made at a mass rally, this rift ultimately led to the PWOC's defeat. In March, when Swift workers turned out to vote, disaffected blacks stayed away from the polls, allowing a narrow company union victory.[20]

In a separate election at the Armour plant, however, the results demonstrated overwhelming support for the CIO. Without competition from a company union, and building upon four years of interracial organizing activity, the PWOC sailed to an easy victory.[21] The union contract that now covered the plant's two thousand workers allowed blacks to register significant advances. Shop-floor rights embodied in the union contract, while resembling those of thousands of other agreements, had radical implications within the context of traditional southern race relations. Carefully enforced seniority eliminated the practice of discriminatory layoffs and enabled black and Hispanic workers to rise into many skilled jobs previously reserved for whites. Similarly, by directing the company to "pay the job not the man," the agreement abolished at a single stroke the 8-cent wage differential between white and black workers. And the grievance system provided minorities with a collective means of addressing discriminatory practices. The industrial "citizenship" and implied egalitarianism of the union contract generated a rights consciousness that encouraged black workers to utilize these new institutional mechanisms.[22]

The PWOC relied upon its power at the point of production to enforce the contract. Despite the labor movement's national wartime no-strike pledge, workers repeatedly engaged in stoppages to force Armour to respect the agreement. If the company lagged in processing grievances, refused to adjust the speed of the line, or violated seniority rights, job actions pressured management to resolve the problem. In August 1944, for instance, when a foreman on the sheep kill discharged a steward for leaving his place on the line to investigate a dispute, all 650 workers in the department walked out of the plant. Similarly, the following month a reduction in the agreed-upon piece rate in the beef-boning department sparked a two-day work stoppage. In contrast to the spontaneous nature of many of the wartime wildcats that swept other industries, local officials sanctioned these actions and stewards in the plant planned and executed them. They tended to promote interracial solidarity, not just through the active involvement of the membership but because white workers throughout the plant depended upon the predominantly black killing floors for crucial support. "They really had the push," one white worker recalled; "we had a strong union because of the black people."[23]

White workers tended to back attacks on discrimination as long as they were articulated through the union in terms of seniority and job rights. Thus in the summer of 1945 when Armour unfairly discharged seven black butchers, the entire plant walked out to force their reinstatement. "What management does to Negroes today it will do to white workers tomorrow," the union paper announced. Yet there existed clear limits to this kind of interracialism. While blacks continued to move with little resistance into skilled jobs in already integrated departments, other areas of the plant remained white preserves. When two black women transferred into the sliced-bacon department, for example, angry whites engaged in a sit-down strike, demanding their removal. Management complied and union leadership, fearing a white backlash, acquiesced. The canning department and the maintenance and mechanical gangs remained all white as well; and the stockyards continued to turn away minority applicants.[24]

Similarly, there were boundaries to the social integration practiced by the union. Committees contained representatives from all groups; and meetings were conducted on a nonsegregated basis. The union even held mixed dances and picnics, in brazen violation of local custom, without incident. Yet at the same time, the union declined to challenge the company's practice of maintaining separate dressing rooms for black and white workers, Jim Crow water fountains, and a partitioned plant cafeteria. When pressured by the international (the PWOC became an autonomous union, the United Packinghouse Workers of America, in 1943), white district officials demurred, claiming that southern workers would not tolerate union attacks upon established racial etiquette.[25]

Many black workers blamed district director Pittman for the union's limited approach to the problem of discrimination. Pointing to Pittman's maintenance of an all-white staff, his opposition to the formation of a civil rights committee, and his refusal to support the membership's selection of a black chief steward, they questioned Pittman's commitment to racial equality. "I wouldn't call him a racist, but I would say he'd lean toward the racists' ideas," concluded Eddie Humphrey. International officials also tended to fault Pittman for the district's lackadaisical response to the union's anti-discrimination program. UPWA president Ralph Helstein believed that "his claim that we had to go slow in order to prevent all hell from breaking loose was just a rationalization, a cover for his belief that segregation was the proper order of things." And Steve Mauser, one of the union's southern field representatives, noted that Pittman "never raised his hand" against segregation in the Armour plant and "was supporting this kind of stuff because he never came out into the open to contest the thing."[26]

Yet, on the other hand, Pittman had proven his ability to accept blacks on an equal footing both in St. Joseph and during the organizing drive in Fort Worth. Moreover, he served on the Texas CIO Council's Human Rights Committee and had been an outspoken critic of the discriminatory practices of other CIO affiliates in the state. His gradualism on civil rights issues was born out of a bureaucratic pragmatism, rather than a commitment to white supremacy. Dependent upon white votes to remain in office, Pittman had no desire to jeopardize that support by offending southern sensibilities. "Pitt was no racist, he just didn't want to rock the boat," an ally stated. "Pittman was in a bad position here. I don't knock him about his cautiousness," another white unionist averred. "This was Texas and you just didn't jack with it. You tried to do small things," he added.[27]

The relationship between Fort Worth's black and white packinghouse workers in this period was an accommodation rather than an alliance. Each group needed the other. A minority of the labor force, blacks required that white workers support the union in at least a tacit manner, while whites needed the power supplied by the predominantly black killing floors. The interests of blacks and whites thus converged around the material benefits that union membership afforded. As long as union goals and civil rights aims ran parallel, a delicate equilibrium prevailed. Attempts to push beyond the fairly narrow language of the contrast met with resistance. Because blacks in Fort Worth did not push too hard during the 1940s, the racial accommodation did not collapse.

The Weight of the International Union, 1948–1952

1948 was a watershed year for the United Packinghouse Workers. In March the union engaged in a national strike against the four largest packing companies—Armour, Swift, Wilson, and Cudahy. Impeded by the recently passed Taft-Hartley Act, and weakened in critical spots by court injunctions and the determined opposition of local governments, the walkout ended in failure after thirteen grueling weeks. In the months following the defeat, with close to 600 local leaders discharged and unable to pay salaries or settle grievances, the UPWA all but ceased functioning as a union. In a remarkable recovery, however, the Packinghouse Workers repaired its shattered organization, regaining within a year much of its former vigor and effectiveness. It did so, at least in part, by rebuilding the union around its black membership. This policy profoundly altered the balance of power in Fort Worth. Again, the actions of the national office determined the course of events in Texas.[28]

In rebuilding, union leaders stressed the importance of racial concerns. The UPWA stepped up its civil rights activities in this period as the union bureaucracy itself moved to demonstrate positive activity to the demoralized rank and file. By late June 1948, just weeks after the strike defeat, the International Executive Board arranged for Fisk University's Race Relations Institute to conduct a series of "self-surveys" of racial attitudes and practices among packinghouse workers. Designed to involve the union's members, and prevent the fragmentation of hard-earned racial unity, the surveys also helped keep workers' interest alive. Queried about the rationale behind this program, President Helstein explained, "I felt there had to be something affirmative going on outside of an area in which the companies could screw us . . . [We] started that program and our people suddenly had something that the union was able to do."[29]

Using renewed civil rights activity as a stepping-stone to strengthen and sustain the union, the UPWA retained the active support of its membership. By September 1949, it had fought off decertification attempts in twenty-four plants, negotiated the rehiring of almost all of the discharged leaders, and secured improved contracts with three of the four packers.[30] More importantly, the self-surveys served as a springboard for the development of a formal civil rights program within the union. Starting in 1949, the UPWA began systematically integrating anti-discrimination activities into its organizational and educational departments. The following year, it directed local unions to establish "AD" committees to oversee the elimination of discriminatory practices in the plants. In this manner, what previously had been a general policy now became a specific program operating at various levels of the union apparatus.[31]

However, the Packinghouse Workers' intensified anti-discrimination effort was not solely the product of bureaucratic initiative. In larger measure, the course of action taken by the international leaders was prompted by the union's Chicago membership. Encouraged by left-wing local leadership, workers in the Chicago plants had always led the union in activism around racial issues. In the postwar period, they pioneered new methods of using the union contract to fight discrimination and involved their locals in a number of community-based and city-wide civil rights struggles.[32] The rapidly expanding black membership base in Chicago also provided the mass constituency for a new bloc of younger black leaders who rose to positions of prominence within the District and the international. They used these positions to agitate for a greater commitment of resources to the struggle for equality, and worked to strengthen the anti-discrimination provisions of the union's contractual agreements with the packing companies.

The insurgency in Chicago affected packinghouse locals in other regions. Soon after the 1948 strike, Fort Worth began to feel the weight of the north. Concerned by incidents of racial violence that had occurred there during the strike, the international commissioned an in-depth survey of racial attitudes in Fort Worth.[33] The completed report provided an unmistakably clear picture of black-white relations. On the positive side, the survey demonstrated that workers of all races strongly supported the union. Nearly 60 percent of the whites in the plant were willing to work with blacks in the same job classification; and an even larger proportion were willing to participate in union programs involving anti-discrimination issues. On the negative side, however, the study found clear evidence of prejudicial attitudes among the white membership. For instance, more than 80 percent of those whites surveyed stated they preferred not to work under a black supervisor, while a clear majority displayed a disturbing lack of appreciation for the broader social problems experienced by blacks.[34]

Encouraged by the international, black workers in Fort Worth be-

came more assertive in their efforts to utilize the contract and grievance machinery to combat discrimination. Frank Wallace recalled how
involvement of the UPWA's field staff helped: "We began to get a
sense of know how . . . then we proceeded to ask for those jobs that in
the past had been off limits to us." These activities clashed with the
sensibilities of many white workers and led to a polarization of the
local. Keenly aware of the backing of the international, and bolstered
by their contacts with Chicago activists, blacks stood their ground.
"That's about the time that we began to recognize the fact that we had
a little bit more muscle, a little bit more people power," Wallace
remembered.[35]

A critical element in this new aggressive stance was the presence in
the plant of a number of young, militant blacks who had entered the
industry well after the initial organization of the union. Many of these
workers were military veterans whose wartime experience had altered
their views about the place of blacks in southern society. Eddie
Humphrey emotionally explained, "We died, our blood had been shed
for this country, and I felt . . . that we should get a better deal out of it.
Instead of crumbs we wanted us a slice of the pie." Less willing than
the older generation to accept segregation and the incremental gains
made by black workers, these militants eagerly took advantage of the
new mechanisms put at their disposal by the UPWA.[36]

In 1952 black activists in Fort Worth received a major boost. The
new contract negotiated between the UPWA and Armour that year
contained a provision mandating the desegregation of all plant facilities. The demand originated in Chicago, at an anti-discrimination conference, and later received formal endorsement at the union's convention. Delegates from the giant Chicago Armour local introduced the
resolution, lobbied for its passage, and engineered its inclusion in
negotiations. Representatives from the major Armour locals supported
the demand. Many of these leaders were southern-born blacks who
had experienced firsthand the injustices of Jim Crow. They had closely
monitored the progress of the union's "AD" program in the South and
believed that the contractual provision would speed its progress.[37]

By narrowing the space for racial prejudice *within* the union, the
new agreement changed the nature of the UPWA's civil rights program
in a fundamental way. Local passivity could no longer block desegregation and implementation could proceed in the face of southern white
opposition. Moreover, the new master contract highlighted the fact

that in the southern context, black workers could find an important ally in the national union bureaucracy. Yet at the same time it empowered this section of the workforce, the 1952 agreement upset the delicate racial equilibrium within the Fort Worth local.

Only a few weeks after the contract took effect, conflict erupted. On the morning of November 11, 1952, management removed signs designating "White Only" and "Colored" facilities. A plasterboard wall partitioning the plant cafeteria was slated for removal ten days later. On the afternoon of the 11th, a crowd of 200 white workers gathered in the union hall demanding a meeting with the officers of the local union. When Dave Nelson, the local president, and W. L. McMahon, a field representative, met with the crowd, they encountered emphatic demands that the signs be replaced and the partition remain in place. When the two men attempted to reason with their members, explaining the importance of the union's anti-discrimination policy and pointing out that delegates from the local had ratified the contract demand, the crowd hooted them down and then stalked out of the building.[38]

The following day, a group designating itself the "Local Rights Committee" leafleted the plant, calling a special meeting for that evening to address the desegregation problem. Despite the appeals of international officers, who had flown down to defuse the potentially explosive situation, the meeting went badly. "There were knives and guns all over the place. There was screaming and hollering. It was impossible to keep order," Helstein recalled. Led by C. H. "Moon" Mullins, an ex-president of the local and a fundamentalist minister, the assembled members blamed Communists in the Chicago office for the union's AD program, demanded the resignation of their local officers, and passed a resolution instructing the bargaining committee of the local union to contact plant management and direct them to replace the signs.[39]

Two days later the signs reappeared. Seething, black workers threatened a walkout. The crisis intensified as rumors spread to other southern plants and a regional "local rights" movement began to form. The international responded with a two-pronged strategy. At the national level, it pressured Armour to abide by the contract, threatening to strike other plants in the chain if the company reneged on its agreement. At the local level, the international cultivated an alternative leadership, throwing its considerable weight behind black veteran unionists. Both steps worked. The first measure resolved the immediate problem of contractual compliance. After initially balking, Armour directed its plant superintendent to proceed with the desegregation plans. Carried out over a two-year period, the second measure ultimately neutralized the racist opposition in Fort Worth, but not before a regional revolt rocked the union and culminated in the disaffiliation of a number of locals.[40]

Revolt and Resolution, 1952–1954

The international union brought its full weight to bear in Fort Worth. It appointed union founder George Thomas as a field representative and transferred a progressive white, Steve Mauser, to Fort Worth. Despite stiff opposition from district director Pittman, who tacitly supported the rebels, the two men molded the black and Hispanic work force into a political force capable of seizing power from the dissident whites. They did this by pressing forward the union's civil rights program, persuading previously indifferent black workers to attend meetings and voice their opinions, and building support for their program through black community institutions. These efforts bore fruit in early 1953 when Armour workers defeated an all-white slate headed by Moon Mullins, which had campaigned around an openly white-supremacist platform.[41]

Although the election marked the end of organized white opposition within the Fort Worth Armour local, it coincided with the start of a more serious regional resistance to the union's civil rights program. Allying with whites in other southern packinghouses, Fort Worth's dissidents turned to the CIO for support. Cloaking their racist motivations in political rhetoric, they complained about Communist domination of the UPWA. Pointing to well-known leftists on the union staff, the union's long-standing relationship with the integrationist Highlander Folk School, and its recent publication and distribution of a booklet critical of U.S. foreign policy, they demanded that the labor federation either "clean out the Reds" in the international or establish a rival union. These pleas fell upon receptive ears. Regional CIO officials in Texas and Georgia pressured new CIO president Walter Reuther to investigate the packinghouse situation. In April 1953 he accommodated them, appointing a committee to assess the validity of these charges. In doing so, he unwittingly played into the hands of the southern racists.[42] The CIO investigation itself lent legitimacy to the dissidents' accusations. Moreover, leading anti-communists within the CIO—most notably Vice-President John Riffe and Secretary-Treasurer James Carey—encouraged packinghouse locals to withhold their per-capita dues payments from the international and, in some cases, promised rebellious local unions new charters.[43]

Helstein and other UPWA officers vainly protested this intervention into their internal affairs. Only in November 1953, when the CIO committee cleared the union, did Reuther move to curb his overzealous colleagues. By that time, the anti-communist hysteria whipped up by the investigation had wrought considerable damage. Many packing locals were deeply divided; and in numerous areas UPWA unions found themselves isolated from the rest of the labor movement. Several locals, including the Fort Worth livestock handlers, disaffiliated themselves from the international. In a number of instances, AFL organizations attempted to raid UPWA locals, directing demagogic appeals to white workers.[44]

While the Fort Worth Armour local remained within the UPWA, many white workers withdrew from active participation in the union. As a result, blacks and Hispanics increasingly filled the local's leadership positions. In 1954 Armour workers elected Mary Salinas, a Hispanic woman, president of the local. The same year, George Thomas replaced the discredited A. J. Pittman as district director. The new balance of power facilitated additional anti-discrimination activity. Within the plant self-segregation was broken down and remaining all-white departments integrated with minimal resistance. In July 1954 a black woman transferred into the sliced-bacon department, once a racist stronghold. When white women protested, the local's new leadership stood firm, pointed to the union contract, and firmly explained that the newcomer had been "laid off out of her department, [and] there are younger women in the plant that she has a right to bump. We don' care whether she's black, brown, blue, polka dot or what. She has that right because her seniority entitles her to this."[45]

The union also succeeded in pushing its civil rights activities beyond the confines of the plant and into the larger community. It forged ties with local branches of the NAACP and Urban League, forced the integration of Fort Worth's Hilton Hotel, fought to desegregate Tarrant County public schools, and joined with other groups in 1955 to protest the brutal lynching in Mississippi of Emmett Till. These activities never involved more than a small portion of the local's membership, and they pale in comparison to the initiatives of packinghouse workers in Chicago and the other northern centers of the meat industry. Nevertheless, they represented an important advance over the practices of the past—an advance made possible by the relationship between Fort Worth and the international union.[46]

Indeed, for a twenty-year period "Chicago" exercised a major influence upon Fort Worth's packinghouse workers. From the onset of organizing activity in the late 1930s, through the arrival at a racial accommodation in the 1940s, and up through the tumultuous period following the desegregation provisions, the weight of the international union was the determining factor in establishing the rights and relationships of white and black workers.

For most of this period, blacks and whites cooperated with one another to achieve certain material benefits. Shared workplace grievances and common concerns tempered traditional racial antagonisms. White workers did not oppose black challenges to economic discrimination as long as they were articulated in traditional trade-union terms. But when black workers questioned racist social customs, the resulting strain ruptured the fragile alliance. Even then, despite the withdrawal of white workers from local union activity, the UPWA maintained a strong, viable bargaining unit in Fort Worth based upon the support of black and Hispanic workers. It thereby demonstrated the possibility of aggressively moving forward with the implementation of a civil rights program under the kinds of unfavorable circumstances that destroyed many CIO unions in the South and caused others to backtrack from their stated commitment to equality.

Notes

1. For discussion of the Amalgamated's 1904 and 1917–22 packinghouse drives, see David Brody, *The Butcher Workmen: A Study of Unionization* (Cambridge, MA: Harvard Univ. Press, 1964), 34–58, 75–105.
2. Walter Galenson, *The CIO Challenge to the AFL: A History of the American Labor Movement, 1935–1941* (Cambridge, MA: Harvard Univ. Press, 1960), 363; Brody, *Butcher Workmen*, 199–206; J. Doherty to Van Bittner, "Memorandum of PWOC Meeting," 10 Nov. 1937, CIO Secretary Treasurer Papers, Box 66, Folder 5, Archives of Labor and Urban Affairs, Wayne State University, Detroit, MI (hereafter cited as CIO-ST).

3. The racial composition of the work force is derived from "Human Relations in Fort Worth Texas," Papers of the United Packinghouse Workers of America, Box 344, Folder 6, State Historical Society of Wisconsin, Madison, (hereafter cited as UPWA Papers); John Hope, "Progress Report," 26 May 1949, UPWA Papers, Box 52, Folder 10.

4. Arthur Kampfert, "History of Meatpacking, Slaughtering and Unionism," unpublished manuscript [c.1949], State Historical Society of Wisconsin, Madison; testimony of Frank McCarty, "Meeting of Delegates Packinghouse Workers Organizing Committee with Alan S. Haywood and James B. Carey, Special Representatives from National CIO Headquarters," Transcripts, vol. 5, p. 78, 16 April 1941, CIO-ST, Box 65, Folder 14; testimony of Kermit Fry, "Meeting of Delegates Packinghouse Workers Organizing Committee," Transcripts vol. 6, pp. 9–11, 16 April 1941, CIO-ST, Box 66, Folder 1; interview with Charlie McCafferty, 20 March 1986, United Packinghouse Workers of America Oral History Project, State Historical Society of Wisconsin, Madison [hereafter cited as UPWAOHP].

5. Interview with Charlie McCafferty; interviews with Kenneth Neidholt, 20 March 1986 and 17 May 1986, UPWAOHP. Some evidence suggests that the Amalgamated local in Fort Worth included butchers from the Swift plant there; see J. Nesbit to Paul Kreuger, 23 Aug. 1934, National Recovery Administration, Consolidated Unapproved Industry Code Files, Box 6380, RG 9, National Archives and Records Administration, Washington, DC.

6. Testimony of K. H. Burson and Wilson Admire, "Meeting of Delegates Packinghouse Workers Organizing Committee," Transcripts vol. 6, pp. 14–15, 32–33, 16 April 1941, CIO-ST, Box 66, Folder 1; interview with Frank Wallace, 17 March 1986, UPWAOHP.

7. Interview with Ralph Helstein, 14 Nov. 1983, in possession of the author; interview with Charlie McCafferty; interview with Eddie Humphrey, 18 March 1986, UPWAOHP. The violence that accompanied the 1921–22 strike in Fort Worth culminated with the lynching of a black strikebreaker who had defended himself against a white mob; "Packers and Union Claim Strike Gains," *New York Times*, 7 Dec. 1921; "Lynch Negro Who Shot Fort Worth Pickets," *New York Times*, 12 Dec. 1921.

8. *CIO News* (Packinghouse Workers Edition), 1 Oct. 1938; interviews with Don Harris, 8 June 1978 and 20 Aug. 1982, Iowa Federation of Labor Oral History Project, Iowa State Historical Society, Iowa City. For Porter's Communist connections, see the Iowa affadavits in the Ralph Helstein Papers, Box 4, State Historical Society of Wisconsin, Madison [hereafter cited as RHP]; and testimony of James Dean, "Meeting of Delgates," Transcripts, vol. 5, 16 April 1941, CIO-ST, Box 65, Folder 14. A WPA interview with Johnson is reproduced in Stephen Brier, "Labor, Politics, and Race: A Black Worker's Life," *Labor History* 23 (Summer 1982): 416–21; interview with Herbert March and Jane March, 25 Nov. 1988, in possession of the author.

9. Kampfert, "History"; interview with Charlie McCafferty; Moses Adedeji,

"Crossing the Colorline: Three Decades of the United Packinghouse Workers of America's Crusade against Racism in the Trans-Mississippi West, 1936–1968" (Ph.D. diss., North Texas State University, 1978), 40; *CIO News* (Packinghouse Workers Edition), 16 Jan. 1939, 27 Jan. 1939, 20 March 1939, 1 May 1939, 21 Aug. 1939.

10. Interview with Frank Wallace; Adedeji, "Crossing the Colorline," 25, 70; *CIO News* (Packinghouse Workers Edition), 20 March 1939, 17 April 1939.

11. *CIO News* (Packinghouse Edition) 24 July 1939, 21 Aug. 1939; interviews with Don Harris. Federal Mediation and Conciliation Service to the Secretary of Labor, 19 July 1939; Frances Perkins to H. S. Eldred, 18 Aug. 1939, both in General Records of the Department of Labor, Records of Secretary Frances Perkins, Box 35, RG 174, National Archives and Record Administration. See also Brody, *Butcher Workmen*, 183, and Galenson, *CIO Challenge*, 365, 374.

12. Quotation in Glenn Weidenheimer to J. Cunningham, 5 Dec. 1939, UPWA Papers, Box 5, Folder 1; minutes of Special Mass Meeting, Local 42, 6 June 1941, UPWA Papers, Box 5, Folder 7; *CIO News* (Packinghouse Workers Edition), 25 Dec. 1939; Adedeji, "Crossing the Colorline," 20. For detailed description of the Armour campaign and the resistance to Bittner's autocratic style, see Eric Brian Halpern, "'Black and White Unite and Fight': Race and Labor in Meatpacking, 1904–1948" (Ph.D. diss., University of Pennsylvania, 1989), ch. 6.

13. *CIO News* (Packinghouse Workers Edition), 2 Oct. 1939; testimony of Wilson Admire, "Meeting of Delegates," Transcripts, vol. 6, pp. 14–15, 16 April 1941, CIO-ST, Box 66, Folder 1; testimony of J. L. Holley and Wilson Admire, "Meeting of Delegates," Transcripts, vol. 2, p. 13, CIO-ST, Box 65, Folder 2.

14. K. H. Burson to J. C. Lewis, 16 Aug. 1941; J. C. Lewis to K. H. Burson 20 Aug. 1941; C. B. McCafferty to J. C. Lewis, 2 Jan. 1942; K. H. Burson to J. C. Lewis, 29 Sept. 1941 and 10 Jan. 1942, all in UPWA Papers, Box 7, Folder 6. For discussion of the protracted negotiations with Armour and the settlement imposed by the NDMB, see Brody, *Butcher Workmen*, 199–205, and Galenson, *CIO Challenge*, 366–67. See also *Packinghouse Worker*, 15 Sept. 1941.

15. J. C. Lewis to K. H. Burson, 6 March 1942, UPWA Papers, Box 7, Folder 6; A. J. Pittman to Lewis J. Clark, 19 Oct. 1943, United Packinghouse Workers of America Collection, 51–1–15, University of Texas at Arlington Archives, Arlington, TX [hereafter cited as UTA]; interview with A. J. Pittman, 23 Aug. 1986, UPWAOHP.

16. Interview with A. J. Pittman; Adedeji, "Crossing the Colorline," 22; quotation from Brody, *Butcher Workmen,* 177; interview with Frank Wallace; interview with Mary Salinas, 18 March 1986, UPWAOHP.

17. Killing-floor dynamics are discussed in several UPWAOHP interviews: Philip Weightman, 7–8 Oct. 1986; Jesse Vaughn, 23 Oct. 1986; Lloyd Achenbach, 19 April 1986. Interview with Frank Wallace.

18. Floyd Brouillard to Sam Sponseller, 16 Jan. 1943, UPWA Papers, Box 2, Folder 3; James P. Dean to Sam Sponseller, 1 Feb. 1943, UPWA Papers, Box 7, Folder 5; interview with Mary Salinas.
19. Hammond quoted in *First-Person America*, ed. Ann Banks (New York: Vintage, 1980), 55; for extended discussion of Swift's paternalism see the UPWAOHP interview with Philip Weightman. Swift's welfare capitalism is discussed in John Calder, *Capital's Duty to the Wage Earner: A Manual of Principles and Practice on Handling the Human Factors in Industry* (New York: Longmans, Green, 1923), esp. 165–72. For the NBPW see Theodore V. Purcell, *Blue Collar Man: Patterns of Dual Allegiance in Industry* (Cambridge, MA: Harvard Univ. Press, 1960), 19–22, 27–28.
20. James Dean to Sam Sponseller, 1 Oct. 1942, UPWA Papers, Box 66, Folder 8; "Northern Dictators" leaflet in UPWA Papers, Box 2, Folder 3; Pittman to Frank Ellis, 7 June 1944, UTA, 51–12–1. On racial tensions at Swift see Floyd Brouillard to Sam Sponseller, 20 March 1943, UPWA Papers, Box 2, Folder 3; and Adedeji "Crossing the Colorline," 23. "Certification of Counting and Tabulating of Ballots," NLRB Case No. XVI–R–597, 17 March 1943, UTA, 51–2–5.
21. "Certification of Counting and Tabulating of Ballots," NLRB Case No. XVI–R–279, 10 March 1943, UTA, 51–1–18; *Packinghouse Worker*, 12 March 1943.
22. For a compelling statement of the implications for racial justice contained in militant industrial unionism in another industry, see Robert Korstad and Nelson Lichtenstein, "Opportunities Found and Lost: Labor, Radicals, and the Early Civil Rights Movement," *Journal of American History 75*:3 (Dec. 1988): 787, 790. For the wage differential, see "Earnings and Hours in the Meat-Packing Industry," *Monthly Labor Review* 49 (Oct. 1939): 953. The racial differential for skilled labor was as high as 14 cents an hour.
23. Armour and Co., Fort Worth, TX, "Slow-downs, Work Stoppages, and Strikes since August 11, 1944," UPWA Papers, Box 196, Folder 1. Stoppages became so endemic throughout the Armour chain that the company requested that the War Labor Board revoke union security measures in its plants under contract with the Packinghouse Workers. For this situation as it pertained to Fort Worth, see Ralph Helstein to Dorothy Bobo, 23 Nov. 1943; and A. J. Pittman to Ralph Helstein, 8 Dec. 1943, both in UPWA Papers, Box 1, Folder 6; interview with Frank Wallace; interview with Mary Salinas.
    A steward in the beef-cutting department, Salinas explained that the no-strike pledge "wasn't just a one-way street . . . if they [were] able to violate their commitment, what would be wrong with us violating ours, too. And we did have quite a bit of stoppages, and in fact I would encourage them. I encouraged them because of the number of hours they were working the people with the number of employees. Some of the employees had to be doubling up into three jobs, and that was unreasonable . . . they wasn't going to work those people day and night and we wasn't going to do nothing about it."

24. *Packinghouse Worker*, 20 July 1945; "Race Relations in the UPWA," n.d. [1947?], UPWA Papers, Box 345, Folder 23; Adedeji, "Crossing the Color-line," 41, 43, 68; interview with Eddie Humphrey, 18 March 1986, UPWAOHP.

25. Adedeji, "Crossing the Colorline," 40–43; interviews with Wallace, Humphrey, and Pittman; interview with Ralph Helstein, 14 Nov. 1983, in possession of the author.

26. Interview with Eddie Humphrey; interview with Ralph Helstein; interview with Steve Mauser, 15 May 1973, UTA.

27. Murray E. Polakoff, "The Development of the Texas State CIO Council" (Ph.D. diss., Columbia University, 1957), 235, 376; A. J. Pittman to Tim Flynn, 13 March 1944, CIO-ST, Box 67, Folder 4; "Notes from file," n.d. [1952?], UPWA Papers, Box 348, Folder 2; interview with Charlie McCafferty.

28. For discussion of the 1948 strike see Roger Horowitz. "'It Is Harder To Struggle Than To Surrender': The Rank and File Unionism of the United Packinghouse Workers of America, 1933–1948," *Studies in History and Politics* 5 (1986): 83–96. For the paralysis of the union in the strike's aftermath, see Frank Ellis to all officers, 25 May 1948, UPWA Papers, Box 50, Folder 3, and "Report of Grievance Department," 16 March 1949, UPWA Papers, Box 58, Folder 8; interview with Jesse Prosten, 18 Dec., 1985, UPWAOHP.

29. Ralph Helstein to John Hope, 21 June 1948; John Hope to Ralph Helstein, 25 June 1948, both in UPWA Papers, Box 45, Folder 9; Hope to Helstein, Lasley, Long, n.d., UPWA Papers, Box 52, Folder 10; interview with Ralph Helstein, 13 July 1983, in possession of the author.

30. Report of Grievance Department, 16 March 1949, UPWA Papers, Box 58, Folder 8; "Jesse Prosten Personal File," UFCW Donation, M80–118, Box 35, State Historical Society of Wisconsin, Madison; interview with Jesse Prosten; interview with Ralph Helstein.

31. John Hope to Lasley, 19 Dec. 1949, UPWA Papers, Box 52, Folder 10; Program Proposal for AD Department, 26 June 1950, UPWA Papers, Box 342, Folder 15. The structural changes made in the union apparatus are summarized in John Hope II, *Equality of Opportunity: A Union Approach to Fair Employment* (Washington, DC: Public Affairs Press, 1956), 110–17.

32. Two examples will suffice: Swift Local 28 successfully attacked inequitable hiring policies, and Armour Local 347 forced the company to employ blacks in its front office staff. See Halpern, "Black and White Unite and Fight," ch. 8, for more detailed discussion. For Swift see Kelly to Lasley and Hayes, 22 June 1950, UPWA Papers, Box 343, Folder 7; *Swift Flash*, 5 July 1950, UPWA Papers, Box 324, Folder 7. For Armour, see Report on District 1 AD Conference, 17 Feb. 1952, UPWA Papers, Box 384, Folder 14; Local 347 Press Release, 11 Dec. 1952, UPWA Papers, Box 98, Folder 3. The Chicago UPWA also played a major role in the Chicago Committee to End Mob

Violence (CEMV), a broad-based community alliance that pressured city officials into extending police protection to besieged black residents who had integrated federally funded housing projects. See Harold Nielsen to all Chicago locals, 22 Nov. 1949; Lasley to Nielsen, 29 Nov. 1949, both in UPWA Papers, Box 52, Folder 10; and the materials in UPWA Papers, Box 342, Folder 10. Particularly insightful on the black insurgency developing in Chicago is the interview with Sam Parks, 3 Oct. 1985, UPWAOHP.

33. The most dramatic of these multiple racial incidents was a firebombing that occurred as the strike began to crumble; see (Fort Worth) *Union Banner*, 9 April 1948. For racial violence on the picket line, see interview with Steve Mauser, 15 May 1973, UTA.

34. "Human Relations in Fort Worth, Texas," UPWA Papers, Box 344, Folder 6. Also see Hope, *Equality of Opportunity*, 10–11, 25–26, 92–93.

35. Russell Lasley to Steve Mauser, 22 March 1950, UPWA Papers, Box 343, Folder 7; "Progress Report AD Program," 19 January 1951, UPWA Papers, Box 344, Folder 15; interviews with Frank Wallace and Eddie Humphrey.

36. Interview with Eddie Humphrey; interview with L. C. Williams, 18 March 1986, UPWAOHP. Other relevant interviews with WWII veterans include those with Earl Carr, 18 April 1986, UPWAOHP, and Charles Pearson, 17 July 1986, UPWAOHP. A packinghouse worker from Cedar Rapids, Iowa, Carr was one of the first black U.S. Marines. Pearson, who came out of the Waterloo, Iowa, Rath plant, was caught in two race riots during his stint in the military. Both speak eloquently about the impact the war had on their future civil rights activities.

37. "Report on District 1 AD Conference," n.d. [1952], UPWA Papers, Box 384, Folder 14; *Packinghouse Worker*, June 1952; *Proceedings*, Eighth Constitutional Convention UPWA-CIO, 110–13; "Major Contract Demands," UPWA Papers, Box 348, Folder 8; Lasley to all Armour Locals, 18 Nov. 1952, UPWA Papers, Box 210, Folder 5.

38. "Report on Local 54," and "Report of W. L. McMahon," 22 Nov. 1952, UPWA Papers, Box 348, Folder 2.

39. Russell Lasley to all Local Unions, 4 Dec. 1952; "Report on Local 54," both in UPWA Papers, Box 348, Folder 2; Helstein quoted in Barbara Griffith, *The Crisis of American Labor: Operation Dixie and the Defeat of the CIO* (Philadelphia: Temple Univ. Press, 1988), 84.

40. Minutes of International Executive Board, 17 May 1953, UPWA Papers, Box 99, Folder 2; Lasley to Helstein, 25 Nov. 1952, UPWA Papers, Box 348, Folder 2; interview with L. C. Williams; interviews with Ralph Helstein, 13 July 1983 and 14 Nov. 1983, both in possession of the author. In an interview with Barbara Griffith, Helstein recalled his conversation with Armour vice-president Frank Green: "You and I got a date to go to Fort Worth. We've got a lot of trouble there." He said, "I understand *you* got some troubles down there, but they're not my troubles." And I said, "Oh, Frank, you're wrong. You've got troubles, too. And you had better *make*

them your troubles; or, if you prefer, I'm going to pick up this telephone and I'm going to call every Armour local in the United States and tell them you are reneging on your agreement about eliminating segregated dining rooms." (*Crisis of American Labor*, 84).

41. Adedeji, "Crossing the Colorline," 70–75; George Thomas to Russell Lasley, 23 Dec. 1952, UPWA Papers, Box 348, Folder 2; Lasley to all Officers and Department Heads, 22 January 1953, UPWA Papers, Box 348, Folder 2; "Notes from file," UPWA Papers, 1 Dec. 1952 and 3 Dec. 1952, UPWA Papers, Box 348, Folder 2; interview with Steve Mauser. For Pittman's opposition to Thomas and Mauser's work, see the correspondence between Pittman and A. T. Stephens in UPWA Papers, Box 107, Folder 11.

42. Untitled document [list of packinghouse locals requesting LIU charters], Walter Reuther Papers, Box 292, Folder 16, Archives of Labor and Urban Affairs, Wayne State University, Detroit, MI [hereafter cited as Reuther Papers]; Robert Oliver to Walter Reuther, 25 Aug. 1953, Reuther Papers, Box 292, Folder 17; Dave Burgess to Walter Reuther, 25 Aug. 1953, CIOST, Box 113, Folder 1; Adedeji, "Crossing the Colorline," 88–94; Polakoff, "Texas State CIO Council," 222ff.

43. John Riffe to all CIO Regional and Sub-Regional Directors, 6 May 1953, RHP, Box 2; Ralph Helstein to John Riffe, 20 May 1953, UPWA Papers, Box 100, Folder 3; Ralph Helstein to Walter Reuther, 20 May 1953, UPWA Papers, Box 100, Folder 3; Dave Burgess to Jack Conway, 4 and 8 Sept. 1953, Reuther Papers, Box 292, Folder 18.

44. For disaffiliation, see "Report on Stockyard Situation," UPWA Papers, Box 210, Folder 13; materials in UPWA Papers, Box 359, Folder 1; *Packinghouse Worker*, Oct. 1954; Adedeji, "Crossing the Colorline," 142; and Herbert Hill, *Black Labor and the American Legal System: Race, Work, and the Law* (Washington, DC: Bureau of National Affairs, 1977), 271–72.

45. C. Brosnan to Durham and Lasley, 26 July 1954, UPWA Papers, Box 354, Folder 10; Richard Durham to John Hope, 27 May 1955, UPWA Papers, Box 367, Folder 2; interview with Mary Salinas; interview with Eddie Humphrey. Especially insightful about the decline of white participation in the local are the candid comments of assistant plant superintendent Kenneth Neidholt; interviews with Kenneth Neidholt, 20 March 1986 and 17 May 1986, UPWAOHP.

46. Interview with Eddie Humphrey; "Anti-Discrimination Department, Two Year Report: 1952–1954," UPWA Papers, Box 354, Folder 5; *Packinghouse Worker*, March 1955. Sept. 1955; press release, 23 Sept. 1955, UTA, 51–79–1.

8. Southern Workers in National Unions

Birmingham Steelworkers, 1936–1951

Judith Stein

When John L. Lewis and the other union leaders of the Committee for Industrial Organization (CIO) created the Steel Workers Organizing Committee (SWOC) in June 1936, expectations for southern workers were modest. The bulk of the steel industry was in the North, where SWOC placed most of its resources and hopes.[1] Lewis's experiences with the fervid anti-unionism of southern coal operators reinforced northern priorities. He told Noel Beddow, the executive director of SWOC's southern region, that he would be satisfied, "if you get results in ten years."[2] Operating on a shoestring and with minimum interaction with northern steel workers, the southerners exceeded Lewis's predictions. Between 1936 and 1942, workers at the Tennessee Coal, Iron and Railroad Company (TCI), a subsidiary of United States Steel (USS), overcame a local tradition of racially divided trade unions and survived a major recession, an AFL offensive, and a corporate effort to foster multiple unionism. During this period, SWOC's national contracts sustained the union and southerners barely altered shop-floor practices.

Between 1945 and 1951, however, a new generation of workers mounted a militant campaign to bring TCI in line with national patterns. In a series of episodes stretching from the 1947 rebellion over wage classification to a 1951 wildcat in the coke plant, which became a plantwide strike, Birmingham workers transcended racial and workplace divisions to forge a genuine grass-roots presence in the mills and shops of TCI. By 1951 they began making meaningful inroads into managerial decision making. The contract, an empowering device with profound racial implications, encouraged the articulation of new standards and rights hitherto unknown in the South, where workers faced not only the arbitrary power of bosses, but a culture where impersonal law often took a back seat to extralegal power.

The international union, enmeshed in the turbulent postwar relations with the steel industry, was slow to respond to the local militancy. But in 1947 Birmingham workers forced the United Steelworkers of America (USW) to begin a serious assault on the southern wage
differential. In 1951 they compelled the international to make key staff
changes to facilitate the transition to northern wage classifications and
trade-union practices. USS functioned well in what Gavin Wright has
called the South's "isolated labor market,"[3] but the workers and their
union could not.

SWOC's early commitment to organize southern workers in 1936,
coinciding with the most favorable conditions nationally and locally,
was crucial. But the South's secondary importance, the resistance of
key parts of the industry in the North, and the social isolation of
southern workers and leaders explain why the commitment to organize
translated only slowly into a genuine union presence. This scenario,
which counters the common notion of working-class militancy tamed
by the CIO's wartime bureaucracy, reflected the history of the southern steel industry and its workers and SWOC's national strategy.[4]

Southern Workers and the Steel Industry: The Non-union Era

The southern steel industry developed thirty years later than the northern industry. Although a center of pig iron, Birmingham did not begin
making steel until the turn of the century, when, prodded by low pig-
iron prices during the 1890s, engineers discovered how to use its local
red ore for steel.[5] In 1899 the Tennessee Coal, Iron and Railroad
Company (TCI) produced its first open hearth steel for rails at Ensley,
a section of Birmingham.[6] Taken over by United States Steel (USS) in
1907, TCI built a new steel complex at Fairfield to produce plate for
the corporation's shipbuilding operations during World War I. Subsequent expansion took place at Fairfield, a physical extension of Ensley, but an independent municipality.[7]

The steel industry was the motor for the growth of the region. By
1930 the population of the metropolitan region reached 431,493 when
nearly 70 percent of the state was still rural.[8] For other firms and
thousands of workers in the area, TCI, the only steel producer in the
city, set the pace. It convinced Pullman-Standard to manufacture railroad cars in nearby Bessemer in 1929. It supplemented its pig iron

with purchases from local producers. Herman Taylor, a black who worked at Ensley, recalled that people "had a tendency to look up to the folk that worked for the big Tennessee company. . . . TCI was the big boy on the block."[9]

TCI's advantage lay in its proximity to raw materials: it owned ore and coal mines within ten miles of its mills. Wages were lower than those in the North, but the productivity of labor was also lower.[10] Inferior Alabama ore and the smaller capacity of Birmingham's blast furnaces and open hearths, reflecting TCI's limited markets, reduced efficiencies.[11] As a result, TCI lagged behind USS's northern facilities in installing new technologies and processes and in making the more profitable, lighter steel products. Compared to locally owned iron companies, however, its technology was advanced.[12]

TCI's work force was both racially mixed and largely native Alabaman. Although TCI imported skilled workers from the North when it introduced new technologies, it obtained most of its labor in-state. The blacks migrated from the Black Belt south of Jefferson County, the whites from the northern counties.[13] Totaling slightly less than 40 percent of the city's population, blacks accounted for over half the work force in iron production and slightly under 40 percent in steel. Actually, as TCI began to produce more and varied steel—sheet in 1926, tin in 1938—the proportion of white workers increased.[14] Improvements in Alabama's rural schools, the agricultural crisis beginning in the 1920s, and the closing of many coal mines in the northern part of the state provided a growing supply of relatively well-educated and work-experienced whites for the new jobs in a modernizing steel industry that now required more formal education than the older sectors of the industry.[15]

Most blacks came directly from Alabama's Black Belt. At the beginning of World War II, TCI employed blacks on any job, except crafts requiring the ability to read blueprints, and authority jobs such as roller. Most Birmingham employers followed similar patterns of racial assignment. The works manager of the American Cast Iron and Pipe Co. justified keeping blacks out of skilled and supervisory positions because "southern Negroes . . . do not want much responsibility." The owner of Stockham Pipe Fittings believed that "Negroes as a rule cannot have first class skills."[16] Individual blacks advanced and held well-paying jobs, but they were usually paid less than whites doing the same work.[17]

The continuing black migration from the plantations sustained the employers' assumption that blacks were best for hard, unskilled labor. Herod White believed he was hired because "they liked my size," probably the criterion for most blacks. Like the goals of foreign-born workers in an earlier period in the North, the goals of workers sometimes coincided with those of capitalists. White's only thought on his first day at Ensley in 1937 was that he was now earning $3.60 a day when he had been receiving 75 cents for a ten-hour day on a farm in Dallas County. King Chandler was glad "to see [a] pay stub," something he had never received as a sharecropper.[18]

Blacks valued the superior schools and housing provided by TCI.[19] But the company did not offer them the mechanical subjects taught in the white schools.[20] Birmingham industrialists, like Alabama plantation owners, required a "dependent, easily controlled, docile, and cheap labor force" and were not about to jeopardize their supply by providing blacks advanced training.[21]

Manning patterns in each TCI mill, which hired independently, varied. Family members and friends usually recruited new workers. In general, the older the facility, the higher percentage of black workers. Thus, the rolling mill in Bessemer, constructed in the nineteenth century, employed a large majority of blacks and the older coke plant and wire mill were 50 percent black at the beginning of World War II. Even as these mills modernized, blacks retained their positions. But in the steel industry generally, a whitening process was taking place. The opening of new mills in the 1920s and 1930s, employing the latest technology and processes, coincided with the growing supply of native white and literate, if not necessarily more skilled, workers. The Ensley rail mill was 50 percent white and the newer Fairfield steel complex was slightly more than 60 percent white. The tin mill, which opened in 1938, was over 80 percent white; the newest ore-conditioning plant constructed in 1942 employed only a handful of black workers. The racially divided work force was always a factor in the union history, but it was always connected with other factors—union objectives, the distinctive circumstances of specific work groups, the specific functions of the facility or department in TCI's overall production scheme—in complex patterns of cooperation and conflict among workers and between workers and the company.

In 1936 the crucial characteristic of the work force was not its racial divisions but its inexperience: southerners were mainly first-generation steelworkers. They worked for a company composed of different plants, using old and new technologies, brought together by a series of mergers. Each plant was a series of small shops, employing workers of diverse skill, often with little or no contact with one another. And, except for the skilled northerners, TCI workers had no experience with steel unions.

The creation of the Birmingham steel industry in the early twentieth century coincided with the final elimination of the Amalgamated Association of Iron, Steel, and Tin Workers (AA) from the steel industry. The AA had only a nominal presence in Birmingham and could do little to counter the isolation of southern workers. Thus, the World War I strike in steel, led by machinists, took place here in 1918 reflecting local militancy in other industries, not with the rest of the steel industry in 1919.[22] But the leaders of the union initiative under the National Industrial Recovery Act were AA members, northern-born rollers hired in the 1920s. Its leading figure, W. H. Crawford, was a Socialist and son of a United Mine Workers (UMW) official. Crawford was a roller in Warren, Ohio, in 1926, when he went to work in the new sheet mill in Fairfield.[23]

From the very beginning, the AA organized industrially. This had clear racial implications in the area because the local, industrial unions, the UMW and the International Union of Mine, Mill, and Smelter Workers (Mine Mill), included blacks while most of the trades did not.[24] The initial organization joined ore and steel workers. The AA was not forced to negotiate across the chasms of separate trade unions, as the machinists did during World War I.[25] Its associations with other industrial unions inoculated steel workers from some of the prevailing racial attitudes of Birmingham's craft unions. But laws prohibiting interracial meetings[26] and the firing of the white and black leaders ended the initiative. Although the organizational legacy was meager, the AA leaders were the first SWOC recruits.

SWOC Era: 1936–1942

The birth of the CIO in 1935 rekindled steelworkers' organization in Birmingham. Gaining a contract with TCI as part of John L. Lewis's agreement with parent USS in 1937, SWOC battled for the next five years to expand the organization, improve both the contents and enforcement of the original contract, and to fight off a company-sponsored AFL challenge. Winning exclusive bargaining power in a December 1942 NLRB election solidified the CIO steelworkers' union in Alabama.

In June 1936, Lewis selected UMW veteran William Mitch as southern regional director of SWOC. A former Socialist, Mitch had been sent to Alabama in 1933 to organize coal miners and quickly became the leading labor official in Alabama, gaining the presidency of the state federation of labor in 1936.[27] Although he supervised, Mitch did not personally direct the steel campaign. He chose Noel Beddow, a metallurgical engineer and lawyer, who had become an enthusiastic supporter of organized labor while serving on an Alabama NRA compliance board. Beddow's knowledge of the steel industry and his legal training, Mitch believed, would make him an effective advocate.[28] Even more important, however, were his local roots. Although Beddow had worked in steel plants all over the country, he was born in Birmingham. "Alabama . . . ," Mitch observed, "is a peculiar territory . . . [W]e have that old prejudice against outsiders . . . , meaning men out of some other state."[29]

SWOC's efforts to build a union in Birmingham in the late 1930s and early 1940s took place amid a hostile public climate. The sympathy of the middle classes found in the North was absent here. Coal and ore strikes in 1934 had identified industrial unionism with blacks, violence, and sometimes communism. "Afraid of trouble," many realtors refused to rent space to SWOC.[30] A part of the middle class supported the New Deal's consumption-oriented policies. But even liberals such as Sen. Hugo Black extended no active support to the CIO. Because President Roosevelt deferred to southern power, New Deal agencies in the state were headed by men from the local governing class, who held traditional views on union and race. Thus, the antiunion vice-president of DeBardeleden Coal Company, Milton Fies, endorsed both by the conservative Sen. John Bankhead and the liberal Sen. Hugo Black, headed the Public Works Administration in Alabama. Thad Holt, formerly a manager at TCI, first headed the Reconstruction Finance Commission and then the Works Progress Administration in the state.[31]

Yet 1936 was not 1918, nor 1934. National politics, particularly the LaFollette hearings, placed TCI and the city on the defensive. Moreover, Gov. Bibb Graves, elected by the loose coalition that had often opposed the plantation and industrial interests of the state, was a benevolent neutral in the state's labor controversies. Graves mediated the ore strikes of 1936; his predecessor had helped the corporations combat those of 1934.[32] But after Graves's term, ending in 1938, conservatives held the governorship until 1946. (Alabama law did not permit a governor to succeed himself.)

Election laws, the one-party system, and disfranchisement made it difficult for the majority to dislodge the Black Belt's control of the legislature and party apparatus.[33] Locally, workers in Jefferson County were fragmented in various political entities—Fairfield, Bessemer, Birmingham, and small industrial towns. Because Black Belt whites and industrial elites were so entrenched in the party and the ultimate power governing labor relations was located in USS offices in Pittsburgh, politics was secondary, initially. But the decision had costs. Alabama's unreformed politics both narrowed the impact of SWOC and limited its political leverage on politicians in the state.

SWOC's initial contract came on 17 March 1937, as a result of the decision of USS head Myron Taylor to recognize the steel union for its members only. Although TCI had not been merged into the parent company during its great reorganization of 1935, USS insisted that the Alabama company sign this agreement, despite the weakness of the CIO union in its mills and shops. Even after the agreement, however, SWOC's foothold in TCI remained tenuous, with membership rarely exceeding one-half until the war years.[34]

Local and national SWOC strategy reduced the resources available to convert a contract into a genuine union at TCI. Mitch and Beddow sent local organizers to other sections of the South. This unofficial Operation Dixie was generated more by southern enthusiasm than by national CIO strategy. Yet local optimism was informed with the correct assumptions that unionism in one company and in one industry would be weak and that the unionization of the South would end the region's poverty and racial discrimination and transform its politics. Although SWOC concentrated on the iron and steel industry, organizers aided workers in many other industries. Most national unions had not begun to organize their southern plants.[35]

At the same time, SWOC head Philip Murray concentrated on the Republic and Bethlehem campaigns in the North. Although understandable, the decision had important effects on southern organizing. The small southern staff was trimmed in July 1937.[36] Beddow wanted to file charges against TCI, but SWOC, consumed with the Republic

Steel cases before the National Labor Relations Board (NLRB), tried to avoid using the Board for USS. SWOC leaders thought they could bring TCI up to minimum standards through the agency of top USS officials.[37]

From the start, TCI managers harassed the new SWOC locals. They had been unwilling signers. Moreover, they were under increasing pressure from USS to cut labor costs and rationalize production, the result of a critical evaluation of the whole corporation produced by an industrial engineering firm in the mid-1930s.[38] Whatever the motivation of Myron Taylor, the decision to recognize SWOC and directives to cut costs produced inevitable conflicts.[39] TCI plants were overrun with industrial engineers.[40] Managers imposed arbitrary changes in wage rates and job assignments, attempting to exclude the union from such questions and from even representing skilled workers.[41]

TCI took advantage of the 1937–38 recession to inflict heavy lay-offs among union activists.[42] Between June and September, operations at TCI were reduced by at least one-third.[43] Membership in the Ensley local plummeted from about 1,000 to 200 in 1939. The wire mill local became defunct. The fear of losing a job undercut the boost the union received when the contract was renewed in 1938 without the wage cut that white-collar workers and management suffered.[44]

The unifying promise of a contract or a general wage increase was not an option after 1937. Workers possessed the first; the recession ruled out the second. There was to be no grand battle at TCI, only guerrilla warfare through the grievance process, job by job, department by department, a slow and difficult way to build a union. Until 1941 there was no staffman at TCI. Beddow helped from his office in Birmingham, but the men were mainly on their own.[45] This meant that skilled and strategic workers, those with more bargaining power, would have more success than others. Uncoordinated job actions in small shops and specific departments, especially those undergoing technological change and "rationalization," kept the spirit of collective action alive, but also reinforced the social divisions within and between the plants.[46]

Changing technology badly affected the sheet mill, the engine of unionism since 1933. Automatic tables, installed in the sheet mill in 1936 or 1937, had eliminated the roughers and catchers from the rolling-mill crew.[47] Some of the mill's work had been transferred to the new tin mill. The introduction of the continuous strip mill, a national phenomenon, reduced the number of rollers.[48] The rollers had been the heart of the union. Now, reductions encouraged an inward and defensive posture, as they tried to protect their jobs and rates. Union leadership would shift to the open-hearth workers, who were more provincial than the men from the sheet mill. The era of the rollers was over.

At times, though, these local struggles could galvanize workers into impressive solidarity. The company actively opposed the union in the Bessemer Rolling Mill.[49] Managers told new men that "if [they] joined that damn shit [CIO], [they] didn't have any job." In one characteristic example of TCI's efforts to continue its dominance despite the contract, managers forced black workers on the night shift to remain in the plant for four uncompensated hours after a power failure had forced a shutdown.[50]

It was only after Ed Hosey, white head roller in the guide mill, was fired in April 1941 that workers faced down their imperious bosses. Backed by his entire black crew, Hosey gained reinstatement and SWOC compelled the company to post a notice of its action on the bulletin board.[51] After the victory, the Bessemer local's membership mushroomed, soon embracing 90 percent of the mill's workers.[52]

Workers in other mills, taking advantage of the tightening labor markets of the defense production period, also became more aggressive. In general, skilled men fared better in these piecemeal protests than other workers but the national contracts in 1941 and 1942 provided greater protection to all steelworkers seeking to resist TCI's efforts to impose unilateral conditions.

Meanwhile, the AFL, sometimes in collusion with TCI managers and public officials, launched a drive against SWOC.[53] Through 1941 and into 1942, encouraged by rulings by the NLRB[54] and the National Defense Mediation Board[55] that sanctioned craft units in some area plants, the Birmingham Trades Council supported a wide-ranging effort to oust SWOC or at least to carve out large craft jurisdictions.[56] TCI was bargaining informally with AFL unions up until the exclusive bargaining election of 1942.[57] This challenge had racial, as well as strictly organizational, overtones, as the craft unions courted public favor and governmental support by depicting SWOC and the CIO as agents of race mixing and radicalism.[58] Although the AFL tried to organize industrially at TCI, its strength was among skilled craftsmen, who were mostly white. Blacks working in craft shops were CIO. Henry Holston explained: In "the [machine] shop they didn't have any union there for the colored people. They had some craft unions . . . We [were] paying to the union but they wasn't able to represent us. Then the CIO came in . . . and they would represent everybody."[59]

Through 1941 local steel unionists were confident that they could defeat the AFL drive.[60] Indeed, a plantwide strike over TCI's refusal to resolve grievances in Ensley in October 1941 brought out Fairfield workers when Gov. Frank Dixon called in the National Guard.[61] But they had to defer the national union's struggle to achieve recognition in the Little Steel companies. Lacking the resources to do both, SWOC put USS on hold. When attention returned to USS in 1942, after the victory at Little Steel in 1941, organizing proceeded with the disabilities of the no-strike pledge.

The national leadership was aware of the relative weakness at TCI. In April 1942 it sent in four men, previously working in the Bethlehem campaign, to help at TCI. It scheduled TCI's exclusive bargaining election in December, hoping that victories earlier in the year in the better-organized USS plants in the North and after the June constitutional convention of the international union would swell the vote. By a 9–1 majority, the AFL and "independent" threat were removed and the United Steelworkers of America (USW) was now firmly planted in Birmingham.[62]

District 36 during World War II

Victory in 1942 did not end the isolation of Alabama's USW locals, now part of District 36. The USW assigned only one representative to Birmingham to deal with Herculean task of resolving grievances, extending organization, and representing the CIO on the National War Labor Board (NWLB) in Atlanta.[63] Throughout the war, the locals pressed the international to add staff for grievance cases, organizing, and, perhaps most important, to "unionize the members we now have."[64] But to national officials, constantly involved in new and complex relationships with federal bodies, Birmingham was of secondary importance.

Thus it was left to local unionists to transform a fledgling labor organization into a cohesive instrument of worker empowerment. And in the 1940s no issue was more revealing in this process than that of race. When the Fair Employment Practices Committee (FEPC) conducted hearings in Birmingham in the spring of 1942, the implicit CIO alterations in race relations became explicit. FEPC targeted southern industries which either did not hire blacks or employed them only as laborers. Using this calculus, FEPC ignored TCI's racial ceilings and focused upon the more severe restrictions in the new war industries, especially Mobile's expanding shipyards and the AFL unions which supplied much of their labor.[65]

FEPC considered SWOC an ally. Steel union leaders and the Alabama CIO applauded FEPC, hailing its exposé of the "Negro-hating AFL unions in Mobile."[66] Birmingham's elites, led by Gov. Dixon, local politicians, and TCI officials, on the other hand, mounted a bitter attack. Even though FEPC had not criticized TCI, the company's chief of police believed that the CIO had enlisted FEPC to aid the SWOC campaign. He complained that SWOC sound trucks were "preach[ing] equal rights and exhort[ing] the negroes to exert themselves." Southern businessmen and politicians used the FEPC hearings to denounce the CIO, charging that "the colored are trying to get as much money as white men, through the labor organizations."[67]

Indeed, here was the central racial issue during the war. The actual meaning and measures of racial discrimination changed over time and were determined by the national government, company policies, local industrial practices, black objectives and organization, white tolerance, and union strength. During the 1930s, the key issue had been inclusion in one union. During the war, it was equal pay for equal work. The few southern businessmen prepared to concede the point, used language that reinforced discriminatory practices (and reaffirmed their own unilateral power to decide), conceding that equal wages would prevail only where the skill of the black man doing the job was equal to that of a white man.[68] One TCI black employee succinctly stated the union definition when he said the USW forced the company to pay "the job not the man."[69]

Reflecting the southern labor market, TCI paid skilled blacks less than whites and often blacks performing semiskilled work earned only the basic labor rate.[70] During the war, blacks upgraded to jobs formerly performed by whites usually earned less than their predecessors.[71] Sometimes, the issue emerged subtly. Robert Nelson, a black in the plate mill, claimed that he was operating a new and more complicated end shears and supervising a crew of men, but was paid only his old rate of 63 cents. The plant manager thought the job would be filled with a white at $1.15, but after he put Nelson on the job, the rate was reduced.[72] TCI's calculation of job rates was still determined by race. In a period of changing technology, the racial determination of wage rates became transparent. When there was a union, blacks could protest the injustice.

Nelson was a grievanceman. But black departments often initially chose whites to represent them because they thought that managers would pay more attention to white spokesmen.[73] Indeed, many firms in the city would not meet with a grievance committee that included blacks; in 1943, Mine, Mill workers in the Harbison-Walker brickmaking plant struck when managers refused to provide chairs to blacks on the committee.[74]

The source of most black improvement during the war came from the general wage and incentive increases, job security, paid vacations, and the other benefits of the national contracts. But general disputes over incentives and wage rates accompanying increased production and plant expansions raised qualitatively different issues that blacks often applied to strictly racial questions. TCI's opportunistic awarding of incentives to electricians in 1941 generated demands for fairness from other craftsmen. Chester Ray, a white worker in the sheet mill, said "men don't begrudge others who receive money but when men are working together and one receives incentives and others do not it is unjust."[75] Incentives in the open hearth led blast-furnace workers to demand the same. Higher incentives for blast-furnace workers in Fairfield led to a strike among the blast-furnace workers at Ensley. While incentives encouraged speedup, they also undercut TCI's claims of a rational wage policy. The incentive for electricians was no true incentive, but only a way to keep the men at TCI. Implicitly, the protests of craftsmen and production workers with less bargaining power than the electricians had the effect of challenging the market determination of wages.

Racial issues grew concretely out of this specific workplace claim of fairness. One group of blacks argued, "if other groups can get wage adjustments . . . [we] should be allowed the same privilege."[76] In the abstract, no black expected to be treated as white in Alabama. But when experiencing poor or different treatment, blacks increasingly expected the essence of equal treatment. Thus blacks often began complaints with "we know that we are here in the South but . . . ," or equivalents.[77]

The extension of the notion of fairness to job assignments was also begun during the war. Changes were initiated by blacks themselves with local white aid but without the prodding of the district leadership, Communists, the government, or race organizations. Black voting in union affairs was the key to producing change and CIO principles narrowed the grounds of white opposition.

The process went furthest in the wire mill, where blacks possessed the numbers and leadership to effect changes. During the war, blacks became a majority in the wire mill and they mobilized their votes to ensure that the white leadership represented their interests. M. D. Knoblock, Tom Howard, and Webb Daniel, skilled whites working in the rod department and machine shop, led the mill union, Local 1700.[78] In 1943, with the aid of a tight labor market, Daniel, chairman of the grievance committee, and a sympathetic manager from the North, who was subsequently removed and retrained in southern mores, opened all the wire-drawing machines to blacks.

In 1945 some whites protested to Philip Murray. They had devised a separate learning route to the machines for whites, which was acceptable to management. They explained that "young white returning veterans . . . would rather learn under a white person," but "the negro committeeman with aid from certain White Officers" refused. The protesters maintained that "no one will be discriminated against on account of RACE or COLOR." Daniel stood firm and told Murray that he was "very sorry we have members in our Union that will not bear true allegiance to. And keep inviolate the principles of the United Steel Workers of America [sic]."[79] District leader Reuben Farr supported Daniel, talked to the men, and the incident ended. (One of the white protesters was eventually made a foreman, but by that time he could do nothing.)[80]

CIO principles afforded blacks considerable room for progress and narrowed the ideological basis of white resistance. The whites argued their case in the union language of nondiscrimination, which was difficult. Nevertheless, the wide gap between union principles, TCI manning practices, and attitudes prevailing in the surrounding city, diluted practice. Both blacks and whites measured what was desirable and possible on the basis of what they saw around them. The politics and ideology of black promotion proceeded in this manner through the 1950s. In none of these cases was there a wall of white solidarity. Each white was confronted with a concrete case where the race issue was enmeshed with the specific man, the position of the company, the implication for the union, the organization, skill, and political strength of blacks, and union principles.

After the war, the atmosphere in Local 1700 facilitated the emergence of a new generation of black leaders. Initially, the boldest were those who were less educated. However, they were joined by World War II veterans and high-school graduates, some imbued with white-collar aspirations that were unfulfilled in Birmingham in the 1950s. This group entered the mills because of the superior wages, but brought broader aspiration and leadership skills.[81] The influx of new men and the increased articulation of black grievances that came with union protection was visible to whites, too. One white veteran, returning to TCI after four and one-half years at war, noticed "how much the negro people had advanced" during his absence. He added, "but not far enough."[82]

Because they were younger, the new black leaders did not compare their situation to that of pre-union workers at TCI. Because most were born in Birmingham, they did not weigh conditions with the measure of the plantation. The key leaders were home owners in Fairfield and members of the First Baptist Church. Although the minister was unsympathetic to unions, the church was a social center. The men acted pragmatically. They decided to control the chairmanship of the grievance committee only in 1947, after Webb Daniel took a supervisory position, reasoning that a black would enjoy long tenure because TCI would never make *him* a foreman. Until the late 1960s, they elected white presidents, usually Knoblock.[83]

Immediately after the war, company intransigence limited their success. In the barbed-wire department, the union demanded the appointment of either Mark Harris, a black, or Emanuel Lucia, an Italian-American, to the position of machine adjuster. The job was filled by a white man brought in from the outside. Management argued, correctly, that machine adjuster was not in the line of promotion for either man. Without negotiations, in 1942, the position was set apart, giving the company complete freedom in filling it. Many key jobs like machine adjuster were outside any line of promotion. But there were customary patterns for filling these jobs which the company frequently violated when it came to advancing a black. Blacks used the precedent of customary manning practices and the principle of limiting management's freedom to promote, which often won white support.[84]

Workers' demands and expectations were growing while the company insisted on the narrowly defined letter of the 1939 agreement, agreed to when the union was small and weak and fighting for its institutional life. The seniority system simply reaffirmed the company's traditional system of job progression, left many jobs unconnected to others, and in the end gave management the power to determine ability, its first principle on promotions.[85] TCI's overriding concern was to limit the principle of seniority. Thus, it opposed shift seniority because certain shifts provided opportunities to fill temporary vacancies in more skilled occupations, which were not fully manned on one or two of the three shifts. According to the union, the senior man should have the opportunity to gain experience that could give him an edge on promotions. Although often a customary practice, TCI argued that the practice was not a right for workers but an example of "management determination of what was considered best for the operation of the mill."[86] Similarly, the company opposed transfer rights out of lines of promotion, arguing that keeping men within a line, and there were many in each department, produced the best workers. Indeed, TCI's unique system of job seniority existed to ensure the transfer of skills, but by determining the limits of advancement at the moment of hire, limited the opportunity of all workers, especially blacks.

Local 1700 appealed to the international, which asked USS to intervene because "the local grievance committee . . . has made repeated and futile efforts to work out lines of promotion. . . . On every occasion the local has been rebuffed."[87] In the midst of the postwar attempt to limit the power of the USW, USS refused.

The local asked for the international's help because Reuben Farr and his staff offered little help although they supported changes the men could win on their own. Elected head of District 36 at the USW's constitutional convention in June 1942, Farr was the only director born on a farm. He had been a member of Mine, Mill during a brief stint in the ore mines during the 1920s and was one of the first members of SWOC, often a decisive qualification in the selection of early union officials. He was a first helper in the open hearth and president of the large and politically significant Fairfield Steel Local 1013.

Farr was so overwhelmed by his tasks as district director that he examined no issue comprehensively.[88] He disliked attending international executive board meetings and avoided those he could. At the meetings, Farr sat silently, commenting only when asked about southern conditions. His self-imposed provincialism froze the union to wartime capacities. At the same time, he cannily wielded the power possessed by all district leaders to combat criticism. As the union grew, men in the mills became more experienced and knowledgeable. But their link with the international was mediated through Farr and his staff who filtered directives through their own narrow beliefs and prejudices.

Throughout the war, there had been some criticism of Farr. But increasing militancy did not develop into an organized opposition or an alternative vision of the union even though Farr's inadequacies contributed to the delays of the NWLB and the tolerance of TCI's wage and labor policies. Most men liked Farr, who was fundamentally decent, but their frustrations led some to believe that he "was too close to the company."[89] However, they had strong criticisms of the staff, Bob Poarch from the tin mill, William Shewmake from the open hearth, and Ben Gage from the sheet mill. The three were early activists but also men with limited experiences. Gage, who often disappeared for weeks, Poarch, and Shewmake drank heavily. Paul Bowron, former head of labor relations for TCI, said "from my point of view, they [the staff] were all right."[90]

Thus, through the 1940s and 1950s, black workers, especially in facilities in which they predominated, conducted effective, if limited campaigns to achieve a measure of shop-floor equality. Using the collective bargaining contract resourcefully and employing the language of fairness rather than that of all-embracing racial equality, they found some white allies in the mills. But black progress was not simply dependent upon removing racial barriers. Racial progress was frustrated by the overall success of TCI in maintaining control of the workplace, often in violation of the national contract. It required a broader worker challenge to alter company practices and convince the international to support the growing insurgency.

Postwar Struggles, 1945–1951

It was not until the wage inequity crisis, peaking in 1951, that workers had an issue that transcended the insularities of race, department, and plant. Rank-and-file activists of both races challenged the company's job and wage classifications, which were completely out of line with the negotiated changes taking place in northern plants. With local activists keeping the pressure on the USW, TCI signed agreements in 1951 that mitigated regional wage differentials and specified job classification procedures and categories that coincided with the industry.

USS viewed wage classification as part of its rationalization program begun in the 1930s. The international's interest stemmed from workers' changing objectives and wartime political constraints. During the 1930s, SWOC had attempted to raise the historic low wages of the industry. The most efficient and unifying solution was general wage increases. Having achieved basic gains, workers during the war began to articulate new notions of fairness. Sixty percent of all grievances involved questions of intraplant inequalities as workers, empowered as they were by the collective bargaining contract, began to protest the notoriously chaotic wage structure in the industry.[91] Moreover, during the war the union found that concentration on these concerns freed it from some of the constraints imposed by the Little Steel formula, which severely limited general wage advances but permitted considerable leeway in incentives and in the adjusting of inequities.[92]

In 1944, the NWLB approved the union's goal of eliminating intraplant inequities. However, at the same time it rejected the principle of "equal pay for similar work throughout the industry," which would have ended geographical differentials. Still, the board's acceptance of the principle that classification of jobs (in terms of their difficulty, skill levels, responsibility, and danger) should be made in comparisons with other plants in the industry, without recognition of strictly regional factors, provided an entering wedge for ending of regional differentials.

The NWLB created the tripartite Steel Commission to implement its directive, but in 1945 TCI refused to join the other USS plants on it. Because many southern companies had successfully resisted other NWLB rulings and because the board had specifically sanctioned regional wage differentials in steel, Murray resisted an impulse to challenge TCI before the board.[93] Instead, while working with USS to rationalize wage and classification patterns on an industrywide basis, the international, Murray concluded, would have to be content with close monitoring of the separate TCI negotiations.[94]

But TCI did precious little negotiating. Instead, in the fall of 1945, it simply submitted to local union officials the results of its own revamped classification system, which entailed no comparison of TCI ratings with those of other USS plants.[95] Inevitably, TCI's new system involved little upgrading of wages. Although the NWLB had sanctioned an increase of 5 cents an hour to permit the readjustments, TCI's plan called for a 1.5-cents increase. TCI finally agreed to negotiate the classifications but refused to accept the principle of comparability with other USS companies. But when TCI released the new rates in February 1947, the workers discovered that between 35 and 50 percent faced wage cuts. One rank-and-file activist recalled that the men "almost went to war." Ignoring the objections of district director Farr, they quickly elected a delegation to go to Pittsburgh to see Murray.[96]

Representing every TCI plant, the dissenters were critical of the union as well as the company.[97] The breadth of discontent called into question the character of the district leadership and the relationship between the TCI locals and the international union. There had been no rank-and-file participation in the bargaining. Few workers knew about the procedure of job classification. Bob Poarch, the staffman handling the job inequities program, covering up his own inadequacy and possible corruption, had told the men that the "program wasn't worth a damn," and was just a way for Pittsburgh to remove local control.[98]

It was Farr and Poarch, not local members, who had appointed men in each plant to negotiate with the company. Only the designated men could obtain copies of TCI's job description manual. Prior to the astonishing February announcement, there had been no meetings or discussions with the rank and file. Even afterwards, Robert Lynn, a machinist and member of the dissident delegation, had a difficult time obtaining a copy of the classification report. When he and other local activists did obtain copies, they were aghast at the document and at their district leadership's passive and ill-informed role in the "negotiations" that produced it.[99]

The delegation forced Murray to confront the issue of the southern wage differential. In all mills under contract the entry wage established the floor on which higher classifications were determined. But in the South, basic labor was 17.5 cents per hour lower than in the North. Although the wage gap in the higher categories was less than the basic labor differential, most skilled and semiskilled rates were lower than those in the North.[100] Thus a system beginning with the base rate reduced the higher rates as well.

Eliminating the differential had always been a union goal, but after the southern rebellion, Murray concluded that it was "extremely critical."[101] USS officials thought the objective "outrageous," although union economists had estimated that it would cost the corporation only one cent per hour.[102] In the subsequent negotiations, the USW was victorious. True, the regional differential remained in the 1947 contract, but it was reduced and scheduled for complete elimination in 1954. Some of the edge had been taken off the wage issue.

The question of job classification was not resolved so easily. Using the Gary plant as a model, the NWLB-initiated tripartite commission established criteria for benchmark jobs to be applied to other jobs throughout the USS facilities. TCI refused to adopt these Gary standards. As a result, its classfications reflected the southern labor market more than it did the steel industry. In 1948 USW staff in Pittsburgh found no job in TCI's coke plant classified in line with other coke plants. No job had the highest value of 3.0 for noxious surroundings in the plant with the worst environment of any phase of steel production. Workers could appeal specific examples of misclassification to the commission, but most, unaware of industrywide standards, yielded to TCI.[103]

But as in the case of the wire mill, the postwar period brought new leadership. Impatient with TCI's intransigence and with Farr's inept performance, younger whites, mainly high school graduates, now took the lead. For example, Roland Goodwin began working as an electrician in the sheet mill in 1939. A member of the electricians' union, he had not joined the USW until 1945.[104] Robert Lynn, a machinist in Fairfield Steel, and James Swindle, a strip-mill operator in the tin mill, were also defense-period hires and now began to assume leadership in the rank-and-file effort to bring TCI in line with national standards. Ernest McLin, a black wire bundler and chairman of the grievance committee in the wire mill, although slightly older, was part of the dissident group. They formed ad hoc committees, independent of Farr and the staff, holding meetings in Fairfield. Communicating with Murray and the Pittsburgh staff, they served as direct links between the international union and the men in the plants.[105]

Although by the end of 1948 the men had convinced Murray that TCI's inequities program had to be reviewed totally, not merely tinkered with, it was only after the TCI locals threatened to strike in April 1951, that the company agreed to this project.[106] The resulting wage classification program aided all unskilled workers, for it recognized dirty and dangerous surroundings, along with skill levels, as relevant factors in determining job descriptions and wage rates. And, of course, it was black workers who disproportionately toiled in these noisome tasks.

Blacks gained as well by removal of the regional differentials. Previously, jobs filled predominantly by blacks at TCI were rated lower than comparable work in the North. Removing steel wages from the local labor market and placing them squarely in the context of industrywide standards had the effect of removing racial, as well as regional, wage differences.

Thus TCI and USS accepted what they had rejected in 1945. TCI had not yielded easily, clinging to its regional and racial wage advantages long after its technology was state of the art and industrywide standards covered steelworkers elsewhere. In the end, it was a combination of biracial rank-and-file activism, reflective of specific workplace conditions and dynamics, and direct, if tardy, intervention by the international union that ended TCI's long-standing regional practices.

New Leaders and "New" Workers:
The Coke Strike of 1951

Throughout the 1950s and into the 1960s, the combination of local militancy and pressure by skilled international representatives dismantled much of TCI's traditional regime. Murray followed up on the controversy over classification by sending his most trusted troubleshooter to Alabama and then by replacing complacent and inept international representatives with vigorous new leadership. Meanwhile, coke workers, hitherto among TCI's less vocal employees, rebelled against discriminatory manning policies. Murray's new appointees, supported by the international, transformed the wildcat into a companywide strike. Emboldened by this success, TCI workers through the late 1950s used the grievance machinery and the strike threat effectively to expand workplace rights. By 1961, when John F. Kennedy issued an executive order banning discrimination in defense contracts, TCI workers and their international representatives had already done much to integrate TCI's production operations.

Originally, Murray had viewed the dissidents at TCI skeptically. He had accepted Farr's analysis that the men were "causing lots of confusion" and showing little "cooperation with the District office." But the legitimacy of the rank-and-file complaints soon became apparent. The lengthy nationwide steel strike of 1949 deflected his attention from the South but in April 1951, he sent USW Vice-President James Thimmes to Birmingham for a first-hand look at the situation in TCI's mills. (Previously, Secretary-Treasurer David McDonald had handled the South.)[107]

Thimmes quickly affirmed the local complaints: "The inequity program had been so distorted and abused that many of our people are . . . being deprived of wages which . . . rightfully belong to them. Evidence . . . support[s] practically every complaint which has been brought to you regarding the handling of grievances." And Thimmes laid blame squarely on the shoulders of international representatives William Shewmake and Bob Poarch, who had been servicing TCI locals and had been the object of rank-and-file criticism.[108]

Few blamed Farr, even though both men had been his choices. James Swindle said we were "not against them," but for "new blood and ideas."[109] Robert Washington, a black organizer and subsequently a union president, concluded that Farr was "soft spoken" and a "very loyal union man," but "Strevel [Farr's successor] was "more forceful."[110]

Murray quickly followed his lieutenant's advice, appointing Bill Kessler and Howard Strevel to service TCI locals. Previously, McDonald had accepted Farr's nominees. Murray broke precedent by appointing men who were not native Alabamans. Kessler, a West Virginian, was thoroughly familiar with the international union's inequity program and served primarily as a technical expert and grievance coordinator. It was Strevel, however, who quickly asserted leadership and who demonstrated to skeptical local workers that the changing of the guard had indeed brought a new dispensation to the district.

The thirty-five-year-old Strevel was a native of eastern Tennessee. He had been head of his local union at Alcoa and president of the Tennessee State CIO Council. Like many from this region, he belonged to a family that was part of that "other South." His great-grandfather had fought and died for the Union and the family had remained Republican. Eastern Tennessee did not practice the rigid segregation and subordination of blacks characteristic of Alabama and Strevel had grown up in an area where black police officers were common. During his long tenure in Birmingham, he proved willing to challenge Alabama's racial etiquette. At the same time, his detailed knowledge of steel processes, very similar to those in aluminum, and his vigorous defense of local activists of both colors enabled him to retain white support.[111]

At the outset of the new appointments, Farr and some local presidents close to him attempted to persuade Murray to rescind the new appointments. Strevel quickly reassured Farr that the newcomers had no intention of challenging his official position. Pacified, Farr retained his directorship, confining his activities to symbolic and official functions.[112]

Soon after Kessler and Strevel arrived in Alabama they faced an immediate challenge. Black workers in the coke plant walked out in protest over the company's unresponsiveness to their complaints about manning practices. When TCI moved swiftly to punish the strike leaders, the walkout quickly transcended these local issues and, with Kessler and Strevel coordinating activities, soon mushroomed into a general strike of TCI workers. Blacks had participated in virtually every significant strike at TCI, but this was the first one sparked by their specific concerns.

The coke plant had been among the last to become organized at TCI. Coke plant jobs were not desirable, demanding as they did the ability to sustain long bouts of hard work in intense heat. The ovens department was filled with the least-educated blacks, who had few alternatives. Perhaps because of the low education levels of the labor force in the coke plant, the men were inactive.[113] But the local leadership, dominated by the white maintenance departments, had little interest in encouraging participation. One white who worked in the ovens department recalled that when he was hired it took him a few days to locate anyone who could give him a union application. No officer came from the coke batteries, a circumstance reflected in the results of the postwar inequity program, which systematically undervalued the jobs there. Thus, for example, the top production job in the coke plant, held by a white man, obtained an "11" rating, whereas in coke plants elsewhere in the steel industry, it was classified at "18."[114]

The grievances in the coke plant were not confined to questions of wage classifications. Blacks had been dissatisfied with the manning levels in the ovens department.[115] During the summer, when the outside heat pushed the temperature in the plants to unendurable levels, TCI assigned additional men to crews transporting coal into the ovens. Earlier protests had been confined to efforts to retain the summer manning levels year-round but the current protest demonstrated that coke workers, in common with workers in TCI's mills, were assessing their position within the context of national patterns of manning and classification.

Thus, in July 1951, TCI coke workers sent a delegation to USS's coke plant in Clairton, Pennsylvania. They discovered that the number of men in Clairton's *regular* crew equaled the number in TCI's *summer* crew and that, in addition, USS supplemented the regular crew in Clairton with still more workers in the summer. Thus, northern workers, the majority of whom were black, too, who did not have to endure the much hotter and more humid Alabama summer, enjoyed far more advantageous manning levels than their southern counterparts. Returning home, the men petitioned the plant superintendent to increase manning to the level found in Clairton. When he failed to respond, the aroused coke workers, believing on the basis of past experiences that their union would not help them, resolved to strike.[116]

Kessler and Strevel acted quickly to support the coke workers, rally workers at other TCI facilities in their behalf, and give notice to the company that the days of union passivity were over. Kessler convinced TCI industrial relations head Johnny Williamson that an injunction against the wildcat would only inflame the situation, but Williamson proceeded to suspend thirty-seven of the strikers. Continued negotiations resulted in the reinstatement of twenty-five, but, ignoring the grievance process, TCI fired eight blacks and four whites, who soon became known as "the Twelve Disciples," around whom TCI workers rallied.

Strevel discovered that the company was actively trying to convince white workers to abandon the blacks. Consequently, he decided to use the coke strike as a galvanizing event and to bring all TCI workers out on strike.[117] At a mass meeting on November 1, chaired by Roland Goodwin, one of the stalwarts in the inequity battles and now president of the sheet mill local, Strevel did not have to do much convincing. Workers representing all locals, including ore and quarry miners, overwhelmingly endorsed the strike, which was supported by the international as well. Finally, on November 11, TCI agreed to process the discharges through the grievance process, leading to arbitration.[118]

Strevel's decision to have blacks and whites picket together was a bold and successful stroke.[119] Traditionally, in all unions in the region, blacks confronted black scabs and whites, the white ones. Clearly, this would not work in a situation where the company was soliciting whites to scab on blacks. Integrated picket lines would defuse the racial component of the conflict, Strevel believed, and would pit union men of both races against union wreckers, thus making the issue union solidarity rather than racial identity. This decision revealed his method of making racial changes: concrete union goals, not abstract egalitarian principles, were the decisive factor.

The strike won national attention. The NAACP's Walter White saw a "new union unity" overcoming "race prejudice."[120] The local power structure was less enthusiastic. At a large public meeting attended by leading politicians, the Birmingham Chamber of Commerce condemned the strike and attributed it to Communists.[121] The FBI tapped the phones of some of the Twelve Disciples, and sheriffs, state troopers, and local police menaced pickets. On occasion, law officers pulled guns on the strikers, but, despite these provocations, there was no violence.[122]

In the end, the arbitration process sustained the workers. The newly-appointed USS arbitrator, Sylvester Garrett, heard the case quickly and found on December 31 that the men had been unjustly penalized, ordering reinstatement of the Twelve Disciples. At the same time, however, Garrett left the immediate cause of the strike—manning patterns in the coke plant—unchanged. He rejected the union arguments that TCI manning levels endangered the men's health and that local crew size must meet the higher national standard. (The men won the improved manning pattern in the late 1950s.)[123]

The strike had an immediate effect on the local. Leaders who had scabbed or advocated scabbing, were replaced. The initial militancy remained strong, as men who had been cautious and skeptical became more active. Those in the ovens department now began to exert leadership and soon won for production men a lunch break, previously a privilege enjoyed only by maintenance men.[124]

Strevel's vigorous defense of the fired men impressed workers in other plants. Gone were the days of Farr's uncertain and indecisive response to traditional TCI workplace practices and "illegal" strikes.[125] Clearly, the 1951 job action was a turning point in the union's relations with TCI, which for years had relied on racial division and cautious local leadership to ensure that unionism remained within easily manageable limits. Indeed, it was in this episode of postwar militancy and not in the fabled days of the 1930s, that the "company's Waterloo" occurred.[126]

In 1952, Strevel, threatening to strike again, strengthened general seniority principles, simultaneously increasing opportunities for black promotion. He won the right for each plant to determine its own seniority rules, ending the stranglehold of the 1939 agreement mandating each plant to limit seniority to the actual job in the specific department. Chester Ray, a white worker at the sheet mill, was correct when he complained that "the Tennessee Company was the only company in the Steel Corporation where department occupational seniority was applied."[127] Because it was impossible to obtain companywide agreement on any kind of seniority system, before any change could take place, it was crucial to free TCI workers from the mandatory system. This enabled Strevel to work plant by plant, where he had favorable majorities or could create them.

Strevel also encouraged black assertiveness in the grievance process. He brought and won at arbitration numerous discipline cases, which undermined the company's autocratic treatment of its workers generally. Blacks, traditionally the most powerless of TCI's employees, benefited especially from this invigorated grievance handling.

Equally important, Strevel ended customs that inhibited the growth of black leadership. Even as black participation in the grievance process grew, it had been the practice that cases reaching the fourth-step meeting stage be turned over to white advocates. Even for whites, it was intimidating to take on the company's fourth-step man, Paul Bowron, the son of the founder of TCI and a member of Birmingham's industrial aristocracy. Much was at stake in any fourth-step encounter, since only those cases with broad implications and involving basic contractual relationships unresolvable at the plant level went this far. Thus, Strevel's insistence, for example, that Ernest McLin, the black chairman of the grievance committee in the wire mill, speak at these proceedings had important meanings for the union, the industrial relations regime at TCI, and the community. And in a city where elite whites met blacks nowhere on the basis of equality, the empowerment inherent in the union contract was translated into a kind of formal equality that had far-reaching practical and symbolic meanings.

In the 1960s, the growth of local union democracy meshed with national events to speed change. John F. Kennedy's presidential order of March 1961 banned discrimination in defense contracts, giving Strevel an additional weapon. The civil rights movement itself, while it produced some divisive effects among steelworkers, did not impede the completion of merging promotion lines.[128] These important victories built upon a whole generation of earlier struggles, first among isolated groups of workers in particular departments and plants and eventually on the part of the USW in Birmingham generally, with Howard Strevel expanding the heritage of protest to lay the basis for the achievement of an unprecedented degree of formal equality in the mills and shops of TCI by the mid-1960s.

Conclusion: Structure, Time, and Southern Unionization

In their 1942 paean to the virtues of stable and mature unionism, USW officials Clinton Golden and Harold Ruttenberg reassured corporate America that the militancy of the 1930s was giving way to "responsible unionism." Bare-knuckled shop-floor battlers, they believed, were being replaced in positions of union power by sober and responsible labor statesmen.[129] But whatever the truth of this widely circulated characterization of general trends in American industrial relations, it had little relevance to the situation in Alabama. Here, Golden's and Ruttenberg's model, as well as the standard mythologies of much recent labor history scholarship, were reversed. Thus, in the iron and steel industry of Alabama, militant and effective industrial unionism emerged only after World War II. And it did so through the vehicle of the collective bargaining contract, which proved an instrument of empowerment, not one of constraint and bureaucratization.

In Alabama, "the turbulent years" occurred in the late 1940s and early fifties. This was, in part, because TCI clung to traditional and regional labor policies despite its recognition of a steelworkers' union. Additionally the international could pay little attention to southern problems while it fought to attain industrywide collective bargaining. Perhaps the key factor, however, was the inexperience of Alabama workers during the 1930s. Only after the war did a new generation of relatively sophisticated and well-educated union activists emerge.

Moreover, the union contract, was a source of standards unknown to southern labor relations. Far from serving to bind workers to bureaucratic and restrictive rules, as an emerging body of historical scholarship and legal commentary suggests, the contract provided the arena in which workplace struggles could be translated into specific gains and, more broadly, a vehicle by which previously voiceless workers, particularly blacks, could begin to exert influence on the shop floor, in the union, and eventually in the community.

The national organizing drives in steel, coal, and ore of the 1930s, in contrast to those in other industries, included southern workers. In steel, SWOC's early breakthrough, a result of the Lewis-Taylor agreement, was crucial, coming in the brief period in which anti-union forces were temporarily neutralized, nationally and locally. Yet for SWOC/USW, national priorities superseded the claims of its southern membership, during the difficult thirties, through the war years, and into the strike-filled postwar period. The union's weak shop-floor power at TCI through World War II reflected the weak bargaining positions of all southern workers, trapped as they were in a regionally and racially defined labor market. First-generation Alabama steelworkers lacked the industrial and union experience that northern workers possessed, thus further retarding the development of vigorous and effective local unions.

But by 1951, a second generation of TCI workers measured their rights by national, not southern standards. In 1947 it was their protest against the locally negotiated inequity program that forced Philip Murray to recognize the importance of southern differentials. Southern black workers began to calculate their circumstances not with reference to provincial standards of life in the Black Belt or conditions in other Birmingham industries but by the standards of white workers in comparable jobs and black or white workers in northern plants with comparable functions.

Second-generation leaders in the South were schooled by TCI's resistance to the union. In the main, they did not have to parry the company thugs, hostile sheriffs, or violent "citizens" groups. But to gain implementation of their abstract contractual rights, they did have to force TCI to bargain with the local union. Success now required not the courage to face goons, but rather the self-confidence and skill to negotiate with a shrewd and powerful corporation. The union founders were militant, but when confronted with corporate expertise they deferred on complex questions of job analysis, manning policies, and wage determination.

After the war, TCI, like the rest of the steel industry, attempted to resist union intrusion on the "rights of management." But TCI's labor relations reflected surrounding southern conditions more than national steel standards despite equivalent technology. Created in the late nineteenth century when southern capitalists attempted to industrialize in ways compatible with southern history, TCI continued the autocratic methods of that project. Indeed, southern iron makers and other industrialists thought TCI's labor relations were too liberal, as their own workers began demanding what TCI workers had won.[130] USS had implicitly accepted the TCI system when it excluded the company from the merger of its steel works in 1935. TCI refusal, supported by USS, to participate with the rest of the subsidiaries in the inequity program in 1945 and the seniority study in 1947[131] revealed its allegiance to regional standards, which affected nearly every measure of working-class power. In 1946, for example, when most northern locals required companies to post job openings, TCI workers had only just gained the right to have the names of successful applications posted.[132]

Technological changes undercut the old system, based upon labor-intensive industry. But while providing an opportunity, the national technology of the steel industry did not automatically change labor relations at TCI. A union was necessary and in that struggle the national contract was an empowering weapon, not the frequently portrayed corset. It established procedures and rights that overcame decades of local practices. And the same men who cited it understood the value of the slowdown and quickie strike, which became more common in the 1950s than they had been in the 1930s.[133] Class consciousness and militancy are often the result of organization, not the cause of it. Black demands were strengthened by contractual provisions, grievance rights, and the attainment of standard rates. In the period before these rights were codified, racial injustice was buried in the entangled web of customary behavior, thus blunting protest against it. It was only through the evolving contract that black workers could identify specific cases of injustice and, on the basis of union-sanctioned claims, build coalitions with white workers to effect change.

At TCI, the intervention of the national union did not stifle local dissent but rather facilitated it. Belatedly to be sure, and at first reluctantly, Murray recognized the justice of the dissidents' complaints and Thimmes endorsed the rank-and-filers' criticism of the district leadership in 1947. Moreover, it was the international representatives Kessler and Strevel who effectively translated uncoordinated local protest into companywide action and who skillfully advanced the claims of racial justice by promoting job-centered union strategies.

Most workers had resented TCI, but a sense of alternatives, necessary for effective resistance, could not be found in Alabama, where most workers were born and spent their lives. Primitive labor relations, an unsympathetic middle class, weak racial organizations, and unreconstructed politics provided little local nourishment. Overcoming the South's isolated labor market required the power of a national union. It also required the coming of age of a new generation of steelworkers, products of a unionized worker culture, forged on the plant floor and tempered by TCI intransigence. Union experiences—where blacks and whites met together, where black voting was uncontested, where blacks could even represent whites—and union principles of equity pushed them away from the general cultural reflex of race relations that surrounded them and continued to influence their lives.

After the war, the decline of coal and ore mining weakened the CIO in Jefferson County. Nothing replaced the mining base and critics accused TCI of stifling the entry of new industries. All the while, the hidebound racial practices of other southern industries and the profoundly segregationist influences of other local institutions—churches, schools, fraternals, the Democratic party—ensured that union principles would be confined to the workplace. Indeed, the civil rights politics of the 1960s, in which Birmingham and other Alabama communities were at the epicenter, strained the biracial solidarity so difficultly achieved and maintained in the workplace. But the continued strength of the steelworkers' union demonstrated that blacks and whites had learned that whatever happened outside the plants, a biracial union was necessary inside them.

Notes

The research for this paper was made possible by a fellowship from the National Endowment for the Humanities and grants from the Research Foundation of the City University of New York. I am grateful to the unstinting generosity and unique integrity of Sub-district Director E. B. Rich, who allowed me full access to crucial records. Rich played an important role in the subsequent history of the union, the subject of my forthcoming work.

1. In 1929, Alabama produced 6.2 percent of the nation's pig iron, 3.1 percent of its steel ingots, and 2.8 percent of its finished hot-rolled products. The state was the sixth-largest producer of these products. C. R. Daugherty, M. G. DeChazeau, and S. S. Stratton, *The Economics of the Iron and Steel Industry*, 2 vols. (New York: McGraw-Hill, 1937), 1:29.

2. "Minutes of Meeting of CIO Directors and Representatives of the South," June 14, 1942, p. 10, Box 1, File 10, District 36, United Steelworkers of America Papers, Historical Collections and Labor Archives, Pennsylvania State University (hereafter cited as Dist. 36).

3. Gavin Wright, *Old South, New South: Revolutions in the Southern Economy since the Civil War* (New York: Basic Books, 1986). Wright roots southern distinctiveness in regional labor markets that originated in plantation slavery and continued into mining and manufacturing. He offers a useful tool for understanding the development of the steel industry and union. Other frameworks are less useful. Because "segmented labor market" theory privileges sociological divisions and operates at a high level of abstraction, it cannot account for the success of unionization. By concentrating upon racial/ethnic divisions, the underlying economies of the North and South disappear. Work inspired by comparisons with other biracial work forces, notably those of South Africa, addresses southern distinctiveness. But it abstracts the South from the nation and abstracts black workers from the labor process by analyzing them simply in terms of power ("dominated") and status ("subordinate"). One of the leading theorists of this school, Stanley Greenberg, acknowledged that his work "requires a broader conceptual framework, one more sensitive to problems of proletarianization generally." Stanley Greenberg, *Race, and State in Capitalist Development* (New Haven, CT: Yale Univ. Press, 1980), esp. 399.

    Moreover, the literature inspired by this work slights the working-class experiences of whites. The three major pieces on Birmingham workers are devoted to blacks only: Paul B. Worthman, "Black Workers and Labor Unions in Birmingham, Alabama, 1897–1904" *Labor History*, 10 (Summer 1969), 375–407; Gary Kulick, "Black Workers and Technological Change in the Birmingham Iron Industry, 1881–1931," in *Southern Workers and Their Unions*, ed. Merl E. Reed, Leslie S. Hough, and Gary M. Fink (Westport, CT: Greenwood Press, 1981), 22–42; Robert J. Norrell, "Caste in Steel: Jim Crow Careers in Birmingham, Alabama," *Journal of American History*, 73 (Dec. 1986), 669–94.

    Norrell's article in particular applies Greenberg's model but ignores his warning. Demonstrating that the CIO was not as egalitarian in actuality as in its rhetoric is not a good starting point for studying labor or black history. It is equivalent to demonstrating that abolitionists did not hold current views on race. One can prove the proposition but one misses the major issue of the period, the ending of slavery. The method encourages an unfortunate conflation of discrimination, caste, Jim Crow, and apartheid, which are not synonymous terms.

    This essay begins with the question of how CIO ideology and organization contested with southern ideas and institutions. To understand racial issues in work and unions requires systematic examination of work structures, labor processes, corporate behavior, and union politics. Research in the papers of

District 35 and related material is essential for such matters. The different conclusions resulting from the above assumptions and the use of these critical sources appear throughout this paper.

4. This pattern was probably common in the North as well as the South and in other industries besides steel.

5. Albert Burton Moore, *History of Alabama* (1934; rpt. ed., Tuscaloosa: Univ of Alabama Press, 1951), 706.

6. Ethel Armes, *The Story of Coal and Iron in Alabama* (1910; rptd., NY: Arno Press, 1973), 407–10, 462.

7. H. H. Chapman et al., *The Iron and Steel Industries of the South* (University: Univ. of Alabama Press, 1953), 11–17; A. V. Wiebel, *Biography of a Business* (Tennessee, Coal & Iron Division, USS, 1960), 44–62.

8. Blaine A. Brownell, "Birmingham, Alabama: New South City in the 1920's," *Journal of Southern History*, 38 (Feb. 1972), 21–22.

9. Herman Taylor interview, "Working Lives," W. S. Hoole Special Collections Library, University of Alabama, Tuscaloosa.

10. In 1929, it took 2.72 man hours to produce a ton of pig iron in Birmingham, 1.38 in Chicago, 1.67 in Pittsburgh. Even with the South's low wages, wage costs were a larger percentage of the cost of production than in the North. Wages composed 8.07 percent of the costs of producing southern pig iron; the nation's average was 4.87 percent. Nevertheless, wages were insignificant factors in pig iron, although they composed 27.9 percent of the cost of making finished steel. Because regional wage differences were greatest in the pig-iron industry, they reflected the southern labor market more than the cost of production. Daugherty, DeChazeau, Stratton, *The Economics of the Iron and Steel Industry*, 1:387.

11. *The Economics of the Iron and Steel Industry*,1:374–86.

12. TCI obtained a continuous strip mill in 1938, later than the USS plants in the North. Gavin Wright's argument (*Old South, New South*, 172–77) that USS did not deliberately suppress southern steel development is persuasive. For the traditional view see George W. Stocking's *Base Point Pricing and Regional Development: A Case Study of the Iron and Steel Industry* (Chapel Hill: Univ of North Carolina Press, 1954). On the backwardness of the city's merchant iron producers, see Kulick, "Black Workers and Technological Change."

13. In 1930, 1.7 percent of the county's population was foreign-born, although the figure was higher at the beginning of the century. In 1941 only 5 percent of TCI's new employees were from areas beyond commuting distance; most of this group, moreover, was from Alabama. "Survey of Employment Situation in the Birmingham, Alabama Area," Oct. 9, 1941, pp. 12–13, Box 6, Records of the Bureau of Employment Security, RG 183, National Archives, Washington, DC.

14. "Birmingham Labor Market Survey," Sept. 1944, pp. 21–22, Box 1, RG 183.

15. George B. Tindall, *Emergence of the New South, 1913-1945* (Baton Rouge: Louisiana Univ. Press, 1967), 113–42; author's interviews, A. C. Burtramm,

July 7, 1988; James Swindle, July 15, 1988; R. B. Murphee, July 16, 1988; Howard Strevel, July 12, 1988; William E. Gilbert, "Bibb Graves as a Progressive, 1927–1930," *Alabama Review* 10 (Jan. 1957), 17–21.

16. E. Q. Hawk, "Defense Training for Negroes, Birmingham, Ala.," Jan. 27, 1942, Box 470, Records of the Fair Employment Practices Committee, RG 228, NA.

17. Wright (*Old South, New South*, 194–95) overstates the size of the black work force at TCI. From the very beginning, the racial hierarchy revealed company preferences. As more whites became available in the 1920s, they were hired. And Alabama was not a "black-majority" state. TCI was using the Alabama labor market, but it was whiter than Wright and others have assumed. The situations of 1890 and 1910 were not the same as 1920 and after. Similarly, although the entry wage in steel was uniform, it is unlikely that separate wage rates emerged only in the 1920s. The point is that market pressures to upgrade blacks were not as powerful as Wright assumes because of the abundant supply of black labor and growing numbers of whites.

18. Herod White and King Chandler interviews, "Working Lives."

19. Author's interview, William G. Phillips, July 25, 1989.

20. James D. Anderson, *The Education of Blacks in the South, 1860-1935* (Chapel Hill: Univ. of North Carolina Press, 1988) ch. 6, esp. 214. The role of education was more important in steel than Wright observed in textiles. *Old South, New South*, 196–97.

21. Harold Woodman, "Sequel to Slavery: The New History Views the Postbellum South," *Journal of Southern History* 43 (Nov. 1977), 549.

22. For the World War I union effort see Raymond Swing's "The Birmingham Case," July 5, 1918, a report done for the National War Labor Board. I would like to thank Joe McCartin for sending me a copy of this document.

23. Crawford led a brief and losing strike in 1927 when TCI changed the payment of the rollers from tonnage to day rates. He remained, but some of the northern rollers left TCI at that time. Author's interview, Earl Spence, July 9, 1988.

24. Thus as the machinists excluded blacks, the molders organized them, but in separate locals. See Herbert R. Northrup, *Organized Labor and the Negro* (New York: Harper and Row, 1944) for specific union policies.

25. The AFL's southern organizing drive in 1930 brushed Alabama's iron and steel industry. Although the main effort was in textiles, AA locals were created in Anniston at the Kilby Steel Co., the only steel union which achieved recognition during the NRA period, and at Gulf States Steel (later Republic) in Gadsden. Birmingham was untouched until the NRA period. Amalgamated, *Journal*, May 1, 1930.

26. The law in question was not the standard Jim Crow ordinance, but one forbidding interracial meetings. Crawford to ACLU, Dec. 22, 1933, Jan. 9, 1934, American Civil Liberties Union Papers, Seeley G. Mudd Library, Princeton University.

27. There is virtually nothing written about Mitch. The best place to begin is the Dist. 20 files of the UMW Papers, Alexandria, Va.

28. Beddow to Murray Dec. 22, 1936, 10/14, Dist. 36; W. L. Mitchell to Beddow, Aug. 20, Sept. 3, 1935, Box 29, Records of the National Recovery Administration, RG 9, NA, Atlanta, Ga.; author's interview with Mrs. Noel Beddow, Sept. 15, 1987.

At the time of his appointment Beddow was Mine, Mill's lawyer, involved in the negotiations and legal work of its 1936 strike. He had the support of Alabama's labor movement. Robert R. Moore to Mitch, June 19, 1936; A. E. Horn and C. L. Pegues to Mitch, June 19, 1936; W. O. Hare to Murray, June 19, 1936, 14/20, Dist. 36.

29. Mitch to Walter Smethurst, June 7, 1937, 14/20, Dist. 36.

30. Mitch to David J. McDonald, July 3, 1936, 9/32, Dist. 36.

31. C. L. Richardson to H. L. Kerwin, Aug. 21, 1933, 176/112, Records of the U.S. Mediation and Conciliation Service, RG 280, NA.

32. Black to W. Cooper Green, July 2, 1937, Box 79; Robert Wagner to Black, April 20, 1934, Box 165, Hugo L. Black Papers, Library of Congress. The liberal Alabama Policy Conference saw no role for unions in its "Industrial Planning for Alabama," April 2, 3, 1937, copy in 15/8, Dist. 36.

33. More, *History of Alabama*, 503.

34. "Payroll Analysis," Dec. 6, 1936–Jan. 5, 1937, 144/2, David J. McDonald Papers, Penn State.

35. Walter Smethurst, "Special Southern Report," Oct. 29, 1937, Alabama CIO file; Mitch, "Report of Southern Region of Steel Workers Organizing Committee for the C.I.O. Conference," Oct. 11, 1937, SWOC file, UMW Papers. Mitch to Smethurst, June 7, 1937, 2/30, Dist 36.

36. Beddow to D. F. Early, July 6, 1937, 5/16, Dist. 36.

37. Murray to Thomas Moses, June 2, 2939, 10/14; Beddow to Murray, Aug. 2, 1939, 19/16, Dist. 36.

38. Michael J. Hogan, *Economic History of the Iron and Steel Industry in the United States*, 3 vols. (Lexington, MA: Lexington Books, 1971), 3:138–45. The TCI expansion announced in 1936—enlarging steel capacity, modernizing the wire mill, and building a tin mill—was one result of the analysis.

39. Even before SWOC was recognized, USS had called all of its managers to Chicago in the winter of 1936–37 to discuss efficiency. Author's interview, Paul Bowron, July 15, 1989.

40. Beddow to McDonald, March 12, 1941, 19/McD, Dist. 36.

41. Beddow to Murray, May 11, 1937, 10/8; Beddow to Perry, June 15, 1937, 15/21, Dist. 36. Lee Pressman, "Memo to Corcoran and Cohen," July 14, 1938, SWOC Releases, UMW Papers; notes on meeting [SWOC local officers], n. d. [July 13, 1939], 19/21; McDonald to Beddow, Dec. 19, 1939, Beddow to Murray, May 29, 1939; Beddow to Pressman, Apr. 5, 1939, 15/McD, Dist. 36.

42. Ensley Cases, 1937–40, Sub-district office, Dist. 36, United Steel Workers

of America, Fairfield, AL. (Hereafter cited as Sub-district office.)
43. Beddow, report, Sept. 1937, 10/8, Sub-district office.
44. USS had wanted to cut the wages of hourly workers by 10 percent. Edward Stettinius, Jr., to Myron Taylor, July 6, 1938, Box 36, Edward Reilly Stettinius, Jr., Papers, Alderman Library, University of Virginia.
45. Beddow to McDonald, Dec. 31, 1940 19/McD, Dist. 36.
46. Beddow to Harold Ruttenberg, Feb. 26, 1940; Ruttenberg to Beddow, April 3, 1940; Clinton Golden to Beddow, June 10, Sept. 9, 1940; Beddow to John A. Stephens, April 4, 1940; Stephens to Beddow, Sept. 5, 1940; McDonald to Beddow, Sept. 5, 1940; Beddow to Pressman, May 10, 1939; Pressman to Beddow, May 8, 1939, 15/1, Dist. 3.
47. Grievance 152–604, step 3, Jan. 13, 1947, LU 1131 files, Sub-district office; Spence interview.
48. The impact of the hot strip mill was, of course, not limited to the South. In 1938 Murray reported that 500 workers in Republic's sheet mill in Masillon, Ohio, and 450 more in Niles, Ohio, were put out of work as a result of the new mills, a phenomenon that should be considered in understanding the difficulties of SWOC at Republic. Indeed, it may be a broader factor in explaining organizing problems in general, as it was at TCI. While the reduction of the workweek in steel from 48 to 40 hours led to the employment of 58,690 more workers, the number of wage earners from 1937 to 1939 declined from 503,000 to 415,000. Compared to August 1936, there were 30,000 fewer steel workers. SWOC viewed technological unemployment as its major problem and devised some imaginative solutions for it. The defense boom and war ended the unemployment and thus reformed the union's priorities. See Harold Ruttenberg, "85,000 Victims of Progress," Feb. 16, 1938, 1/5, Harold Ruttenberg Papers, Penn State.
49. The mill made plates and shapes for the Pullman-Standard plant. Author's interview, Harold Strevel, July 12, 1988.
50. "Statement by Ed Hosey," May 8, 1941; affidavit, May 17, 1941, 17/21, Dist. 36.
51. Grievance committee meetings, May 15, 19, 1941, 17/21; Beddow to Walter J. Kelly, Nov. 13, 1941, 16/1, Dist. 36.
52. Beddow to McDonald, Sept. 16, 1941, 16/1, Dist. 36.
53. W. Cooper Green to Hugo Black, June 16, 1937, Box 79, Black Papers, LC.
54. Locally, the personnel director of Pullman-Standard, who also was president of the Bessemer City Council, encouraged the electricians and machinists, leading to the NLRB certification of separate elections for the two crafts, which won in October, 1941. SWOC was victorious among the remainder of the workers. Beddow to Pressman, Sept. 14, 1941, 12/12, Dist. 36; V. C. Finch to J. R. Steelman, Jan. 15, 1942, 196–8934, U.S. Conciliation Service, RG 280.
55. Concerned about maintaining defense production and sensitive to AFL power, the National Defense Mediation Board in 1941 recognized the International Brotherhood of Electrical Workers' (IBEW) claims to represent

electrical workers at TCI and recommended an incentive. Mitch feared that the Labor Department was backing the AFL determination "to tear up CIO unions in steel." He also blamed Sidney Hillman. Mitch to Murray, Aug. 18, 1941. Mitch expressed his outrage to Lee Pressman, Emil Rieve, Frances Perkins, and McDonald on Aug. 30, 92/11, McDonald Papers; Mitch to Lewis, Oct. 9, 1941, Dist. 20, UMW Papers.

56. Leaflet, "To TCI Employees," 15/6, Dist 36.
57. Mitch to McDonald April 6, 1942, 16/17, McDonald Papers; Beddow to Murray, Mar. 30, 1942, 15/9, Dist. 36. TCI pursued the same policy in its coal mines. Mitch believed that TCI's encouragement of an AFL group composed of most of the whites was an attempt to divide the union on racial lines. Mitch to Lewis and Murray, Feb. 8, 1941, Dist. 20, UMW Papers. In 1942 the Alabama Department of Industrial Relations unsuccessfully tried to convince Beddow to agree to an AFL local for whites and CIO for blacks in the refurbished TCI plant at Holt, near Tuscaloosa. M. C. Hughes to William Ivey, Dec. 11, 1942, 16/1, Dist. 36.
58. Author's interview, Robert C. Lynn, July 9, 1988. John Altman, formerly general counsel for the Alabama State Federation of Labor, openly appealed to white supremacy to attack William Mitch and the CIO. Birmingham's business community claimed that the AFL expelled the CIO because the new organization was dominated by Communists. *Alabama News Digest*, May 21, 1936, Nov. 24, 1938.
59. Henry Holston interview, "Working Lives."
60. See July 19, 1941, petition, Box 16/1, Dist 36; George Baker and all TCI local presidents to Beddow, Aug. 14, 1941, TCI. McDonald responded that "we must be absolutely certain that we can win such an election. . . . Anything short of complete victory would be a total disgrace." Sept. 9, 1941, 2/18, Dist. 36.
61. W. C. Agee to Dixon, Sept. 29, 1941; Mitch and Beddow to Dixon, Sept. 28, 1941, Gov. Frank Dixon Papers, Alabama State Archives. Dixon brought in the Home Guard "to prevent bloodshed and preserve order." Although there was no sign of disorder, General Smith conferred with TCI officials before he gave the order that only three pickets were allowed at each gate. The next day all the locals voted to strike unless the military was removed. Because the CIO lacked confidence in Dixon's state labor conciliator, the U.S. Conciliation Service negotiated the withdrawal of the troops and convinced the company to begin grievance negotiations the next day.
62. Yet the union vote was only 10,611 (57 percent) out of an eligible 18,527. Other USS plants were higher: Carnegie-Illinois, 72 percent, American Steel and Wire, 75 percent. Yet the newer plants, like Geneva Steel, in 1944, had only 55 percent. Farr to McDonald, May 10, 1943, 8/35, Dist. 36.
63. Beddow to McDonald, April 19, 1943, 18/Beddow, McDonald Papers.
64. H. Tinney to R. E. Farr, May 3, 1943; minutes, Local 1700, May 4, 1943, Sub-district Office.
65. The FEPC ignored Birmingham because in 1942 the city did not contain new

industries requiring the employment of large numbers of new men, one FEPC criterion. The city obtained two new plants in 1943, after the hearings, when the $5 million expansion of steel-making facilities at TCI was completed. "Alabama Labor Market Survey," May 26, Oct. 15, 1942, Box 6, Records of the Bureau of Labor Statistics, RG 183; John Beecher to George Johnson, April 15, 1942; Lawrence Cramer to Johnson, June 1, 1942, file Birm., Ala., Box 370, Records of the Fair Employment Practices Committee, RG 228.

66. *Alabama News Digest*, April 16, 1942.
67. Dixon to J. F. Brawner, Aug. 31, 1942, Gov. Frank Dixon Papers, drawer 162, Ala. State Archives; Oliver T. McDuff, "Report on Racial Conditions," Sept. 8, 1942, 15–782, Records of the War Manpower Division, RG 211; "Threats of National Unity in the South," copy in file Birm-Bess, Labor Unions, 1942, Box 345, NAACP Papers.
68. At Fairfield Steel, black truck drivers were paid 55 cents per hour to whites' 66.5. Although TCI claimed that one of the blacks was nearly blind and the other illiterate, the union insisted that if the company put the men on the job, the implication was that they were doing it. Beddow to TCI locals, May 10, 1941, 8/18, Dist. 36. The principle behind such discrimination was consistently espoused by business representatives on the NWLB in Atlanta. See Harold McDermott to Reuben B. Robertson, June 19, 1943, Box 2806, Ser. 412, Records of the National War Labor Board, RG 202, Atlanta.
69. Herbert Hill, "Confidential Memorandum to Walter White," May 8–17, 1953, copy in A4–105, Philip Murray Papers, Catholic University of America.
70. See Charles S. Johnson, *Patterns of Negro Segregation* (New York: Harper and Brothers, 1943).
71. Grievance 152–275, Step 4, May 5, 1943, Sub-district office; John W. Brown to Murray, Aug. 26, 1945, 4/13, Dist. 36.
72. "Minutes of Plant Management with Gr. Comm. 1013 and 1587," Nov. 9, 1943, 16/16, Dist. 36.
73. Author's interview, Marion Martin, July 23, 1989.
74. Author's interview, Charles Wilson, July 13, 1989.
75. Chester Ray to Beddow, Aug. 12, 1941, 15/1, Dist. 36.
76. Claude Adams to Murray, Aug. 8, 1943, Murray Papers.
77. J. T. Ward et al. to Murray Aug. 8, 1943, A-2, Murray Papers.
78. The local had been dominated by the company union. After its charter was removed in 1937, remaining members were part of the open hearth local until Local 1700 was reborn in 1940. James Blair to Vincent Sweeney, April 1, 1941; minutes, June 17, 1941, Minute Books, Local 1700, Sub-district Office.
79. Rev. H. W. Daniel to Philip Murry [sic], Sept. 1946, 20/17. Dist. 36.
80. Kenneth Armstrong et al. to Murray, July 25, 1946; Murray to Farr, Aug. 8, 1946; Farr to Murray, Aug. 30, 1946; Murray to Miles T. Otwell, Aug. 15,

1946; Farr to Murray, Sept. 19, 1946, 20/17, Dist. 36; author's interview, William G. Phillips, July 25, 1989.

81. Author's interview, Virgil Pearson, July 15, 1988.

82. Charles Roestridge to Murray, June 1, 1950, A-78, Murray Papers.

83. Phillips interview.

84. Grievance 154–190, Sept. 3, Mar. 20, 1946; Gr. 154–234, Jan. 10, 1949, Sub-district Office.

85. Thus TCI's rules "recognized that certain positions involve special knowledge, training, and abilities and Management may, where necessity arises and where qualified personnel within the bargaining unit is not available, introduce specially qualified personnel, or promote, or retain with due regard to potential ability of employees." This paragraph gave the company nearly full freedom. TCI, "Seniority practices and procedures, 1939" 17/3, Dist. 36.

86. Grievance 151–1160, Step 4, Aug. 25, 1953.

87. Frank Donner to Stephens, June 18, 1945, 12/9, Dist. 36. Corporate policy was not uniform on the race issue in the South. The most cooperative companies were the southern affiliates of northern corporations who had sympathetic national executives. Thus, International Harvester was relatively progressive; Standard Oil was not. TCI did not fit the model at all. It was not a creation of a national corporation and USS executives were not sympathetic. See Minutes, CIO Committee to Abolish Racial Discrimination, Oct. 5, 1954, 109–10, James B. Carey Papers, Archives of Labor and Urban Affairs, Wayne State University, Detroit, Mich.

88. Farr to Murray, Nov. 20, 1943, 10/16; Beddow to Farr, nd [1943], 5/10; McDonald to Farr, March 14, 1944, 35/8, Dist. 36.

89. They frequently sought help from the union's new Birmingham lawyer, Jerome Cooper, also lawyer for Operation Dixie. Author's interview, Jerome Cooper, July 13, 1988; Jimmie Lee Williams interview.

90. Bowron interview.

91. David H. Kelly, "Labor Relations in the Steel Industry: Management, Ideas, Proposals, and Programs, 1920–1950" (Ph.D. diss., Indiana University, 1976), 246.

92. For a discussion of the inequities program see Jack Stieber, *The Steel Industry Wage Structure* (Cambridge, MA: Harvard Univ. Press, 1959).

93. "Before the National Wage Stabilization Board," NSC–44, 1 May 1946, A4-37, Murray Papers. The NWLB had approved lower rates for Atlantic Steel in Atlanta, and the Hold furnace of TCI, near Tuscaloosa. TCI also resisted NWLB directives. Although it checked off members' dues, according to the NWLB directive, TCI eliminated members without informing the union or explaining its reasons. Every other USS company transmitted names to the union and discussed removals. TCI claimed that it was not the union's "bookkeeper." It took an appeal to the board to win compliance. TCI and USA, Aug. 10, 1945; Farr to Pressman, Aug. 21, 1945, 10/11, Dist. 36.

94. Murray to Elmer F. Maloy, April 2, 1945, 18/9, Dist. 36.

95. Maloy, Steve Levitsky, Ben Fischer to Murray, April 12, 1950, A4-19, Murray Papers; minutes, SWOC-TCI, April 30, 1945, 7/15, Dist. 36.

96. Frank Fernbach and Ben Fischer, "Report on Wage Inequity Negotiations at TCI," Sept. 15, 1945; Fernbach and Fischer to Murray, Sept. 18, 1945; Alvin M. Mosley to Murray, Oct. 16, 1945, A4-19, Murray Papers; minutes of the International Executive Board (IEB), Sept. 11, 1945, Penn State; Lynn interview.

97. LU 1489, 2421, 2405, 1131, 2122, 1700, 2405, 1013 to Murray, Feb. 13, 14, 1947, A4–43, Murray Papers.

98. Author's interview, A. C. Burtramm, July 7, 1988.

99. Lynn interview.

100. Pressman to Murray, March 4, 1947, A4–43, Murray Papers.

101. Memorandum, March 6, 1947, 58/Inequities, 1943–48, McDonald Papers.

102. Murray, "Confidential Memorandum," March 7, 1947, A4–35, Murray Papers.

103. Meeting, March 10, 1947; Marion Martin to Murray, July 1, 1951, A4–102, Murray Papers.

104. Goodwin had been a member of the electricians' union despite the fact that his father was an original member of SWOC at the Fairfield blast furnace. Williams interview; author's interview, Iva Watts Goodwin, July 12, 1988.

105. Swindle interview; Local 1013 minutes, Feb. 5, 1951, Local 1013 office, Fairfield, Ala.

106. Maloy to Conrad Cooper, March 27, 1952, 155/11; "Resolution on the Wage Rate Inequity Program," April 12, 1951; McDonald to F. W Huey et al. April 25, 1951; "Memorandum of Understanding," April 26, 1951, 147/13, McDonald Papers.

107. Beddow to Murray, May 23, 1949, July 7, 1949; Murray to Beddow, July 18, 1949, A-78, Murray Papers.

108. Thimmes to Murray, Apr. 19, 1951, A4–87, Murray Papers.

109. Swindle interview. Farr had been challenged for the presidency of the district in 1946 by Tom Howard. Of the same generation as Farr, he was less intimidated. Although some protested electoral procedures, Howard was not well enough known outside the wire mill to overcome the power of incumbency. Knobloch et al. to Murray, Dec. 4, 1946, A-78, Murray Papers; Lynn interview.

110. Robert Washington interview, "Working Lives."

111. LU 1013 minutes, May 21, 1951; Strevel interview. While Strevel grew up in an area with different race relations, simply experiencing different race relations was very effective with white Southerners. An organizer reported that a white local president's attendance at the steelworkers' convention "helped him lots especialy [sic] on the race situation . . ." and took "lots of that foolishness out of him." Although blacks, of course, were more sensitive to the injustices of segregation, many believed that it was part of a given, if not natural, order. Jess Gross, when asked about Jim Crow cars

said, "When you get used to a thing, . . . it don't go so hard with you." William Dunn to Beddow, May 16, 1943, 5/file Dunn, Dist. 36. Jess Gross interview, "Working Lives."

112. Strevel became district president in 1965 when Farr retired.

113. Jimmie Lee Williams interview.

114. Author's telephone interview, J. F. Williams, Jan. 30, 1989. J. P. Worthy to Maloy, Sept. 15, 1948, LU 2405, Sub-district Office.

115. Gr. 153–627, Nov. 6, 1946, Sub-district Office.

116. Jimmie Lee Williams interview.

117. Archie Jennings, grievance committeeman of the shipping department in the wire mill, tried to rally support against the strike. He failed and he was removed from his union position and from all others for a year. "Appeal of Archie Jennings," March 11, 1953, 100–103, IEB Papers, Penn State.

118. A. V. Weibel to Murray, Nov. 6, 1951; Murray to Weibel, Nov. 7, 1951, A4–78, Murray Papers. Evidently, McDonald had agreed to a compromise involving suspensions. Murray intervened and demanded exoneration. J. F. Williams interview.

119. Strevel, J. F. Williams interviews. Many blacks and whites feared that if they integrated the picket lines, Commissioner Eugene "Bull" Connor would break up the line. The fear was not fanciful because Connor had arrested a black and a white playing checkers on a picket line. Cooper interview.

120. Clipping, n.d. [1951], Farr file, Correspondence of Vice-President James Thimmes, microfilm roll 859, Penn State.

121. Bull Connor to Farr, Nov. 23, 1951, Dist. 36 office, Birmingham, Ala.

122. J. F. Williams interview.

123. Jimmie Lee Williams observed men doubled up in cramps and taking salt pills. Williams, subsequently a union staffman, helped integrate the lines of promotion in the coke plant and organized fearful fertilizer workers in the Mississippi Delta. But he believed the improvement of the working conditions in the coke plant was his most important accomplishment. Williams interview.

124. Jimmie Lee Williams, who had not been active in the coke strike, became its first black officer in 1953. J. F. Williams interview.

125. Farr, however, supported this strike. When a policeman menaced a striker with a gun, Farr, a big man with a soft manner, simply told him, "Sir, if I were you, I would put that gun down." He did. J. F. Williams interview.

126. Author's interview, Bruce Thrasher, July 10, 1989.

127. Gr. 152–604, Step 3, Jan. 13, 1947, Sub-district office.

128. Strevel, Cooper, J. L. Williams interviews. The merging of lines of promotion took place in 1962 and 1963. Seniority was placed on a plantwide basis in the Consent Decree of 1973, motivated by the effort to remedy the victims of past discrimination, that is, those hired before 1964 when TCI ended its assignments on the basis of race. This potentially divisive issue

was defused because the new rules applied to black and white workers and the group with temporary special rights was clearly defined and clearly victims of discrimination: the pre–1964 hirees.

129. Lee Pressman observed that Golden never understood why a company did not want a union. Golden and his assistant Joseph Scanlon left the USW in 1946 to teach, advise, and implement their notion of cooperation. The problem with their ideas, embodied in the Scanlon plan, was that they did not fit the industry they worked in. Some small companies were attracted to the idea, but the major corporations were bent on retaining and expanding managerial prerogatives. During the war, Murray had attempted cooperation but was rebuffed by the government and industry. "Reminiscences of Lee Pressman," 137, Oral History Project, Columbia University, New York; Clinton S. Golden and Harold J. Ruttenberg, *The Dynamics of Industrial Democracy* (New York, 1942). See Clinton S. Golden Papers at Penn State on the Scanlon plan.

130. "Conflict of Philosophies," n.d., [1956], Records of the Woodward Iron Company, Birmingham Public Library, Birmingham, AL.

131. "Memorandum of Meeting . . . " May 5, 1947, Dist. 36 office, Birm., Ala. No one interviewed, black or white, recalled any discussion of the subject.

132. "Agreement between Tennessee Coal & Iron . . . and United Steelworkers of America CIO," 1947, Fairfield, Ala., Sub-district office.

133. Swindle interview.

9. Southern Industrial Workers and Anti-Union Sentiment

Arkansas and Florida in 1944

Gilbert J. Gall

Southern industrial workers have often been portrayed as either indifferent or hostile toward unionization. Commentators have variously pictured this category of the southern working class as either wholehearted adherents of the economic individualism expressed by the business elites of their communities, or as workers who at times could show impressive labor militancy but lacked an understanding of union building. In the 1940s, though, contrary to the impressions of some union organizers and social observers, southern industrial workers—at least in Arkansas and Florida—were no less union-minded than their non-southern counterparts. In 1944 both those states, as well as California, held statewide referendums on right-to-work proposals. Though the measures passed in the South, it was not because of an anti-union industrial working-class vote. Using the three right-to-work votes as an index of union sentiment, a statistical analysis of county-level voting patterns demonstrates that southern workers in the industrial sector were no more "anti-union" than similarly situated workers in California.[1]

In December 1944, AFL president William Green received an informational copy of a letter sent to the Bakery and Confectionery Workers' international union from Wesley High, a member then in the armed forces. "As you have most likely forgotten who I am," wrote High to one of his union's top officers, "I will just tell you I am the little short guy who was business agent for Local #442, Little Rock, Ark. . . . now trying to do my bit for Uncle Sam." His friends in the local had written that the state's recent passage of a right-to-work law prohibiting union membership as a condition of employment had already prompted the Colonial Baking Company to inform new employees "that they had better not join [the] local" and that they did not have to attend union meetings. The business agent asked his union's officers to render whatever aid they could to the local in his absence. "When we guys get back we will know how to deal with such rats, but until then, we will have to leave everything on your shoulders," he wrote. Moreover, he thought, in addition to fighting the new law all the way to the Supreme Court, organized labor should take up this amendment "with every local in the country, to let them see how the people from Arkansas have been put back into slavery." "Please don't let our local down," High wrote in conclusion, "we guys want something to come back to—we don't want to be slaves of a few big business men."[2]

While the business agent's sentiments succinctly described the reaction of most *union leaders* to state legislation restricting union security arrangements in labor agreements, exactly how representative High's pro-union feelings were, at that time, in relation to *southern industrial workers* generally, has been much more problematical. Indeed, arriving at a satisfactory answer about the overall receptivity of southern workers themselves toward unionization, both during and after World War II, is critical to any assessment of the quality of modern union leadership. Southern industry was a post–World War II organizing target of both the AFL and the CIO. Each of the federations' campaigns failed, however. The seeming inability of unions in the South to establish themselves as economically powerful interests resulted in a sharp ghettoization of labor in the region. This hampered union efforts to act as broad "liberalizing" political influences, as had been done in so many areas in the North after the successful organizing victories of the 1930s. Consequently, conservative southern politicians were thus easily able to maintain their power bases in both state and national political arenas.

Largely as a result of these developments, conservative southern Democrats with long tenure in Congress, in combination with Republicans, repeatedly frustrated labor's efforts to reform the nation's labor policy in a pro-union direction subsequent to the passage of the Taft-Hartley Act in 1947. Having been beaten in those legislative engagements, labor leaders eventually came to experience national labor policy, especially when interpreted by "unfriendly" political appointees, as not only hamstringing their efforts to organize the unorganized, but also as severely restricting their use of self-help measures in collective bargaining. In this way, labor relations law came to hinder the expansion of union power even outside the South. The debate on the responsibility of union leaders in the erosion of labor's power and influence in the post–World War II years remains sharp and unresolved.[3]

Because the potential organization of the South was so crucial to labor leaders' national postwar hopes in politics, uncovering the sentiments of southern workers toward unionization looms as a historical investigation of significance. If southern workers were somehow more "immune" to pro-union sentiment than non-southern workers, as one line of argument suggests, then there was little that top officials in the CIO or AFL could have done to effect mass organizing and subsequent political mobilization. The unfortunate results for the labor movement could then not fairly be laid on the shoulders of union chieftains. On the other hand—despite the intense hostile response of the South's power elite toward unions—if there was significant pro-union sentiment in the southern industrial working class, of if southern sentiment was not remarkably different from that of non-southern workers, then the ultimate failure of both federations' organizing efforts might be seen as more "tragic." That is, union leaders might be viewed as being at least partially culpable for the defeats, either by virtue of a refusal to commit adequate organizational resources to the task, by falling prey to rampant anti-communist ideological factionalism, or by virtue of incompetence and lethargy.

In trying to come to terms with this larger question about working-class attitudes toward unionism in the South, it is useful to broaden the historical investigation by examining quantitative evidence of such attitudes during this critical period.[4] When Arkansas and Florida both passed the country's first right-to-work laws by statewide referendums in November 1944, they unintentionally provided historians with a way to make at least an initial comparative assessment based upon fairly broad data. The essential element of the model under investigation is the contention that pro-union consciousness among industrial workers was less intense in the South than in other parts of the country. The hypothesis to be tested is that the voting behavior of industrial workers on a union-related measure in Florida and Arkansas was different from the same categories of workers in California because workers in the former states had regionally based anti-union sentiments. Specifically, if the "percent-no" vote at the county level can be accurately termed an index of pro-union sentiment in 1944, and the percentage of industrial working-class occupational distributions at the county level can be accurately termed an indicator of self-conscious working-class membership, then a comparison of the relationship between these two variables, as descriptively revealed by a bivariate regression analysis of different categories of industrial workers, should reflect the degree of pro-union sentiment of the industrial working class in a given county.[5]

Thus, if the percent-no vote on right-to-work tends to rise as the percentage of industrial working-class occupations in a county rises, this will support the contention that there is a positive relationship between the two variables, and that the nature of that positive relationship to some degree reflects the aggregate "union-mindedness" or union sympathies of that county's industrial working class. Conversely, a negative relationship or no relationship at all between the two variables can serve as an indicator that the industrial working class is either opposed to, or indifferent to, unionization. Finally, a comparison of regression analysis results in the southern states of Arkansas and Florida with the results in the non-southern state of California, will yield generalizations about the similarities and/or differences in pro-union sentiment between southern and non-southern industrial workers in 1944. If, for example, the strength of a positive linear relationship between the two variables in California is markedly stronger than in either Arkansas or Florida, it tends to support the idea that southern industrial workers were perhaps culturally unsympathetic toward unions. On the other hand, if the regression relationship is at least relatively equivalent between California and Arkansas/Florida, or if one southern state had a stronger pro-union association than California, then empirical evidence exists to argue against the idea that there was an inherent "anti-union" belief system among southern industrial workers, although of course such evidence should be analyzed with caution.[6] Before proceeding further with the quantitative analysis, however, it is helpful to outline the economic and political climates in which the elections occurred.

Wartime Economies

All three of the 1944 state right-to-work referendums were fought in the context of vast changes to each state's economy wrought by wartime production. Though defense-related spending in California dwarfed the funds that poured into Arkansas and Florida, in relative terms, the latter two states perhaps experienced the greater amount of social change stemming from the investment. Overall, about 20 percent of the $20 billion in federal war-related spending ended up in the South. While neither Arkansas or Florida led as recipients in the southern states, each did obtain its share of monies for the construction of military and shipbuilding installations, as well as ordnance and munitions plants.[7]

In this respect, the war brought fundamental changes to southern industry and society. Prior to 1940, the region's industries were largely concentrated in four areas: textiles, lumber, furniture, and tobacco, with some oil refining in the Southwest. Starting in 1940, the mix changed as most of the federal investment found its way into durable goods like transportation equipment (jeeps, trucks, tanks, ships, aircraft). Aluminum and synthetic rubber plants sprang up in Pine Bluff and Eldorado, Arkansas, for instance, while the shipbuilding facilities at Jacksonville, Miami, Tampa, and Panama City, Florida, worked at a feverish pace. By 1944, Florida manufacturing alone employed approximately 135,000 workers, according to the U.S. Bureau of Labor Statistics, and Arkansas had 77,000 people on its manufacturing payrolls. Growth in the new areas was not at the expense of the older industries, though; textile and tobacco production reached record levels at the same time.

Although the production of durables declined sharply at the war's end, the initial investment for them either produced or quickened social and demographic changes. Foremost among those effects was labor migration, both internal and external. Here, Florida and Arkansas differed. From 1940 to 1945, Florida experienced a rapid in-migration of 219,000 people, while Arkansas lost, through out-migration, 265,000 citizens to the North and West. Both patterns followed prewar tendencies, but were greatly accelerated. Perhaps even more importantly, wartime production spending stimulated rural-to-urban population shifts in both states.[8]

Operating in this context, the union movements of each state, largely consisting of AFL affiliates, the railroad brotherhoods, and a few CIO adherents, found themselves in an advantageous situation. Many wartime production agreements were negotiated on a regional basis, and unions participated as interested parties. Union security agreements such as the closed shop, particularly in the building trades, often became part and parcel of wartime labor relations in the South.[9] And most likely, it was the specter of facing a strong and reinvigorated union movement at the end of the war—one that could reach into the traditional southern manufacturing areas and maybe even into agriculturally related processing and low-wage extractive industries—that provided the impetus for the drive for right-to-work legislation in 1944.

The 1944 Right-to-Work Elections

Arkansas first began to feel the pressure for restrictive labor legislation from a coalition of businessmen and large landowners calling themselves the Arkansas Free Enterprise Association. Politically, Arkansas was a one-party Democratic state, as were other areas of the South. But unlike some other states, Razorback politics was excessively factional. Over the course of its history, no dominant political machine had emerged to dominate the entire state, perhaps because of the quite different regional characteristics of the northern Ozark region and the eastern Mississippi Delta cotton areas. Moreover, corruption plagued its atomized politics; the purchase of votes by competing politicians was a common occurrence in Arkansas elections. Thus on the national level, the state and its citizens were subject to periodic derision for backwardness. War industries, however, threatened to change the social landscape. As elsewhere, they caused great labor shortages, many times to labor's advantage. For example, at their peak, defense construction projects from 1940–1945 employed over 27,000 people. Military installations and other war-related industries were scattered across the state, stimulating the production of aluminum, chemicals, paper/pulp, and petroleum, which then and afterwards became important additions to the Arkansas economy and became attractive targets for unionization.

Nevertheless, most fearsome to Arkansas business and agribusiness interests were the public threats of CIO organizers to begin a campaign among the state's poverty-stricken tenant farmers in the east, many of whom were black. Even AFL organizers had become interested in trying to organize Arkansas's burgeoning lumber industry camps, another haven of low-wage workers. In combination, the state's landowners in the delta areas and Little Rock business interests agitated for passage of an anti-union violence law in the 1943 session of the legislature. In the debates over that measure, labor opponents excoriated the supposedly radical and racially egalitarian CIO. Though Arkansas politicians' rhetoric toward the AFL was less heated, even the older federation eventually found itself under assault when an initiative petition to restrict union security, successfully circulated by the Arkansas Free Enterprise Association, found its way onto the state general election ballot in 1944.[10]

Agricultural business interests had good reason for concern because despite the war production, Arkansas was still far and away the most agricultural of the three states in terms of workers engaged in certain types of occupations. According to the 1940 U.S. Census, 32.8 percent (191,607) of the Arkansas labor force consisted of farm owners, and 10.6 percent (62,020) were paid farm laborers. Correspondingly, its nonagricultural working class (both industrial and nonindustrial) was smaller: about 20.3 percent (118,585) of the labor force was involved in industrially related production and 17.2 percent (100,056) nonindustrial. Middle-class occupations just barely outstripped the category of paid farm laborers with 10.9 percent (63,856). Predictably, the number of workers belonging to the unions was substantially smaller than the number of laborers that made up the industrial working class. In 1939 the Razorback state had an estimated total of 25,000 union members (14,600 in AFL-affiliated unions, 5,400 in CIO organizations, and 5,000 in unaffiliated or railroad organizations). By 1944, though, union membership had grown to embrace approximately 43,000 workers, who constituted about 17 percent of the labor force.[11]

The Arkansas State Federation of Labor and CIO unions fought the electoral initiative as best they could. Prior to the vote, political observers remarked not long afterward, the referendum "was a storm center of state politics . . ." and attracted widespread publicity. Even the governor of the state, Ben Laney, was circumspect in deciding whether to endorse the anti-labor position. "We have started advertisements once a week in all of the 28 daily papers in the state, 7 sunday [*sic*] dailies and 128 weeklies," wrote Arkansas AFL functionary E. H. Williams to William Green on October 19, 1944. "We have arranged several radio broadcasts and have outlined and publicised [*sic*] mass meetings to be held in all of the principal cities of the state beginning today and continuing to the election date," he also informed the AFL president.[12]

Table 1. Arkansas, Florida, California Right-to-Work Elections, 1944

State	Yes RTW	No RTW	Total	% Ratio	Y/N County Ratio
Arkansas	105,300	87,652	192,942	55/45	52/23
Florida	147,860	122,770	270,630	55/45	57/10
California	1,304,430	1,893,630	3,198,060	41/59	21/37

Source: Gall, *The Politics of Right to Work*, Tables 2.1 and 2.6

Despite these efforts, the voters of Arkansas passed the union secu-rity restriction in November 1944, as indicated in Table 1. The break-down in the right-to-work victory ended up at a 55 percent to 45 percent yes/no spilt; in absolute terms, 105,300 citizens agreed with the proposal, while 87,652 did not, a difference of 17,648. The com-bined vote totaled approximately 91 percent of all votes cast for the highest office (president of the United States) on the ballot in the election. In geographic terms, 52 counties had a majority of votes in the "yes" column while 23 favored prohibiting the measure; however, 25 of the 75 counties were in the marginal range (between 45 and 55 percent, in either direction). Unsurprisingly, the counties of the state that had been most affected by wartime production seemed to be the ones most against the anti-union measure. A group of lower-north-western counties were clearly against the right to work: Crawford, Sebastian, Madison, Franklin, Johnson, Logan, Scott, and Yell—sur-rounding and contiguous to Fort Smith (where Camp Chafee, the main campus of the University of Arkansas, and much aluminum production were located). While Pulaski and Faulkner counties in the Little Rock area in the center of the state were less strongly against it, the counties in the industrial corridor from there directly southwest toward Hot Springs (Saline and Garland), and the counties to the southeast in the direction of Pine Bluff (Jefferson, Desha, and Cleveland), which had numerous war industries, formed another anti-right-to-work bloc. Fi-nally, several counties in southern Arkansas that had benefited from defense production (Ouachita, Dallas, Bradley, and Ashley, among others) provided an additional base of support to the labor move-ment.[13]

Though Florida unionists faced the most serious challenge to their union security practices in 1944, the issue had been percolating in state

No. of Marginal Counties	% of Vote for Highest Office in Election	Approximate Union Membership, 1944	
25	91	43,386	17.1%
10	56	83,000	13.8%
24	86	796,893	29.2%

politics for several years. The state had a much more diversified economy than was common in the South, with lumbering, citrus growing, phosphate mining, tobacco farming, fishing, cattle raising, and tourism all being important. In politics, Florida was similar to Arkansas in some ways. Though still a solidly Democratic state, it had more of a Republican presence. As in its sister southern state, factionalism dominated Florida politics and no one group could put together an effective statewide political machine. In this, the state's far-flung geography had a profound impact; the distance between the northern and southern urban areas was imposing and hampered effective political coalition building. Moreover, the distinct character of each region amplified the problems. South Florida emphasized the economics of tourism and was somewhat more cosmopolitan, the central portion of the state concentrated on large-scale agricultural production, and the northern tier was very similar to the Deep South in its economy as well as its social composition and attitudes. It was quickly apparent that the labor relations climate fostered by war industries had stimulated indigenous industrial and agricultural forces to launch an anti-union security attack.

In 1941, not long after his election as the state's attorney general, conservative Democrat J. Tom Watson, surprised a state AFL convention during a speech by denouncing closed-shop practices, to the very vocal displeasure of the assembled delegates. In subsequent legislative efforts to undercut union security clauses, Watson cited the union security arrangements during the building of the cantonment at Camp Blanding as being anathema to democracy. The legislative debates surrounding this first attempt, defeated in committee, castigated the CIO as a *bête noir*. In these denunciations, even AFL partisans took part in the red-baiting. An AFL attorney, for example, asked the legislators to make qualitative distinctions between the "good" and "American" AFL form of unionism and "these communists and vultures of the CIO who are causing trouble." In addition, a state representative voted against the bill, he claimed, because getting rid of the closed shop would "open the door to the CIO to come into Florida and create discord and unrest as it has in other states."[14]

Watson continued his crusade into 1942 and 1943. In alliance with the Associated Industries of Florida, a National Association of Manufacturers affiliate, he first attempted to challenge legally the constitutionality of the union security clauses attached to several of the AFL metal trades' working agreements with the Tampa Shipbuilding Company. After the national AFL's general counsel, Joseph Padway, defeated this court suit, the attorney general altered his tack and assisted in lobbying a state right-to-work constitutional amendment through the legislature in 1943. The submission of the question to the voters for the 1944 general election had the backing of a wide range of Florida business and agribusiness interests. After the resolution passed the legislature, disgusted state AFL president Leo Hill, a Jacksonville plumber, predicted "a long period of unrest and upheaval in Florida" if voters passed the proposal. "Naturally, it will mean the end of conservative [union] leadership, for an outraged labor population will turn to a leadership of a more radical nature. Radicalism always begets radicalism," he warned.[15]

Florida labor, which for all intents and purposes consisted of AFL affiliates and the railroad brotherhoods, set about to face its opponents. Since it was a larger and more populous state, Florida had more union members than Arkansas in absolute terms, though less in terms of percent of labor force organized. In 1939 the state movement consisted of 39,500 workers in AFL unions, 1,100 in CIO locals, and 3,000 in independent units. By 1944, membership had risen considerably because of war production. Union membership had climbed to approximately 83,000 workers which, as Table 1 shows, represented nearly 14 percent of the labor force. There were more industrial workers than in Arkansas, however; in this respect, Florida's occupational distribution was much closer to California's than an "Old South's" economic structure. About 32.7 percent (223,372) of the Florida workers toiled in the industrial sector. Nonindustrial working-class occupations just exceeded the industrial sector with 33.8 percent (230,185), and the Sunshine state's middle class was larger at 16.9 percent (111,735). While the number of paid farm laborers was slightly smaller at 8.9 percent (61,044), Florida's total number of farm owners was substantially fewer than Arkansas's at 6.1 percent (41,938) of the labor force. Given that the state had more industrial workers, and that more of its population was in urban areas, right-to-workers believed they would have to marshall the rural vote. In this, the state's Farm Bureau Federation led the way by proselytizing for the cause in its statewide farm publications, urging rural voters to "leave your sow, [and] leave your plow" to vote for union security restrictions on election day. The bureau even conducted door-to-door canvasses—not an easy task in agricultural regions. And significantly, as the *Miami Citizen* noted, the most vigorous right-to-work backers represented the low-wage lumber, turpentine, and citrus sections of the state. For good measure, Watson also made the issue the centerpiece of his primary and general reelection campaigns.[16]

Florida unionists responded with equal emotional vigor but with less in terms of electoral resources. Together they formed a committee to conduct an educational drive and raise money. The strong union movement in Tampa, buttressed by the large number of union members in the cigar industry, attracted 700 rank-and-filers in an anti-right-to-work rally in the summer of 1944. Led by Teamsters' business agent W. E. Sullivan, also a vice-president of the state federation, unionists adopted a public-relations stance that tied the currently high union wage scales to the state's future business prosperity. It was no surprise, they charged, that the right-to-workers hailed primarily from the low-wage industries of the state. The state federation's publicity committee put heavy emphasis on radio advertisements, with daily broadcasts late in the campaign in major cities such as Tampa, Miami, West Palm Beach, Jacksonville, St. Petersburg, Lakeland, Daytona, and Pensacola. Lengthier, twenty-minute segments were scheduled immediately prior to the election. And, in addition to leaflets and labor papers, state unionists used sound trucks to reach voters in rural regions. Unfortunately, the efforts that the state labor movement succeeded in putting together seemed to fall short, and Sullivan began making desperate but unsuccessful entreaties to William Green to rouse the financial assistance of international unions.[17]

Ultimately, the electoral activities that Florida unionists were able to muster were not enough to offset the effective Farm Bureau campaign (see Table 1). While winning in the urban areas, which made up

71 percent of the votes on the referendum, labor lost badly, 67 percent to 33 percent, in the agricultural regions. Overall, Florida passed the legislation by a relatively modest margin of 55 percent to 45 percent, representing roughly the same split as evidenced in Arkansas. Unlike its sister southern state, however, the geographic spread of the victory was greater, with 57 of Florida's 67 counties assenting to the right-to-work constitutional amendment, and only 10 of the 67 falling in the marginal range. Also unlike Arkansas, Florida voters were apparently more confused or uninterested than their Razorback counterparts, since the referendum drew only 56 percent of the total votes cast in the election. In total votes cast, the measure won by 25,090 votes out of 270,630 cast (compared to a margin of 17,648 in Arkansas), 147,860 "yes" to 122,770 "no." Again, evidence of the impact of wartime industries is clear from a survey of the counties that did vote with labor. The two highest margins were in areas with heavy concentrations of defense-related facilities in the Panama City area, Bay and Gulf counties. Each voted down the proposition by a 69 percent margin. Nearby Escambia County (Pensacola) did so by 61 percent. Dade and Monroe counties at the southernmost tip of the peninsula also backed the labor movement. Even a few rural, or small-town industrial counties, such as Holmes in the northernmost panhandle tier, and Gilchrist in the north-central region, did the same. More disappointing, however, were the relatively modest pro-labor margins in the heavily urbanized counties of Hillsborough (Tampa) and Duval (Jacksonville), which returned 55 percent and 51 percent "no" votes, respectively.[18]

In comparison, California labor leaders fared better than their brothers and sisters in the South. Of course, as a two-party, heavily industrialized state, California differed from Arkansas and Florida in the fact that it had had a powerful labor movement in existence for many years prior to the war. Total union membership in 1939 was estimated at 434,000, about 25 percent of the labor force. While the state's CIO membership was larger than in any southern state, with about 52,000 enrolled, the AFL again far outstripped the newer federation with 334,200 members. In addition, 37,800 unionists were in independent organizations such as the railroad brotherhoods. By 1944, defense spending in California pushed these figures upward to approximately 770,000, or 29 percent of the labor force (see Table 1 for approximate union membership figures). Structurally, the California economy reflected the sharp historical drop in the percentage of the labor force working in the farm sector. The corresponding percentage and absolute figures for California's occupational categories yielded an industrial working class of about 34 percent (858,260) and a nonindustrial working class of 34.9 percent (880,136). The Middle-class-occupations category was the largest of the three states at 20.8 percent (523,987), as might be expected. Paid farm laborers took up 5.2 percent (130,550) of the work force and farm owners constituted 4 percent (101,532). Thus while agriculture was critically important in all three states, its structure in both Florida and California tended to be that of "agribusiness," while Arkansas was a "small farm" state.[19]

Early in 1944, the California State Federation of Labor appointed a committee of vice-presidents to oversee a projected electoral fight against a right-to-work petition drive sponsored by the Merchants and Manufacturers Association. Initially fearing the popularity of the measure with the state's voters, state federation secretary C. J. Haggerty recommended an intense, unified response to the threat. "The outsider" in the pro-labor political community "will let us use their names but they will not get out and work," he informed the body's executive council. "The one thing against us is the apathy of our movement. Our union people have become executives and cannot be bothered," he contended. "The most important thing is to rouse the people to get [the] outside help we need."[20]

Fortunately, California union leaders were able to obtain statements opposing the initiative proposal from prominent state politicians, including Republican governor Earl Warren. Even more significant, however, was the fact the California business community was not united in pressing for the measure, more than likely because the business sectors that were benefiting from wartime profits were not eager to disrupt the flow. The state's chamber of commerce, for example, announced that it was critical to continued war production to maintain industrial peace, and adopting a right-to-work law would work in the opposite direction. Religious leaders and many other civic groups joined with the California labor movement in opposing restrictions on union security.[21]

Despite influential opponents, the proposal, though defeated, still attracted a significant number of votes; 1,304,430 citizens backed the concept, while 1,893,630 agreed with labor. In terms of percentages, unionists won by 59 percent to 41 percent, as shown in Table 1. The center of strong labor support, predictably, emanated from the heavily unionized San Francisco Bay area and radiated northeastward and, to a lesser extent, to the counties due east. The geographic distribution of the county votes was more even than the overall percentages indicated, however, with 21 counties having "yes" majorities and 37, "no," with 24 of the 58 counties falling in the marginal range. Unsurprisingly, traditionally conservative California areas such as Orange County tended to be outposts of labor opposition.[22]

Results of Regression Analysis

But, in terms of worker support, what did the voting figures in the three elections mean? In order to deepen the analysis, an examination of the three main components of the industrial working class—craft workers, operatives, and laborers—was undertaken. These three categories are viewed in turn in cross-state comparisons. They are then combined into the broader industrial working-class variable and analyzed.

Table 2 lists the regression coefficients (b), the correlation coefficients (r), the standard error of estimate (s), and the coefficient of determination (r^2), and additional related statistics from a regression and correlation analysis conducted on the percent-no right-to-work vote and the percentages of several categories of industrial workers in Arkansas, Florida, and California counties. The craft census category in 1940 contained the most concentrated listing of occupational designations normally considered union prone. For example, it included boilermakers, brickmasons, machinists, locomotive firemen, millwrights, molders, sheet-metal workers, and pressmen, among many others. Of the three states, Arkansas's regression coefficient (slope of the least squares line) was the highest at 3.23, followed by Florida at 2.20, and California at 1.62. In Arkansas, then, a change of one percentage point in the number of skilled workers in a county was associated with an increase of 3.23 percent in the percent-no level of the county's right-to-work vote. For Florida and California, the associated change was an increase of 2.2 percent and 1.62 percent increase in the "no" vote per 1 percent increase in craft workers, respectively. California's simple correlation coefficient, on the other hand, was the highest of the three states at .51, signifying a slightly stronger clustering of the variable pairings around the regression line than Arkansas's

Table 2. Bivariate Regression and Correlation Results, Arkansas, Florida, and California Right-to-Work Elections, 1944

State/ Worker Category	Number of Workers	County Percent Range	b	r	r^2	s
Arkansas (N=75)						
Craft	32,524	2/09	3.23	.42	.18	3.5
Operative	42,722	2/14	2.22	.50	.25	2.7
Laborer	43,321	2/20	1.06	.34	.12	2.7
IWC	118,567	6/35	.92	.51	.26	3.2
Florida (N=67)						
Craft	61,891	2/12	2.21	.36	.13	4.7
Operative	86,800	2/20	0.68	.19	.03	4.1
Laborer	74,681	5/44	-.26	-.16	.02	3.4
IWC	223,372	14/63	.03	.02	.0003	5.5
California (N=58)						
Craft	322,964	4/17	1.62	.51	.26	3.6
Operative	383,938	5/35	0.27	.20	.04	2.7
Laborer	151,358	3/21	.49	.22	.05	2.3
IWC	858,260	13/59	.29	.35	.12	3.4

*Key:*IWC = Industrial Working Class; n = No. of Counties

Source: Occupational Distributions—U.S. Census, 1940. Right-to-Work Election Statistics—Arkansas, Florida, and California Secretaries of State.

Note: No tests of significance are reported in this paper since the correlations and regression coefficients are based upon a complete enumeration rather than a sample.

comparable figure of .42. Florida showed the most dispersion with a correlation statistic of .36.

The operative classification of the 1940 census also contained many occupations traditionally having significant union penetration—railroad switchmen, mine operatives, drivers—as well as others not likely to be unionized at that time. Again, Arkansas evidenced the sharpest association between the two variables with a regression coefficient of 2.21 and a correlation coefficient of .50. The percentage of workers in the operative category in both Florida and California, though, had a much weaker relationship to the percent "no" vote. In Florida the regression coefficient totaled .68 versus .27 in California, with correlations .19 and .20, respectively.

The final distinct category taken directly from census compilations is the laborer classification, with a much more limited range of occupations. It included some unskilled general laborer occupations probably untouched by unionism, as well as others, such as longshoremen and stevedores, which more than likely had experienced some union influence. Here the strongest linear trend was again in Arkansas, where the regression coefficient was 1.06 with a correlation of .34 as listed in Table 2. This represented a little better than one-to-one ration: for every percentage point increase in laborers in the county, there occurred an associated 1.06 percent increase in the "no" right-to-work vote. California had a regression number of .49 with a correlation coefficient of .22, indicating a weak linear trend. The response of Florida counties, of all the categories and states examined thus far, was the only instance of a segment of the industrial working class being negatively associated with the percent "no" right-to-work vote, though that association was indeed a weak one. The regression coefficient was -.26 and the correlation coefficient was -.16.

When all industrial working-class occupations are combined (the total of the craft, operative, and laborer classifications in each county) and transformed into percentages, a regression and correlation analysis yields the following results: Arkansas again shows a positive linear trend, as shown in table 2. The coefficients for the regression and correlation were .92 and .51 respectively. California's result also indicates a positive linear trend with a regression of .29. Here, however, the dispersion or error about the regression line is far greater, as the lower correlation coefficient of .35 supports. Last, Florida provides little evidence at all of any linear trend when its industrial working-class categories are combined; its regression and correlation figures are both negligible at .03 and .02. More than likely, the inclusion of the negative linear results in the laborer category in Florida offset the positive trend noted in the craft and operative categories.

Conclusions

What conclusions can be drawn from the above analysis? Admittedly, the positive association of craft-worker occupations to an increase in the "no" vote level is not unexpected; more surprising is the seeming lack of cohesive response in the operative and laborer categories in California and Florida. Exactly what this signifies is open to speculation.[23] However, those speculations are not the central concerns of this paper. Here, the central question is the *comparative* response of the southern and non-southern states. And in regards to *that* relationship the conclusion must be drawn that California counties showed no marked superiority over the southern states in positive associations between percentages of the industrial working class in a county and the percent increase in the "no" right-to-work vote. In fact, Arkansas—the least industrialized state of the three—evidenced the strongest overall measure of a positive relationship in all the categories of variables examined. Craft-worker percentages in both California and Florida were comparable, as was the general response in the operative classification. In only one category—laborer—did California percentages show discernible superiority over Florida's negative regression and correlation response, and even then the coefficients for California's laborer grouping were quite weak in terms of a positive association.

Thus this examination of the quantitative dimension of the aggregate response of the southern industrial working class to a pro-union electoral measure indicates that simple generalizations about the existence of an indigenous "anti-union" culture in the South's working class are overdrawn. Southern workers in Arkansas and Florida collectively were no more culturally "anti-union" than their counterparts in California on the eve of both the AFL's and the CIO's postwar organizing drives. Moreover, as the measures in Arkansas imply, they could at times be even *more* sympathetic toward trade-union goals such as preventing the prohibition of union security restrictions. By inference, this suggests that the primary reason and/or reasons for organized labor's failure to breach the South in organizing might be more strongly associated with factors extraneous to the supposed anti-union bias of southern industrial workers.[24]

Notes

1. For example, see W. J. Cash, *The Mind of the South* (New York: Vintage, 1941); Liston Pope, *Millhands and Preachers: A Study of Gastonia* (New Haven, CT: Yale Univ. Press, 1942). The most recent attempt to examine this problem in the context of the 1940s is Barbara S. Griffith, *The Crisis of*

American Labor: Operation Dixie and the Defeat of the CIO (Philadelphia: Temple Univ. Press, 1988). Griffith's study, as well as many others, approaches the historiographical problems of the susceptibility, or lack thereof, of the southern worker toward unionization from the perspective of the textile industry. Interestingly, a recent dissertation by William E. Regensburger, "'Ground Into Our Blood': The Origins of Working Class Consciousness and Organization in Durably Unionized Southern Industries, 1930–1946" (Ph.D., diss., UCLA, 1987), suggestively challenges the predominant view of the infertile nature of southern culture toward lasting unionization. In essence, while southern culture as portrayed by Cash, Pope, and others stresses how paternalism and authoritarianism could undercut union sentiment, Regensburger maintains that other strains of southern culture—community consciousness, concern for kin and group, feelings of social entitlement, and combative individualism—could and *did*, in the coal, nonferrous, maritime, oil, and steel industries, interact to produce lasting commitments to unionism. Thus, according to Regensburger (31), the "southern 'character structure' had the potential to be either a barrier or a catalyst to union and class consciousness."

2. Wesley High to Joseph Schmidt, 3 Dec. 1944, and Herman Winter to William Green, 13 Dec. 1944, Box 1, AFL State Legislation Files (hereafter AFL State Legislation Files), State Historical Society of Wisconsin, Madison. For a survey of organized labor's efforts to influence political parties on the right-to-work issue, see Gilbert J. Gall, *The Politics of Right to Work: The Labor Federations as Special Interests, 1943–1979* (Westport, CT: Greenwood, 1988).

3. For example Mike Davis, in *Prisoners of the American Dream: Politics and Economy in the History of the U.S. Working Class*(London: Verso, 1986), 91–101, directly ties the defeat of the CIO in the South, along with the negative national consequences, to the organization's anti-communist factionalism of the late 1940s. The best analysis of the negative impact of the historical development of American labor relations law on unions and unionization is Christopher L. Tomlins, *The State and the Unions: Labor Relations, Law, and the Organized Labor Movement in America, 1880–1960* (New York: Oxford Univ. Press, 1985).

4. The traditional method of approaching this problem is to cite "qualitative" historical evidence: organizers' written reports, oral history interviews, and archival collections. An alternative, empirically based strategy is to analyze the representative election statistics of the National Labor Relations Board in the South. This technique, though, is also idiosyncratic, for elections would not usually be held unless an organizer was "working" the target and had succeeded in converting enough workers to obtain an NLRB election. This method ignores those workers who would have been sympathetic but for one reason or another were not approached. A broader design, therefore, would assist in extending the analysis and generalizability of the impressionistic

evidence regarding the union sentiment among southern industrial workers.

5. Regression analysis is perhaps one of the most widely used statistical methodologies. In social science research it is often employed to assist a researcher in describing the nature of the relationship between two variables. Normally, the investigator assigns some level of responsibility for "causation" to one of the variables (termed the independent variable) according to a preformulated hypothesis. Therefore, it is expected that the other variable (termed the dependent variable) thus in some way "depends" on the independent's value. It is presumed that if there is a relationship between the two variables it is a linear one, either in a positive or negative direction or trend. A measure of no relationship either yields a completely horizontal line or is randomly dispersed. The measure of this direction or trend is termed the regression coefficient (symbolized by b) and signifies the slope of an imaginary line—termed the "least squares" line—that best fits the data collected.

For all of the observations in any given data set, there is almost always some variation from the linear tendency. This variation is the "error" in the hypothesized model, which not only represents deviations from the main tendency but also deficiencies in the quality of the data, mistakes, and so on. Rarely, if ever, does social science research yield data observations where all observations fall tightly along the "least squares" line. Therefore, additional measures of association aid in evaluating the "strength" of the relationship and how much of the variation is explained by the analyzed variable. The first of these is the correlation coefficient (symbolized as r) and is often included in the analysis and reported in tandem, to assist in determining the strength of the relationship. In essence, while the regression coefficient describes the "nature" of the relationship between two variables (in what direction the trend is going and how much increase is occurring in the dependent variable per unit increase in the independent variable), the correlation coefficient describes the "strength" of that relationship. This coefficient varies from 1.0 for a perfect positive relationship to -1.0 for a perfect negative relationship; in each case all observed data would fall exactly on the "least squares" line. A coefficient of zero would indicate no relationship at all. Related to the correlation coefficient is the standard estimate of error (symbolized by s), which is also a measure of how tightly points cluster on the regression line but which is expressed in the units of the variables analyzed. For example, an s of 2.5 would signify that two-thirds of the observations lie in a band 2.5 units above or below the regression line. Finally r-squared, or the coefficient of determination (symbolized as r^2), is the square of the correlation coefficient; it indicates how much of the variation in the dependent variable is accounted for by the independent variable and assists in evaluating the strength of the correlation coefficient. For explanations of regression and correlation techniques, see Hubert M. Blalock, Jr., *Social Statistics*, 2nd ed. (New York: McGraw-Hill, 1972). For further elaboration of how statistical procedures can be applied to electoral history, as well as other methodological concerns, see *Analyzing Electoral History: A Guide to the Study of American Voter Behavior*, ed. Jerome M. Clubb, William H. Flanigan, and Nancy H. Zingale (Beverly Hills, CA: Sage, 1981). For examples of historical studies of electoral politics using quantification, see *The History of American Electoral Behavior*, ed. Joel H. Silbey, Allan G. Bogue, and William H. Flanigan (Princeton, NJ: Princeton Univ. Press, 1978).

6.   There are three areas in which concerns arise. They involve the problem of inferring individual behavior by analyzing aggregate data (often referred to as the "ecological fallacy"), the problem of whether the percentage of negative votes on the right-to-work measures is a valid indicator of union sentiment, and the problem of the limitations of the 1940 census data on occupational distributions. Each deserves some elaboration.

The "ecological fallacy" essentially involves a debate centered around the argument that we cannot logically infer, as quantifiers studying politics often do, that a relationship observed at the aggregate level can be transferred to the individual level. For example, in the context of this study, any association discovered between the percent-no vote and percentage concentrations of industrial-worker categories does not mean that *individual* industrial workers behaved that way when they cast their ballots as the variations could be due to other categories of voters. For more on this position, see William H. Flanigan and Nancy H. Zingale, "Alchemist's Gold: Inferring Individual Relationships from Aggregate Data," *Social Science History* 9:1 (Winter 1985), 71–92. Other analysts believe that the arguments denouncing the "ecological fallacy" are too overdrawn. For the purposes of this study, I agree with the observation that "whether an ecological correlation [or regression] is 'acceptable' depends upon the questions asked in any particular study" (See John L. Shover and John J. Kushma, "Retrieval of Individual Data from Aggregate Units of Analysis: A Case Study Using Twentieth-Century Urban Voting Data," in Silbey et al., *The History of American Electoral Behavior*, 327–42). Thus when the object of theoretical interest is the relationship between aggregates, as it is here, since it is recognized that the assertions pertain only to the observations of the behavior of aggregate groups of workers (counties), then an ecological correlation/regression poses no problems.

In regard to the validity of the right-to-work vote as an index of union sentiment, there are two difficulties. The first involves whether voters actually knew the meaning of their vote. Right-to-work proponents often clouded the wording of the proposals on the ballot for tactical advantage, as in Florida in 1944 (Joint House Resolution No. 13) when voters had to read 50 words before finding out the measure had anything to do with unions. Also, political analysts point to the fact that voters tend to vote no on referendums automatically, under the assumption that the status quo is preferable to any change and that at least "things will not get worse" if they vote no.

As it pertains to the three 1944 elections, only Florida had the wording difficulty. Its major impact had much more to do with the reliability of the yes vote and the fact that many voters who voted on the candidates (44 percent) apparently did not vote on the right-to-work resolution. The specific phrasing of the resolution was constructed in such a way that a voter could vote against the labor position, without realizing it, by voting yes, while a no vote, again given the specific wording of that measure, in all probability signified that the voter was aware of the anti-union intent of the referendum.

The tendency to vote no on referendums is also less problematical than upon first consideration. Current political science research indicates that referendum campaigns of high public salience (such as the Proposition 13 tax limitation proposal in California) do not fit this pattern. Referendum campaigns that attract a good deal of publicity and the backing or opposition of important statewide political figures create a political environment in which most voters *do* know what they are voting on and what their vote signifies (on referendum voting see Thomas E. Cronin, *Direct Democracy: The Politics of Initiative, Referendum, and Recall* (Cambridge, MA: Harvard Univ. Press, 1989), 60–89 and David B. Magleby, *Direct Legislation: Voting on Ballot Proposals in the United States* (Baltimore: Johns Hopkins Univ. Press, 1984), 77–99, 100–144). Impressionistic evidence suggests that this was the case for the three 1944 right-to-work elections. Given that labor relations and unionism had a high public visibility profile in the 1940s (the 1943 coal strikes created intense public debate, for example), and that all three 1944 elections generated a great deal of state political controversy, it is reasonable to assume that they fit the high public salience pattern. Thus, while there may have been a small number of voters who mistakenly voted no or voted no for no apparent reason, on these referendums, it seems logical to conclude that the great majority who did vote no did so for a reason—they had accurately identified the anti-union nature of the provision and were against it, and hence possessed some sympathy for unions.

Assuming that we accept the percent-no vote as a valid indicator of pro-union sentiment within a given county, then, with what confidence can we state that those votes were broadly "representative" of that sentiment? The data do not reflect an entire statistical "universe" for examination, nor are the county-level votes random samples that can be subjected to the laws of probability. First of all, there is the problem of those who did not vote, especially in the South. Voting restrictions such as the white primary, literacy tests, and the poll tax not only effectively disenfranchised black citizens but the poll tax also dampened white working-class political participation. In tandem, this led to a low rate of voter participation in elections throughout the South. Additionally, there is the difficulty that those who did vote on the right-to-work measures were not even identical to those who voted in the general election; in Arkansas they came closest with 91 percent, followed by California's 86 percent, and Florida's much smaller ratio of 56 percent. Pro-

or anti-union sentiment among the working class, or the general populace for that matter, no doubt had a broader existence than among those voters who chose to vote on the question.

There is no reliable way to tell how broad the franchise was among blacks in Arkansas and Florida in 1944, and how many whites in the industrial working class were ready and able to vote. In April of that year the Supreme Court ruled the white primary unconstitutional, opening a "window of opportunity" of sorts for an increase in black voter participation. In addition, the Florida legislature had repealed the poll tax in 1938. Arkansas, though, still had a tax of one dollar but it was not cumulative. By 1944 the industrial workers of both states had experienced three years of a high employment, wartime economy. Money was probably not a difficulty in 1944 as it had been in the depression years, even for blacks. Moreover, the Razorback state had had a long history of voting corruption, with competing candidates paying the poll tax of white workers in order to "buy" a bloc of voters. Thus many white workers may have been able to vote for that reason. A guarded conclusion would be that given the strong adverse social reaction that widespread black voting would have generated, blacks probably did not challenge the white power structure in tremendous numbers in the 1944 general elections. White workers in the two states, however, more than likely could have voted without much difficulty, if they had wanted to do so. For the labor movement this may have proven a disadvantage, because black voters proved strong supporters of the labor position on the right-to-work in the 1958 Ohio referendum election (see Gall, *The Politics of Right to Work*, 140–44). On the other hand, segregationist AFL unions clearly used union security to keep blacks from job opportunities in the Florida shipbuilding industry during the war, and had blacks voted in large numbers in 1944 they may have angrily cast ballots against the AFL position on right to work (see Merl Reed, "The FEPC, the Black Worker, and the Shipyards," *South Atlantic Quarterly* 74:4 (1975), 446–67). For a valuable contemporaneous sociological guide to southern political life see Ralph J. Bunche, *The Political Status of the Negro in the Age of FDR*, ed. Dewey W. Grantham (Chicago: Univ. of Chicago Press, 1973), 181–215, 328–83. This study was originally done under the auspices of Gunnar Myrdal's *An American Dilemma* project and was written by Bunche in 1940.

In conclusion, the percentages of right-to-work votes available can only be said to represent a nonrandom sample of adult voters who chose to cast a ballot on the right-to-work referendum. Still, 192,952 Arkansas citizens, 270,630 Florida voters, and 3,198,060 California balloteers registered their opinions on the question. Even with all of these defects, the votes maintain reliability as historical evidence due to their fairly large numbers, more so than the use of any other political statistic conceivably available.

The question of class identification through occupational designation also poses difficulties. Defining class has always been a problem for sociologists, whether it is done through the assessment of characteristics such as income, residence, education, or occupation. All definitions have limitations that force qualifications. In addition to these conceptual complications, there are difficulties as well with inconsistencies in classification schemes and often with the quality of the data itself. Even so, the information on occupational categories, derived from workers who identified themselves as working in certain occupations, has perhaps the least number of definitional problems and is thus the best indicator available for use at the county level.

Still, the deficiencies should be noted. The first involves the imperfections of categorization. The Census Bureau compiled figures on twelve categories of occupations: professional workers; semi-professional workers; farmers and farm managers; proprietors, managers, and officials, except farm; clerical, sales, and kindred workers; craftsmen, foremen, and kindred workers; operatives and kindred workers; domestic service workers; service workers, except domestic; farm (wage) laborers and farm foremen; farm laborers (unpaid family); and laborers, except farm. The "Industrial Working Class" (IWC) category referred to in this paper is a compilation of three of the census classifications that contained the highest content of industrial workers. These were "craftsmen, foremen, and kindred workers" (Craft), "operatives and kindred workers" (Operative), and "laborers, except farm" (Laborer). While the other classifications no doubt had workers who might have either been unionized or sympathetic to unions—such as telephone operators who fell into the "clerical, sales, and kindred worker" segment and perhaps some of the service-worker category—the Craft, Operative, and Laborer divisions were clearly the most ostensible targets of unionization in any mass organizing drive.

Second, though the census figures are broader than the percentages of "no" right-to-work votes in terms of population coverage, they represent only the ratios of "employed" workers over 14 claiming to be performing work in that occupation at the time of the census of 1940. Obviously, since the dependent variable, percent "no" right-to-work vote at the county level (PNRTW) is a 1944 figure, there is a time gap and no doubt the occupational ratios changed from 1940 to 1944. Most likely, expanding war production and conscription put the unemployed back into the labor force, caused all categories to change in terms of the sex and age of the workers, and perhaps drew nonindustrial workers and some farm laborers into the industrial worker segments.

How these changes affected the county-level ratios by 1944 in Florida, Arkansas, and California, in terms of crossing "class" divisions is difficult if not impossible to determine. The most probable overall result was that the ratios changed somewhat with most growth occurring in the industrial segment. The broader class component of each category, though, likely stayed relatively stable (with possibly the nonindustrial service, domestic, and white-collar working class entering the industrial sector), including the agricultural workers who produced war-related goods. Other types of agriculture, however, more than likely found their labor force siphoned off into wartime industry, particularly in the operative and laborer categories. The gender and age mix of the workers changed the most, as industrial and nonindustrial working-class women, youths, and nonconscriptable males entered the industrial occupation categories. Thus the quality of the 1940 census percentage figures also suffers from the inclusion of an undeterminable number of workers (aged 14–20) who were unable to vote at that time and might not have been able to vote even in 1944. In addition, by 1944 the sexual composition of the labor force undoubtedly changed; the most pronounced difference was probably the incorporation of many women who had previously had not been engaged in industrial work. Still, since the class composition of the ratios had most probably not been extensively disrupted (with the possible exception of an influx of the agricultural working class into the industrial working class), the data maintains validity as an identifier of the industrial working class at the county level.

7. U.S. Department of Labor, Bureau of Labor Statistics, *Labor in the South*, Bulletin No. 898 (Washington: GPO, 1947).

8. Ibid.

9. Florida attorney general Tom Watson's first anti-closed-shop lawsuit against the Tampa Shipbuilding Company in 1943, for example, involved an agreement negotiated during the Gulf Zone Stabilization Conference in New Orleans, wherein representatives of the shipbuilding industry, unions, the War Production Board, the U.S. Navy, and U.S. Maritime Commission had agreed upon wage and labor standards for shipyards. See *State of Florida v. Tampa Shipbuilding Company, 10 Nov. 1943* (Supreme Court of Florida), copy of opinion in Box 1, AFL State Legislation Files. F. Ray Marshall, in *Labor in the South* (Cambridge, MA: Harvard Univ. Press, 1967), cites the fact that the war greatly advanced the cause of organized labor in the South. Virtually all of the urban mass transportation systems were organized by 1944, the AFL's city central in Tampa ostensibly represented 40,000 workers and had three Labor Temples as a result of wartime gains, and the shipyards and defense facilities of Panama City led to the founding of 18 new local unions during the war years (225).

10. C. Calvin Smith, *War and Wartime Changes: The Transformation of Arkansas 1940–1945* (Fayetteville: Univ. of Arkansas Press, 1986), 19–35, 109–18. For a contemporaneous analysis of Arkansas politics see V. O. Key, Jr., *Southern Politics in State and Nation* (New York: Knopf, 1949), 183–204.

11. Statistics on occupational distributions are derived from U.S. Department of Commerce, Bureau of the Census, *Sixteenth Census of the United States, 1940: Characteristics of the Population*, v. 1–2 (Washington: GPO, 1940) (hereafter *Census*, 1940). The classification Industrial Working Class is composed of Craft, Operative, and Laborer, while the category Non-Indus-

trial Working Class consists of Clerical, Service, and Domestic workers. The Middle-Class division is compiled from the occupational classifications of Professional, Semiprofessional, and Proprietor, Managers, and Official. Finally, the agricultural occupation distributions of Farm Laborer and Farm Owner correspond to wage-paid farm laborers and owners of farms, respectively. Union membership statistics are derived from Leo Troy, "Distribution of Union Membership among the States, 1939 and 1953" (Washington, DC: National Bureau of Economic Research, Occasional Paper 56, 1957) and Gall, *The Politics of Right to Work*, 23, 233–35.

12. Alexander Heard and Donald S. Strong, *Southern Primaries and Elections, 1920–1949* (New York: Freeport, 1950), 21, 35. The AFL's electoral efforts are outlined in E. H. Williams to William Green, 19 Oct. 1944, Box 1, AFL State Legislation Files.

13. The election statistics are from county-level tabulations provided by the Arkansas secretary of state's office, and derived in the fashion indicated in Gall, *The Politics of Right to Work*, 233–35. The description of the geographic dispersion of the counties was compiled by comparing the percentage "no" right-to-work votes in the counties with the a county map of the state of Arkansas, and then comparing that with the elaboration of war-related production as chronicled in C. Calvin Smith, *War and Wartime Changes*, 19–35. Also see I. A. Moke, "Distribution of Major Manufacturing Industries in Arkansas," *Journal of Geography* 54 (May 1955), 239–46. For a survey of the subsequent legal interpretation of Arkansas's right-to-work law see James E. Youngdahl, "Thirteen Years of the 'Right to Work' in Arkansas," *Arkansas Law Review and Bar Association Journal* 14 (Fall 1960), 289–301.

14. Key, 82–105; J. William Lowe, "Union Security in Florida Industries under the Right-to-Work Amendment" (Ph.D. diss., University of Florida, 1956), 26–30.

15. Business sponsors of the referendum bill included Florida insurance, financial, manufacturing, restaurant, and hotel associations, in addition to the state chamber of commerce, the Farm Bureau Federation, the Citrus Growers', Canners', and Cattlemen's trade groups. See John G. Shott, *How "Right-to Work Laws" Are Passed: Florida Sets the Pattern* (Washington: Public Affairs Instit., 1956), 23. The Hill quote is cited in Lowe, 41.

16. Statistics on union membership and the state's occupational distributions were derived in the fashion indicated in note 11. The Farm Bureau campaign and Watson's reelection activities are described in Shott, 23–31 and Lowe, 41–45.

17. Shott, 32–37. For Sullivan's exchange with Green see Gilbert J. Gall, "Constant Vigilance: The Heritage of the AFL's Response to Right to Work Legislation, 1943–1949," *Labor Studies Journal* 9 (Fall 1984), 193–96.

18. The rural/urban figures were calculated by Shott, 37–38, 43. The additional statistics for Florida were derived by the identical method as outlined in note

13. AFL unions most active in fighting the right-to-work in Florida were the Machinists, the IBEW, the Teamsters, the Operating Engineers, the Boilermakers, the Carpenters, the Ironworkers, the Painters, the Laborers, and the Sheet Metal Workers—all building trades except for the Teamsters, and all heavily involved in defense industries. The role of the Latino-based Cigarmakers union in Tampa remains unclear. In its 1946 test suit regarding the amendment, the AFL claimed that its affiliates had 500 separate labor agreements in the state, representing nearly 100,000 workers in bargaining. See the "Florida" folder, Box 1, State Legislation Files, especially the AFL complaint filed in the state's Thirteenth Judicial Court of Hillsborough County, *AFL, Florida State Federation of Labor, et al. vs. J. Tom Watson, Attorney General of the State of Florida, et al.*

19. The statistics on California union membership and occupational divisions were derived in the same manner as set forth in note11.

20. Philip Taft, *Labor Politics American Style: The California Federation of Labor* (Cambridge, MA: Harvard Univ. Press, 1968), 232–35.

21. Ibid.

22. The election figures were put together in the same manner as outlined in note 13.

23. The relatively weak positive association between the percentages of workers in the operative and laborer categories is somewhat surprising, especially so for California. This could be due to several factors. The most important might be the change in composition of these occupational classifications by the 1944 vote; for example, many working-class women, both from the industrial and nonindustrial economic sectors, probably entered the operative category from 1940 to 1944. Other works have noted that World War II's impact brought workers into certain industrial job categories who had had little experience with unions, evidencing less union-mindedness and posing a problem for some industrial unions like the Steelworkers. See Nelson Lichtenstein, "Ambiguous Legacy: The Union Security Problem during World War II," *Labor History* 18 (1977), 214–38. In addition, the census data regarding classifications contained workers aged 14 to 20, and most likely they would tend to cluster in operative and laborer categories, probably contributing to the less cohesive response. Similarly, the drawing of former agricultural workers and nonindustrial working-class workers into the industrial class most likely had the same effect.

24. Interestingly, some studies among southern cotton-mill operatives provide a modicum of support to this contention. For example, shortly before 1930, Jennings J. Rhyne surveyed 468 heads of families in Gaston County, NC, on their feelings about unions. Nearly half, 48 percent, supported unionization, while 27.1 percent were against it (with 29.9 percent "unconcerned or indifferent.") Rhyne, *Some Cotton Mill Workers and Their Villages* (Chapel Hill: Univ. of North Carolina Press, 1930), 205–6.

In another, more modern study (1980), Joseph A. McDonald and

Donald A. Clelland surveyed the workers of a nonunion textile operation in Georgia. Among other conclusions, they found that 39 percent claimed they would vote for a union, while 36 percent said they would not, with 25 percent uncertain. The level of union sentiment was about the same for blue-collar workers nationwide at the time. "The popular supposition that southern workers are distinct from non-southern workers in response to unions is not supported in this community," they wrote. Therefore, they contend, "variables other than union attitudes need to be examined in accounting for actual rates of organization in the region." See McDonald and Clelland, "Textile Workers and Union Sentiment," *Social Forces* 63:2 (Dec. 1984), 502–21.

10. Labor Trouble

George Wallace and Union Politics in Alabama

Robert J. Norrell

At a large convention of Alabama unionists in 1958, a middle-aged black worker took the microphone and offered a story to illustrate a sad reality about organized labor. Jesse Thomas of the Molders Union explained that three men appeared at Heaven's gate only to learn that to gain entry each had to ask St. Peter a question that he could not answer. Two of the men were utility company executives and the third was a common laborer, a union man. "The Alabama Power Company man felt like he was the biggest man," Thomas said, "so they let him go first. And he whispered something in St. Peter's ear, and [St. Peter] sent him right back." Exactly the same thing happened to the man from Southern Natural Gas. "So they decided that ain't nobody going to heaven today," but Thomas said, the disappointed businessmen agreed that it was only fair to let the working man have a chance. He too whispered in St. Peter's ear, and the great Divine quickly rose and ushered him into the Kingdom. "These [corporation] fellows was very much surprised," Thomas reported, and they asked St. Peter, about "this ignorant labor man" getting in, saying, 'with the education we have, you turned us down. . . . Tell us, what was [it] that he asked you that was so hard that you couldn't answer?'" Thomas said that, with some exasperation, St. Peter replied, "He asked me when was the labor people going to get together, and I told him I didn't know."[1]

Jesse Thomas's gentle reproach about the divisions within Alabama's labor movement came in the context of racial tensions in the mid-1950s. The Montgomery bus boycott, which began in December 1955, and a mob's attack on a black student, Autherine Lucy, attempting to enter the state university two months later sent racial passions soaring throughout Alabama. Working-class whites were integral in the so-called "massive resistance" to desegregation that followed these events. They indeed composed both the mass *and* the most resistant part of the opposition to changing southern society. Whenever they could, white workers used their union organizations to help their cause, and they harshly condemned the institutional labor movement that supported civil rights for blacks. White unionists reacted angrily against the labor movement's support of the National Association for the Advancement for Colored People (NAACP), the organization credited with "stirring up" integration.[2]

As the movement for civil rights mounted over the next decade and a half, organized labor in Alabama would become preoccupied with the issue of race. The crisis dramatized the profound difficulty with creating effective class-based action in a society that historically had accepted race as the primary social determinant. Many white unionists rejected the class-oriented positions of labor's leadership in favor groups and politicians making a last-ditch defense of segregation. Nowhere were the racial bases of working-class politics more evident than in the ardent support that blue-collar whites gave to the archsegregationist George Wallace. They did so because they believed that they had much to lose economically and socially if white supremacy was undermined. There was enough truth in that belief to cause much trouble for labor in Alabama.[3]

At almost precisely the moment that the Montgomery bus boycott startled white Alabamians awake to the black revolt, the national labor movement announced its increased commitment to racial justice. During their merger negotiations in 1955, the American Federation of Labor (AFL) and the Congress of Industrial Organization (CIO) had been pressured by black unionists, primarily A. Philip Randolph of the Brotherhood of Sleeping Car Porters, to use their influence on behalf of blacks' civil rights. Both President George Meany and Vice-President Walter Reuther of the merged AFL-CIO publicly endorsed civil rights for black Americans, and their consolidated organization lent its considerable political and financial support to the NAACP. At the same time, it pledged to oppose such organizations as the Ku Klux Klan and the White Citizens Councils. In early February 1956, the AFL-CIO executive board denounced the councils as the "new Ku Klux Klan without hoods."[4]

The AFL-CIO's difficulties with this issue in the South emerged at an initial state meeting of its postmerger Committee on Political Education, called to meet in Tuscaloosa, Alabama, on February 17, 1956. Convened at the cafeteria of the local white high school, the meeting attracted the state's labor leaders and national representatives of the United Rubber Workers of America, which had a large contingent of members at the local B. F. Goodrich plant. The poor attendance of the rank-and-file unionists—about 12,000 AFL-CIO members worked in Tuscaloosa—disappointed the meeting's organizers, already highly uncomfortable in the aftermath of the Autherine Lucy incident because of accusations that rubber workers had composed the largest part of the mob attacking her. But conspicuously present were politicians interested in courting labor for support, among them Judge George C. Wallace, who was planning a run for the governor's office in 1958. As a state representative, Wallace had voted against right-to-work legislation and he now told the small if presumably influential group of unionists in Tuscaloosa that the "new South is going to be built on the shoulders of labor."[5]

As it happened, another organizational meeting taking place the same night at the Tuscaloosa County Courthouse a few blocks away probably drew many more unionists. Almost 2,000 people flooded the first meeting of the White Citizens Council of West Alabama and heard several speakers decry the integrationist efforts coming from many quarters. "Nine men sat in Washington and made a decision which we don't feel honor-bound to support," state Sen. Walter C. Givhan of Selma told the throng, referring to the U.S. Supreme Court's recent *Brown* decision. Among those following Givhan to the podium was Edward Robertson, an employee of B. F. Goodrich and a member of the Rubber Workers. Robertson condemned Walter Reuther and George Meany for their support of the NAACP, insisting that the national leadership did not represent the views of organized labor in Tuscaloosa.[6]

An analysis of the membership of the Tuscaloosa White Citizens Council supports Robertson's point. A sample of council members suggests that at least 28 percent were in all likelihood members of a labor union, 10 percent of them being rubber workers. Truck drivers, mechanics, and/or taxi drivers composed another 19 percent. Nine percent worked in the building trades. Blue-collar workers thus accounted for at least 56 percent of council membership. The percentage went considerably higher with the addition of the deliverymen at the local diaries and bakeries and the service workers at the local veterans hospital, the state mental hospital, and the university. But also present in the group were shopkeepers and small businessmen of many varieties and even a few professionals and executives. Perhaps no organization more representative of the various strata of white society existed in Tuscaloosa at the time. That in fact was what the architects of the citizens councils had wanted: an organization in which *all* whites could come together to defend segregation and to uphold a white man's democracy.[7]

In Montgomery, white labor unionists became the vanguard of the opposition to the boycotting blacks. A newspaper typographer named Jack D. Brock announced in his own publication, *Alabama Labor News*, the creation of a "Southern Federation of Labor" to counteract the pro-black policies of the national AFL-CIO office. "The labor movement in the South," he wrote, had been built "*around* Southern traditions, and not *over* them." Formerly the state president of the AFL and now head of his local union, Brock warned that neither "George Meany, Walter Reuther, the President, nor the Supreme Court of the United States shall force the labor movement in the South to discontinue Southern traditions. I am a Southerner, an American, and a Union man, in the order listed." In response to the AFL-CIO board's denunciation of the Citizens Councils, Brock informed George Meany that he and a large portion of labor in Alabama were members of the council and embraced all it stood for. When Gov. James E. "Big Jim" Folsom appointed Brock as labor's representative on a biracial commission formed to address the soaring racial hostilities in Alabama, Brock announced, "We will fight at every turn if the Negro race seeks to mongrelize the white race." "Of all our sovereign rights," Brock wrote in his newspaper in May 1956, "we hold segregation the highest. That right is a part of every southerner. It is his prime philosophy, the basic thought which has remained with him through childhood, a social concept which he has always accepted, and will continue to accept as long as there is an Alabamian left to raise his voice—or his hand."[8]

Brock led a substantial group of angry Montgomery unionists that included, in addition to a few typographers, members from the painters', carpenters', and bus drivers' unions. Lester Hawkins, business agent for the painters' union, was widely suspected of being a Klansman. The carpenters' hall, used by all the other unions for their meetings, became a rallying place for the local Ku Klux Klan, its ritual crosses on full display in the hall. Homer Welch, business agent for the carpenters' union, was a bitter segregationist and probably a Klansman. His brother William Welch was president of the bus drivers' union and a like-minded man on racial matters. The plight of the sixty-five bus drivers laid off as a result of the bus boycott was a source of angry resentment because it demonstrated to these working-class whites who, in fact, suffered most when white supremacy was undermined. In August 1956 members of the carpenters' union constructed a gallows in downtown Montgomery from which the NAACP was hanged in effigy. Attached to the gallows was a sign, "Built by Organized Labor."[9]

Some of their prosegregation actions may have been far more serious. Members of the typographers', carpenters', and painters' unions were widely suspected of being among the group responsible for the terrorist bombings of black churches and homes of boycott leaders, including the home of the Rev. Martin Luther King, Jr. In early 1957 a Montgomery grand jury indicted seven men for the bombings, including a plumber, a foreman at a furniture factory, a mechanic, and a typographer, Eugene S. Hall. Suspicion centered especially on the typographers, because police investigators discovered that the bombs were made with a particular kind of pressure-sensitive tape then used only in hot-type printing.[10]

The indictments appear to have represented part of an effort by the Montgomery political and business elite to stop anti-black violence that was in fact redounding to the benefit of civil rights activists. The Montgomery Citizens Council, to which most city officials and many leading businessmen belonged, had already removed Eugene Hall from its executive committee and from his position as editor of the council's publication, the *States Right Advocate*. The editor of the Montgomery *Advertiser* wrote that the bombers were "small and simple minded . . . a blockhead element that thinks that bombs displease the NAACP. . . . A Negro church blows up and the dangerous civil rights legislation pending in Congress . . . is advanced." The grand jury, composed mostly of middle-class businessmen and professionals—a business executive, Rotarian, and former chairman of the county Democratic Committee—and headed by a foreman whom the judge actually *appointed*, made plain its commitment to segregation in handing down the indictments: "We are determined to maintain racial segregation in Montgomery but also to maintain law and order as it applies to both those who support segregation and those who oppose it. Our action in returning indictments . . . should not be constructed as any weakening in the determination of the people of Montgomery to preserve our segregated institutions." In other words, segregation would be preserved but the decent people would take care of the job of defending it.[11]

Eugene Hall and Jack Brock worked together at the Montgomery *Advertiser*, and Brock immediately began a door-to-door fund-raising effort for the accused bombers' legal defense fund. He and others raised many thousands of dollars in an effort that the Montgomery police chief condemned as Klan-inspired. Brock responded that it was "common knowledge that the NAACP furnishes large sums of money to defend Negroes regardless of whether they be charged with rape, murder, or other [heinous] offenses," and he could not understand why the chief of police was "opposed to white men having competent legal counsel." The city of Montgomery revoked Brock's license to solicit funds. Clearly Montgomery's civic leadership was attempting to distance itself and the Citizens Council from the bombings. By now Brock surely must have questioned how sincere Montgomery's elite had been in the council pledge to white solidarity. But the effort to hang the redneck segregationists did not work because most white Montgomerians, regardless of class, in fact did not want the bombers punished. The accused retained John Blue Hill, Montgomery's most accomplished criminal lawyer and a member of the aristocratic and politically influential family that included U.S. Senator Lister Hill. In the end only two of the seven were brought to trial, and a jury of mostly middle-class white men voted to acquit even them.[12]

In Birmingham, the southern city with the most unionists, labor's disaffection from the national AFL-CIO was virtually complete. The Southern Federation of Labor held a rally at Birmingham's Municipal Auditorium in July 1956 to which were invited all "interested in maintaining the cherished ideals of our Southland." Speakers at the rally included only one unionist but several violent reactionaries, among them a Memphis preacher who cried out, "The die is cast, the flag is raised, the battle is on. Will you do your part in the front line trenches or behind the lines?" Several Birmingham locals were embroiled in race-related struggles. The Birmingham local of the American Federation of Teachers surrendered its charter rather than accept the national organization's position on school desegregation. At Hayes Aircraft, a new union called Southern Aircraft Workers challenged the United Automobile Workers (UAW), its president claiming that the UAW had contributed to a "constant hammering away at Southern traditions and culture by a horde of misguided meddlers, political opportunists, lawless labor leaders and revolutionary agitators, all wittingly or unwittingly accepting direction from the Northern left-wing masterminds." Jack Brock's brother Elmer, a member of the painters' union, helped to raid a small United Steelworkers of America local for a new union called Southern Crafts, whose membership was "confined to the white race, but will represent all races in bargaining and will operate within the pattern of common decency and equality for all." Brock, once the police chief of a small mining community near Birmingham, had been indicted for activities related to Klan floggings in Birmingham in 1949, and his unsavory background facilitated the AFL-CIO's counterattack against him. He soon was expelled from the painters' union, and Southern Crafts failed to catch on.[13]

Nowhere was race a greater problem than among the more than 20,000 members of the Steelworkers' union in Birmingham. The steelworkers segregated their meetings and did relatively little about an all-encompassing system of job discrimination in the mills. The union's district staff in the past had been indifferent if not actively hostile to black members and had managed the purge of the black Communist Hosea Hudson from the union in 1947. They led a successful raid on the locals of the Union of Mine, Mill and Smelter Workers in Birmingham between 1949 and 1951. The rationale for the raids was to reclaim the workers from a Communist union, but the ugly and violent battle on Birmingham's Red Mountain was understood by most involved— black and white—as a racial conflict for control of the union. The Steelworkers' success in the notorious "mountain campaign" was also a victory for white supremacy. The internal affairs of the Steelworkers had a far-reaching effect, because prior to the merger with the AFL the union had dominated the CIO, its more than 30,000 members composing almost half the state's CIO roster. Indeed, Steelworkers' staffmen had run the state CIO council from the early 1940s to the merger.[14]

Philip Murray, the Steelworkers' national president, was bothered by the racist actions of the Alabama membership, and in 1950 he ordered the removal of all Jim Crow signs from union halls. The announcement sparked threats of massive resignations in the biggest Steelworkers local in Birmingham. The local leadership simply ignored the order, and Murray was persuaded to drop the issue in Birmingham. In 1951 Murray did remove three Birmingham staffmen and replaced them with representatives from outside Alabama who had clear directions to clean up the racial problems in Birmingham. One of the new staffmen, Howard Strevel, discovered that the job was going to be extremely difficult. The white majority of Alabama steelworkers adamantly opposed desegregating union halls, opening the lines of promotion to blacks, or encouraging black voting. Strevel would learn that only in the few plants where blacks held a majority could he get a system of fair treatment for blacks in hiring and promotion prior to the mid-1960s.[15]

The AFL-CIO's pro-civil-rights positions created a new uproar in the steel mills. More than 400 men at the U.S. Steel sheet mill wrote to Meany in April 1956 that his financial support of the NAACP had "upset the most harmonious white and black race relationship on earth." Could not Meany see that the NAACP was "dominated by persons, envious of the happiness of the Southern white and black, and ignorantly careless of the consequences of a false and phony philosophy?" Workers at the huge tin mill nearby spared the rhetoric and gave Meany the straight truth: "If we have to choose between staying in the union (or) see our segregated way of life being destroyed, we will pull out and form our own union."[16]

What happened in the labor movement in Tuscaloosa, Montgomery, and Birmingham suggested the basic pattern of experience throughout the South. In Gadsden, where in some of the nation's worst class warfare just over a decade earlier workers had prevailed against Republic Steel and Goodyear Tire, the steel and rubber locals became bastions of segregationist feeling. In Mobile, workers in the paper and shipping industries were similarly adamant. Few groups in the working class were as fiercely white supremacist as the railroad brotherhoods, which had a substantial membership in big cities like Birmingham and Atlanta and smaller towns like Selma, Alabama, and Meridian, Mississippi. Unionists outside Alabama were also rejecting the national leadership. In Chattanooga in 1955, dissidents in the Printing Pressmen's Union, angry over the city central labor body's acceptance of school desegregation, organized the Southern States Conference of Union People to agitate for segregation within the AFL-CIO. In North Carolina an avowedly anti-AFL-CIO organization, the United Southern Employees Association, emerged in 1956 and tried to attract white workers from other unions by appealing to whites' racial anxieties. It reportedly took relatively few members from the AFL-CIO but did agitate racial feelings among the membership in the southern Piedmont.[17]

White unionists defended segregation because they perceived that they would lose economic advantages as well as social status if Jim Crow met his demise. Testimony to this reality would later come from Samuel M. Engelhardt, Jr., who in the mid-1950s led the statewide White Citizens Council movement in Alabama and had connections among segregationist organizations throughout the South. Engelhardt would remember Jack Brock as a large, sincere man, if something of a "loudmouth"; Eugene Hall as a small and "sneaky" Yankee whose loyalty was somewhat suspect; and Tuscaloosa rubber workers and Birmingham steelworkers as the backbone of the council movement in Alabama. "The labor boys played a big part in the segregation fight," the Black Belt planter and politician Engelhardt said, thirty years after the fact. "The business people would give lip service, but the labor people would get out and work. They had more to lose than anybody else."[18]

Some white unionists in Alabama, especially those in leadership positions, rejected the uncompromising segregationist position. They recognized that the segregation question was destructive to the labor movement. Howard Strevel and a few others in the Steelworkers labored diligently if not very successfully to open doors for black workers and to show whites the advantages of interracial solidarity in politics. Carl Griffin, a member of the painters' union, brought charges against Elmer Brock for fomenting disloyalty and got him expelled from the union. Earl C. Pippin of the Communications Workers of America was a forthright liberal in an organization with many reactionary members. Most leaders of labor in Alabama disapproved of Jack Brock and his behavior, even though they usually did not directly address his racial attitudes.[19]

One determined opponent of Brock was a fellow Montgomery typographer, Barney Weeks, who had contended with him for many years in the composing room of the *Advertiser.* A longtime unionist and past president of the local, Weeks witnessed how Brock and Eugene Hall had a disproportionate influence on the typographers because "they were very vocal and very loud" and others were "keeping

their heads low." He believed that the *Advertiser*'s management toler-
ated Brock and Hall because "they were tearing up the union." Although he shared the working-class Alabama background of most
unionists, Weeks abhorred the racial attitudes of Brock and Hall. Finally, in the midst of the post-1954 racial turmoil, he challenged Brock
and regained the presidency of the local. He brought disciplinary
action against Hall for wearing a pistol in the composing room and
against Brock for misuse of the union's "sick" fund. He moved the
local union meeting away from the Klan-infested carpenters' hall.
Brock and Hall's influence in the union soon began to fade.[20]

In 1957 Barney Weeks was elected president of the state AFL-CIO
body, the Alabama Labor Council, to succeed Carl Griffin, who in
effect arranged Weeks's election because of his like-mindedness on
the matters of race and loyalty to the national AFL-CIO leadership.
Weeks began what became a long tenure in office at a time when his
racial views were decidedly more liberal than most working-class
white Alabamans. He would survive as president of the labor council
because he was viewed as an honest man and a good trade unionist,
especially among the AFL organizations who wanted one of their own
to head the merged labor movement. He carefully avoided public
discussions of the race issue in order that he not be easily branded an
integrationist. Once in office, he used the power of incumbency and
the support of the national office, especially that of George Meany, to
shore up his position locally. There would be harsh criticism of Weeks
for his racial liberalism, but most of it came sporadically from local
leaders and the rank and file. The higher-ranking leadership in the
Alabama labor movement rarely spoke against him; most knew that
his position was best for organized labor in the long run and that he
had entrenched support. In the absence of a direct, organized effort to
defeat him, Weeks survived and indeed got stronger over the years.[21]

Weeks immediately began an effort to push the Labor Council's
membership toward a more liberal outlook on race. He organized
integrated meetings of Alabama unionists and brought in speakers to
discuss aspects of race relations, including Phil Weightman, the AFL-
CIO's black expert on minority matters; Dan Powell, the southern
director for AFL-CIO's Committee on Political Education; and, later,
James Silver, the historian at the University of Mississippi who offered
a severe critique of southern race relations in his 1964 book, *Mississippi: The Closed Society*. Weeks distributed dozens of copies of

Silver's work, and others like it, among union leaders throughout Alabama. Most of Weeks's early labor-education meetings were held outside Alabama because of the laws prohibiting integrated meetings, though in 1958 Governor Folsom gave him permission to have an integrated meeting in a state office building despite objections from some segregationists in the Labor Council. At these meetings, Weeks later explained, "we gave them heavy doses of economics in which we showed how the best way in the world to keep the wages of the whites down [was] to keep blacks a little lower." A primary purpose of the meetings was to put white unionists in social situations of equality with black unionists, something that otherwise rarely happened. Whenever possible, black and white workers shared hotels and cafeterias as well as meeting rooms. Gradually, Weeks later said, white unionists began to see that "the world didn't end" with integration.[22]

Improving racial understanding, Weeks believed, was a prerequisite to achieving the council's main purpose, the expansion of labor's influence in Alabama politics. Although Alabama contained a relatively large number of unionists in contrast with other southern states, organized labor had been on the defensive politically since the late 1930s, when a powerful and harsh business reaction in the aftermath of the CIO's organizational triumphs caused an early, well-orchestrated, anti-labor movement in the state's politics. For every pro-labor politician like Sen. Lister Hill and Gov. Big Jim Folsom in the 1940s, there was at least one union-baiting counterpart to stifle any expansion of organized labor's power. The labor federations were fighting a purely defensive battle long before the Taft-Hartley Act, which got support from every Alabama representative in Washington except Hill. In 1953 the legislature passed a right-to-work law. The labor movement mounted a strong repeal effort in 1955 and came within three votes of winning, but five of seven legislators from Jefferson County, where the more than 50,000 unionists held a clear working-class majority, voted against it. Most responsible for the defeat was Rankin Fite, the wily, anti-labor Speaker of the House who had been given his post by that great friend of the common man, Governor Folsom. With friends like Big Jim, organized labor in Alabama hardly needed enemies.[23]

Labor's political weakness owed much to the widespread disfranchisement of workers. Alabama's poll tax historically had kept many citizens from voting, though the removal of the cumulative feature of

Alabama's law in 1953 made it easier for delinquent white voters to regain the franchise. For blacks the big problem was getting past the boards of registrars, which since World War II had generally succeeded in thwarting blacks' increased attempts at registration in most communities. White unionists in Birmingham in the late 1940s had expressed great outrage at the Jefferson County Board of Registrars' indifference to registering "men in overalls," but they offered little complaint about the continuing discrimination against black voters in the 1950s and 1960s. Howard Strevel received criticism from white members of the Steelworkers for scheduling voter-education schools for black workers at union halls. When whites later complained to Strevel about inadequate workmen's or unemployment compensation, he reminded them of their open opposition to black voting. "Half the people who work in this mill," he told white steelworkers, "are black and can't vote. When you get enough of this [government indifference], you'll want them to vote." Most white steelworkers, however, apparently reasoned that their economic self-interest lay in continuing white supremacy.[24]

Labor's internal divisions caused Barney Weeks to move carefully in his early years at the helm of the Alabama Labor Council. It was a period, he later said, "when we spent more time trying to keep everybody pulling together than we did anything else." He discouraged the Council from making a single endorsement in Alabama's 1958 gubernatorial election, even though there were several pro-labor candidates, including George Wallace, in the field. Weeks believed that, given the low repute of the national AFL-CIO, an endorsement would give business interests a propaganda weapon to use against labor's choice. Moreover, he doubted that the rank and file would follow the Council's endorsement. Not only did each of the pro-labor men have strong local followings among unionists, but also many members were attracted to the candidacy of John Patterson, the young attorney general who very effectively exploited racial tensions with his 1956 suit demanding the NAACP's state membership list. Patterson was the favorite of the White Citizens Councils and the Ku Klux Klan; he received the endorsement of Robert M. Shelton, the Imperial Wizard of the Klan and a Tuscaloosa rubber worker. Instead the labor council "favorably recommended" four men, and Wallace but not Patterson was among them. Patterson defeated Wallace in a runoff, taking about two-thirds of the working-class white vote in Birmingham. After the election Wallace reportedly promised never to be "outniggered" again.[25]

Getting organized labor in Alabama to pull together in politics proved to be a difficult task indeed. Weeks developed an extensive direct-mail program to communicate with the high proportion of the almost 200,000 unionists who did not participate actively in their locals. "These members are reading the daily press, and hearing the other side of the issues presented, without labor being able to really reach them during a campaign," he explained. The Labor Council sent out one and one-half million pieces of mail to Alabama unionists in 1960. But the best efforts for racial tolerance and moderation could not overcome the intense feelings engendered that year by the sit-in movement begun by black college students. Then the Freedom Rides in May 1961, which precipitated violent spectacles in Anniston, Birmingham, and Montgomery, heightened tensions even further. News coming later that the AFL-CIO had provided financial support for the Freedom Riders caused another outcry against the national organization.[26]

On the heels of these troubles, George Wallace ran his second campaign for governor, and this time he spared nothing in making himself the staunchest segregationist possible, even promising to "stand in the schoolhouse door" to prevent integration. The Labor Council again refrained from endorsing a candidate but recommended favorably Wallace, Folsom, and a third candidate, Ryan deGraffenried. A business agent for the Operating Engineers, a union that announced its endorsement of Wallace, said that the fighting little judge did not have the support of "New York politicians or the Washington bosses, but he has the support of the true Southerners." Wallace won easily, having taken about 60 percent of the working-class white vote in Birmingham and at least 75 percent in Montgomery. Homer Welch and Lester Hawkins, the suspected Klansmen in the Montgomery building trades, were prominent in Wallace's campaign. Jack Brock claimed sick leave from the *Advertiser* to tour Alabama for Wallace, service that later won him the privilege to sell wines to Alabama's state-controlled liquor stores.[27]

In spite of Weeks's careful approach, many Alabama unionists began to reject the labor council's leadership on politics because of its failure to give full support to Wallace. Some guessed correctly that Weeks disapproved of Wallace's exploitation of the race issue, though

Weeks was careful not to take public or official positions on the race question. When the Labor Council mailed out its candidate endorsements, hundreds were returned with negative remarks about the organization's liberal positions. Some of Weeks's harshest critics were in the big Steelworkers' locals in Birmingham and Gadsden where the white rank and file were wildly enthusiastic about Wallace and had collected money for his campaign at plant gates. Members of the largest Birmingham local took Weeks to task for sitting on the "black" side of the union hall when he visited their meetings. Steelworkers' locals had already begun to withdraw their support from the Labor Council and secessions accelerated rapidly in 1962. Reuben Farr, the Steelworkers' district director, offered no objection when some on his own staff and many local union officers renounced the Labor Council. By mid-1964 thirty-four Steelworkers' locals had withdrawn and the Labor Council had lost 30,000 members, though by no means were all the losses in the steel locals.[28]

Wallace's great popularity among white unionists was based on more than a simple appeal to racial fear. On almost all issues important to labor, Wallace in fact took the correct position, though Barney Weeks would criticize him in the years ahead for his willingness to increase regressive taxes. Wallace was, and always had been, pro-labor on questions like unemployment and workmen's compensation, use of American-made products, and respect for collective bargaining. Labor leaders were hard-pressed to show their rank and file that Wallace was anti-labor; their opposition to him was indeed founded almost entirely on his promotion of racial antagonism. To most white unionists, Wallace was a good labor man defending the position of the white working class from incursions by blacks who intended to take away whites' superior status position.[29]

Wallace's defense of the white working class was all the more important by 1963 because the national government and even many businessmen seemed to be siding with the blacks. The leading industrialists and bankers had abandoned the Citizens Council commitment to interclass solidarity in Montgomery, Birmingham, and Tuscaloosa as highly publicized racial conflicts arising from the Freedom Rides, and the long-delayed desegregation of the university created terrible publicity that damaged business prospects. Business leaders in Birmingham, Tuscaloosa, and Montgomery pushed through compromise settlements with black activists that ended segregation in one place after another. Only Wallace, it seemed to many working-class whites, remained true to their interests. The Tuscaloosa local of the United Papermakers and Paperworkers publicly expressed their full support for Wallace's defiant stand in the schoolhouse door in Tuscaloosa in June 1963 and condemned the merchants and businessmen who begged the governor not to interfere. The paperworkers reminded the businessmen that "their money comes from the laboring people of this area and they could very easily be boycotted by the Southern whites. The white laboring class of people have made industry and business-men of Tuscaloosa who they are today by putting them out front. They are expecting the right kind of leadership from these people by stand-ing together as a majority group." But in fact the upper classes had abandoned working-class whites and the total commitment to white supremacy. Wallace's political support fell drastically among upper-middle-class and upper-class voters, and the lower-class and lower-middle-class bases of his support would become more distinct over the course of the 1960s.[30]

Wallace's popularity among labor was a major finding of a poll of Alabama voters in early 1965. Wallace considered running for the U.S. Senate seat held by John Sparkman, a man who had often supported labor's positions in the past. An Oliver Quayle survey commissioned by Sparkman revealed that voters preferred Wallace over him by al-most two to one. Sixty-five percent of blue-collar Alabamans said they would take Wallace over Sparkman or any other candidate. Among the many demographic, occupational, and economic groups into which Quayle divided the Alabama electorate, organized labor composed Wallace's most devoted following. Seventy-two percent of union members chose Wallace, as opposed to 62 percent of farmers or 63 percent of whites in general.[31]

Wallace's 1964 campaign for president thrilled many working-class whites in Alabama and excited some into a frenzy of political activity. Steel and communication workers collected money for Wallace's pri-mary efforts in Maryland, Indiana, and Wisconsin. Campaigning in the Indiana primary, Wallace claimed that his expenses had been "picked up by thousands of laboring people who send us money—steel work-ers, rubber workers, iron workers." He made a point of including trade unionists in his campaign entourage in these states, an he ran large newspaper advertisements with endorsements from leaders of various unions in Alabama. He did this to counteract criticism from labor leaders in these states, including the Wisconsin AFL-CIO head's condemnation of Wallace as a demagogue. The presence of white unionists also helped to dramatize Wallace's opposition to civil rights legislation then pending in Congress, especially the equal-opportunity provisions that would become Title VII of the Civil Rights Act of 1964. Keenly intuitive to the concerns of working-class people, Wallace knew that whites in the big mills in Baltimore, Gary, and Milwaukee were worried about the damage that Title VII would do to seniority systems that protected whites' superior job opportunities.[32]

Most visible in their support among unionists were men like Homer Welch and Lester Hawkins of the Montgomery building trades; the legislative representative of the Brotherhood of Railroad Trainmen; the president of a paper workers' local near Mobile; the president of an Operating Engineers local in Birmingham, a man Weeks believed was a Klansman; the president of a large Communications Workers local in Birmingham, an enthusiastic member of the John Birch Society; and a group of at least a dozen Birmingham Steelworkers, primarily from the large tin mill local, whom Howard Strevel and others believed were Klansmen or Klan sympathizers. Labor's most enthusiastic Wallaceites had two things in common: They usually had some connection to a far-right racist organization, and they always worked in industries—railroad, construction, steel, paper—where job discrimination historically had given whites substantial material advantages over blacks. The connection to racist organizations was important for giving Wallace's labor cadre a sense of unified commitment outside the institutional labor movement. Employment discrimination gave all white workers a material reason to oppose civil rights for blacks.[33]

Wallace's 1964 presidential campaign further compounded Barney Weeks's problems. The labor council endorsed President Lyndon Johnson's electors in Alabama's Democratic primary, but Wallace's slate won and Johnson did not appear on the state's ballot in November. Weeks advised organized labor to vote a straight Democratic ticket in November in the hope of keeping votes from Sen. Barry Goldwater, but the Republican nominee got almost eight of every ten white working-class votes in Birmingham anyway. In October a member of the Communications Workers in Birmingham wrote to his local newspaper condemning Weeks and the "Washington controlled" Labor Council, from which his local had seceded; praising George Wallace as a "good friend to labor"; and announcing his belief in a "balanced budget, not in free handouts that my children will have to pay . . . and peace through preparedness. This is why I will cast my vote for Sen. Barry Goldwater."[34]

Wallace's success encouraged dissidents within the Steelworkers to join a movement against the union leadership. Wallace's most active supporters in the Steelworkers became the Alabama campaign managers for I. W. Abel's 1965 challenge to the incumbent David McDonald as head of the national union. The district director, Reuben Farr, supported McDonald, as did Howard Strevel, the sub-district director then campaigning to succeed the retiring Farr. The Wallaceites' support of Abel, especially the highly visible role taken in the campaign by Johnny Nichols, the Birmingham Steelworker Wallace had appointed assistant director of the state labor department, injected the race issue into the union election. Abel was portrayed by some in Alabama as the segregationist alternative to the union's liberal leadership, which in fact belied Abel's long-standing public commitment to racial fairness. To Howard Strevel, who was elected district director and was determined to be more aggressive than his predecessor in thwarting the anti-black actions of the "Kluxers" in his union, Abel's acceptance of the Wallaceites' support was extremely destructive. When Abel took his longtime friend Strevel to task for allowing the segregationist label to be hung on him, Strevel replied, "You did that better than I could have done it," thereby casting aspersions on the character of the men representing Abel in Alabama. After he was elected, Abel asked Strevel to hire some of his supporters as union staff representatives in Alabama. "There ain't no way I'll get along with those sons of bitches," Strevel replied. "They ain't nothing, never have been nothing and never will be nothing as far as this union is concerned." Perplexed by the depth of Strevel's anger at the Wallaceites, Abel unhappily accepted the refusal.[35]

The state elections in 1966 would mark the low point for the Labor Council's influence in politics. Prohibited from seeking a second consecutive term, Wallace ran his wife Lurleen for governor. The Council endorsed a former pro-labor congressman, Carl Elliott. This choice earned widespread condemnation from the white rank and file who, according to a Wallace enthusiast in the Birmingham tin mill, would not be "hoodwinked" into supporting candidates "picked by Barney Weeks and company." The president of the Birmingham Building Trades Council said, "Barney Weeks is a puppet controlled by strings, the strings reaching all the way to Washington." Lurleen won easily; she received almost two of every three working-class white votes. Having been rejected in the Democratic primary, the Labor Council made no recommendations in the 1966 general election. "The situation is very simple," Weeks said. "There are no people running to whom organized labor can give an official endorsement." The Council even spurned U.S. Senator John Sparkman's candidacy, though he had often voted with labor in the past. In explanation, Weeks pointed to Sparkman's recent anti-labor votes, but in actuality the council was punishing Sparkman at the behest of the International Brotherhood of Electrical Workers, who had been trying without success to open collective-bargaining negotiations at Sparkman's family-owned radio stations in northern Alabama. Many locals defied the Council and endorsed Sparkman, who had toed the line on segregation and had done abundant constituent favors over the years.[36]

At the end of the 1966 political season, many labor leaders and liberal politicians were profoundly depressed. One defeated candidate reminded unionists at the Labor Council's annual meeting that virtually everyone endorsed by labor had lost that year. "It is a fact of political life that we are pointed to by politicians as people who can be divided, sub-divided and cut up. If you want your voice to be heard economically and politically, you are going to have to do something about these divisions."[37]

Labor's troubles would continue only a few more years before they began to ease. George Wallace's 1968 presidential campaign made an impact similar to the previous one on Alabama unionists, though fewer men from labor played central roles in the effort. The Alabama Labor Council stood behind the Democratic party nominee, Hubert Humphrey, and many locals announced their endorsement of Wallace's third-party bid. Wallace carried Alabama overwhelmingly; he received 77 percent of working-class votes in Birmingham and Montgomery. Almost all the others went to Richard Nixon. Humphrey's meager support was primarily from blacks.[38]

The 1970 Alabama gubernatorial election proved to be a turning point. Lurleen Wallace had died in office in 1968, and her successor, Albert Brewer, was seeking election on his own. George Wallace challenged Brewer, his old ally. Recent changes in the electorate—

especially the registration of several hundred thousand blacks—promised to make things more difficult for Wallace. Organized labor showed "unprecedented unanimity" in its support for Brewer, Barney Weeks said. Howard Strevel had pushed most of the Steelworkers' locals back into the Labor Council, and he and his staff were supporting Brewer strongly. "Our people are finally waking up to the fact that Wallace can't roll back events," Weeks observed. "Integration is a fact of life now, whether they like it or not." Brewer led Wallace in the primary, partly because of strong support from blacks and organized labor. "Our people stuck together real good," Weeks said later, but keeping them together for the runoff against Wallace proved to be a greater challenge. Wallace's runoff campaign made blatant appeals to race, citing the "black bloc" vote that supported Brewer. He even tied the black vote to a Steelworkers' "labor boss" who sent union money to Alabama to help get black voters to the polls.[39]

The tactic worked perfectly. Wallace reclaimed most of his labor support; he carried more than 60 percent of working-class white votes in Birmingham and Montgomery. Something called the Rank and File Labor Committee based in a Birmingham neighborhood populated by Steelworkers ran an advertisement near the end of the campaign asking, "Do you want the Black Block Vote to elect and control the Governor's Office and our State? Think—only 16% of the white voters voted for Brewer." Although the ad made a false claim, such appeals to racial fear helped to put Wallace in the governor's chair again.[40]

After the 1970 election, Wallace recognized that the race issue no longer would have the same potency in politics. He reached out to the Labor Council as a natural ally. Barney Weeks, Howard Strevel, and other labor leaders were perfectly willing to accept his overtures if he stopped exploiting racial fears. They knew that Wallace was fundamentally a liberal with a sincere empathy for working men and women. As governor for three more terms in the 1970s and 1980s, Wallace did indeed cease exploiting race and he even expressed regret about things done in the past. At Weeks's behest, Wallace had the state underwrite the establishment of a center for labor education and research at the University of Alabama in Birmingham. But by the time interracial class solidarity finally became more nearly a reality in Alabama and black workers gained political rights, organized labor had become less influential in the working class. Relatively fewer unionized workers were available to inject a powerful liberal influence into politics. The drastic contraction in mining in the 1960s and steel making in the 1970s had shrunk large segments of organized labor almost to insignificance. Just as important, the national political climate turned more conservative just as Alabama's was becoming more liberal, a change that worked against class-based politics in the state. In one sense labor's trouble had ended, but opportunities for great progress seemed more remote.[41]

Organized labor's experience in Alabama politics in the 1950s and 1960s reveals something of the peculiar way that the American working class has perceived itself in the twentieth century. In a time of rapid change and real crisis, white workers in Alabama insisted on identifying their interests in racial terms. Black workers, whose perspective has not been attended to herein, *ipso facto* understood the world in the same way, if from the opposite side of the racial divide. But working-class whites were hardly ignorant of the class realities of their circumstances. Their support of Wallace was based on his empathy for their class interest in maintaining a racially discriminatory society. However cynical and opportunistic he was, Wallace must be credited with perceiving—better than any other American politician of the day—the ways that race and class interests are intermingled in the American political impulse and how the one interest often mystifies and obscures the other.

Notes

The author wishes to express his appreciation to Professors E. Culpepper Clark of the University of Alabama and J. Mills Thornton III of the University of Michigan for their assistance with the research for this article.

1. "Special Convention of Alabama Labor Council, AFL-CIO," March 15, 1958, in Files of the Alabama Labor Council, Birmingham, Ala.
2. For background on the history of labor in Alabama, see Philip Taft, *Organizing Dixie: Alabama Workers in the Industrial Era* (Westport, CT: Greenwood, 1981); Carl V. Harris, *Political Power in Birmingham, 1871–1921* (Knoxville: Univ. of Tennessee Press, 1977); and Robert J. Norrell, "Caste in Steel: Jim Crow Careers in Birmingham, Alabama," *The Journal of American History* 73 (Dec. 1986), 669–94. The last citation should be consulted in conjunction with the article by Judith Stein in this collection, for it contradicts Stein's interpretation on many points.

3. For an extended explanation of early civil rights activism in Alabama and the white reaction, see Numan V. Bartley, *The Rise of Massive Resistance: Race and Politics in the South during the 1950's* (Baton Rouge: Louisiana State Univ. Press, 1969); J. Mills Thornton III, "Challenge and Response in the Montgomery Bus Boycott of 1955–1956," *The Alabama Review* 3 (July 1980), 163–235.

4. Herbert Hill, "The Racial Practices of Organized Labor: The Contemporary Record," in *The Negro and the American Labor Movement*, ed. Julius Jacobson (Garden City, NY: Doubleday, 1968), 286–357; *New York Times*, Aug. 13, Sept. 9, Nov. 13, 1955, Feb. 11, 1956. For a summary discussion of the impact of the race question on the AFL-CIO, see Alan Draper, *A Rope of Sand: The AFL-CIO Committee on Political Education, 1955–1967* (New York: Praeger, 1989), 106–17.

5. *Tuscaloosa News*, Feb. 18, 1956.

6. Ibid.; *New York Times*, Feb. 26, 1956.

7. Based on a membership list contained in Citizens Council Collection, Special Collections, University of Alabama Library, Tuscaloosa, AL. Members' occupations were identified in the 1956 Tuscaloosa City Directory.

8. *Alabama Labor News*, Feb. 14, 28, May 22, 1956.

9. Transcript of author's interviews with Barney Weeks, Feb. 21, Oct. 18, 26, 1989, in author's possession, Tuscaloosa, Alabama, hereafter cited as Weeks interviews; *Alabama Labor News*, Oct. 23, 1956; *Union Labor News*, Aug. 18, 1956.

10. *Montgomery Advertiser*, Jan. 31, Feb. 1, 2, 1957; Weeks interviews.

11. *Alabama Labor News*, Nov. 6, 1956; *Montgomery Advertiser*, Feb 5, 12, 17, 1957.

12. *Montgomery Advertiser*, Feb. 11, May 21, 27, 31, 1957.

13. *Birmingham News*, July [?] 1956, in clipping scrapbook, 1957–71, Alabama Labor Council News, hereinafter cited ALC scrapbook, 1957–71; *Birmingham News*, July 22, 1956; *Alabama Labor News*, Aug. 28, 1956; *Birmingham Post-Herald*, May 28, 1956; "Introducing Southern Crafts," in ALC scrapbook, 1957–71; *Birmingham News*, July 10, 11, 1949; *Birmingham Post-Herald*, Aug. 10, 1956; Weeks interviews.

14. Norrell, "Caste in Steel."

15. Ibid.

16. *Birmingham News*, April 5, Feb. 23, 1956.

17. Weeks interviews; Bartley, *Massive Resistance*, 307–8; *Labor's Daily*, Nov. 8, 1957; Ray Marshall, *The Negro and Organized Labor* (New York: John Wiley, 1965), 192–96.

18. Transcript of author's interview with Samuel M. Engelhardt, Jr., Oct. 26, 1989, in author's possession, Tuscaloosa, Alabama.

19. Transcript of author's interviews with Howard Strevel, May 25, Aug. 6, 1984, Oct. 27, 1989, in author's possession, Tuscaloosa, Alabama; Weeks interviews.

20. Weeks interviews.
21. Ibid.
22. Ibid.
23. Ibid.; Jim Battles to CIO Members, Oct. 21, 1955, in Philip Taft Papers, Birmingham Public Library Archives, Birmingham, AL; George E. Sims, *The Little Man's Big Friend: James E. Folsom in Alabama Politics, 1946–1958* (Tuscaloosa: Univ. of Alabama Press, 1985), 66, 134, 154–55.
24. Donald S. Strong, "Alabama: Transition and Alienation," in *The Changing Politics of the South*, ed. William C. Havard (Baton Rouge: Louisiana State Univ. Press, 1972), 429–30; *Birmingham Post*, Jan. 26, 1948; Strevel interviews.
25. Weeks interviews; the estimate on Patterson's working-class white vote in Birmingham is based on precinct data for lower- and lower-middle-class white voters in Numan V. Bartley and Hugh D. Graham, *Southern Elections: County and Precinct Data, 1950–1972* (Baton Rouge: Louisiana State Univ. Press, 1978), 349–50.
26. Taft, *Organizing Dixie*, 166; *Montgomery Advertiser*, June 22, 1961.
27. *Birmingham News*, May 8, 1962; Weeks interviews; Bartley and Graham, *Southern Elections*, 349, 347.
28. Weeks interviews; Strevel interviews; *New York Times*, June 4, 1964.
29. Weeks interviews; Strevel interviews.
30. For an analysis of businessmen's acceptance of desegregation, see *Southern Businessmen and Desegregation*, ed. Elizabeth Jacoway and David R. Colburn (Baton Rouge: Louisiana State Univ. Press, 1982); *Tuscaloosa News*, June 4, 1963; Bartley and Graham, *Southern Elections*, 347–50.
31. "A Survey of the Political Climate in Alabama," Report prepared by Oliver Quayle and Co., Feb. 1965, in State Democratic Party Executive Committee Papers, Birmingham Public Library Archives, Birmingham, AL.
32. *Birmingham News*, May 3, April 1, 2, 26, 1964; unidentified newspaper, March 11, 1964, ALC scrapbook, George Wallace.
33. *Louisville Courier-Journal*, April 26, 1964; *Washington Evening Star*, May 13, 1964; *Birmingham News*, May 13, 1964; Strevel interviews..
34. *Birmingham News*, April 26, 1964; unidentified newspaper, Oct. 1964, ALC scrapbook, 1957–1971; *Birmingham News*, Oct. 16, 1964.
35. John Herling, *Right to Challenge: People and Power in the Steelworkers Union* (New York: Harper & Row, 1972), 221–22, 247–48; Strevel interviews.
36. Weeks interviews; *Birmingham Post-Herald*, March 31, 1966; Bartley and Graham, *Southern Elections*, 347, 349; *Birmingham News*, Oct. 11, 1966.
37. *Birmingham News*, Oct. 10, 1966.
38. *Birmingham Post-Herald*, April 11, 1968; *Birmingham News*, Sept. 25, Oct. 22, 1968; *New York Times*, Oct. 19, 1968; Bartley and Graham, *Southern Elections*, 348, 350.
39. *Steel Labor*, April 1970; Strevel interviews; *Wall Street Journal*, April 23,

1970; Weeks interviews; unidentified newspaper advertisement, ALC scrapbook, George Wallace.

40. Unidentified newspaper advertisement, ALC scrapbook, George Wallace; Bartley and Graham, *Southern Elections*, 348, 350.

41. Strevel interviews; Weeks interviews.

Contributors

Colin J. Davis is lecturer of history, Department of Labor Studies, Rutgers University–New Brunswick. He received his Ph.D. from the State University of New York at Binghamton. His most recent publication is "Strategy for Success: The Pennsylvania Railroad and the 1922 National Railroad Shopmen's Strike," *Business and Economic History* 19 (1990).

Gary M. Fink is professor of history and chair of the department at Georgia State University. He received his Ph.D. from the University of Missouri and has published extensively in modern American labor and political history.

Mary E. Frederickson is co-editor (with Joyce Kornbluh) of *Sisterhood and Solidarity: Women's Workers' Education, 1914–1984* (Temple Univ. Press, 1984). She teaches women's history at Miami University of Ohio.

Gilbert J. Gall is an assistant professor of labor studies and industrial relations at Pennsylvania State University. He is the author of *The Politics of Right to Work: The Labor Federations as Special Interests, 1943–1979,* and he has published articles in *The Historian, Labor History, Labor Studies Journal,* and *Labor Law Journal.*

Rick Halpern is lecturer in American history at University College, London. He received his Ph.D. from the University of Pennsylvania and is completing a study of Chicago's packinghouse workers in the CIO era.

Michael Honey teaches American history and labor and ethnic studies at the University of Washington, Tacoma. His book, *Southern Labor and Black Civil Rights: Organizing Memphis Workers, 1929–1955,* is forthcoming (Univ. of Illinois Press).

Robert J. Norrell is associate professor of history and director of the Center for Southern History and Culture at the University of Alabama. His book *Reaping the Whirlwind: The Civil Rights Movement in Tuskeegee* (Knopf, 1985) won the Robert F. Kennedy Book Award. His most recent work is *A Promising Field: Engineering at Alabama, 1837–1987* (Univ. of Alabama Press, 1990), a study of technological education.

Judith Stein is professor of history at the City College of New York and the Graduate School of the City University of New York. She received her Ph.D. from Yale University and has published in the field of African-American and American history. She is the author of *The World of Marcus Garvey: Race and Class in Modern Society* (Louisiana State Univ. Press, 1986).

Joe William Trotter, Jr., associate professor of history at Carnegie-Mellon University, is the author of *Coal, Class, and Color: Blacks in Southern West Virginia, 1915–32* (Univ. of Illinois Press, 1990), and *Black Milwaukee: The Making of an Industrial Proletariat, 1915–45* (Univ. of Illinois Press, 1985). He is now completing an edited volume, *The Great Migration in Historical Perspective: New Dimensions of Race and Class in Industrial America.*

Robert H. Zieger is professor of history, University of Florida. He is the author of *John L. Lewis: Labor Leader* (Twayne, 1988), *American Workers, American Unions, 1920–1985* (Johns Hopkins, 1986), *Rebuilding the Pulp and Paper Workers' Union, 1933–1941* (Univ. of Tennessee Press, 1984), and other works in American labor history.

Index

Abel, Iwor W., 266

African-American workers: Alabama, 183–222; and CIO, 135–57; coal miners, 60–83; in meatpacking industry, 158–72; in Memphis, 135–57; migration north of, 60; Pittsburgh, 8; railroads, 114, 127; in steel industry, 183–222; textile industry, 25, 50, 97; union proclivities of, 50, 70–74, 135, 138–39, 140–41, 143, 146–47, 149–50, 158–59, 161, 162, 164, 165, 167–69, 170–73, 174, 175–76, 187, 191–92, 193–96, 198, 201–2, 204–7, 211, 244–45

Akron, Ohio, 40

Alabama, 102; African-American coal miners in, 78; civil rights in, 8, 265; politics in, 250–72; railroads in, 113; steel industry in, 183–222; textile industry in, 35

Alabama Labor Council, 259, 261, 263, 267, 268

Alabama Labor News, 253

Alabama Power Company, 250

Alabama, University of, 4

Alabama, University of, in Birmingham, 268

Alcoa, 203

Alexandria, Va., 87

Aliquippa, Pa., 41

Amalgamated Association of Iron, Steel, and Tin Workers (AA), 187

Amalgamated Clothing and Textile Workers (ACTW), 50–51

Amalgamated Clothing Workers of America (ACWA), 91–92, 95, 102

Amalgamated Meat Cutters and Butcher Workmen (AMCBW), 158, 160, 164

American Cast Iron and Pipe Company, 185

American Federation of Labor (AFL), 15, 42, 94, 102, 114, 158, 159, 164, 175, 224, 229, 239, 251, 253; in Alabama, 183, 191, 192, 193, 256; in Arkansas, 223–24, 227, 228, 229; in California, 234–35; in Florida, 227, 231–33; in Memphis, 137, 139, 140, 142, 144, 150

American Federation of Labor-Congress of Industrial Organizations (AFL-CIO), 152–53, 251, 252, 253, 255, 256, 257, 258, 259, 261; Committee on Political Education, 251–52, 259

American Federation of Teachers, 255

American Federationist, 95, 105

American Newspaper Guild (ANG), 140, 142, 145, 151

American Snuff Company, 150

Anderson, S. R., 76

Anderson, Sherwood, 95

Anniston, Ala., 262

anti-communism, in CIO, 40, 145–50, 174–75

anti-unionism, 4–6, 7, 52–53, 223–49; in Arkansas, 223–24, 225–26, 228–30, 236–39; in Florida, 223, 225–26, 236–39; in California, 223, 225–26, 234–36, 236–39; in Memphis, 137–40; in textile industry, 39, 51, 87

Arkansas: economic and political patterns in, 1940s, 223, 225–30, 236–39; organized labor in, 223–24,